Peter Caton was born in 1960 and has always lived in Upminster, Essex. He is married with two children. After training as a polymer chemist, he set up his own business testing and manufacturing adhesives. He has a keen interest in walking, the countryside and conservation and is a member of many environmental organisations. His other interests include travelling and football (he is a West Ham season ticket holder) and he is a member of Upminster Methodist Church.

# ESSEX
## COAST WALK

PETER CATON

Matador
9 De Montfort Mews
Leicester LE1 7FW, UK
Tel: (+44) 116 255 9311 / 9312
Email: books@troubador.co.uk
Web: www.troubador.co.uk/matador


ISBN 978 1848761-162


A Cataloguing-in-Publication (CIP) catalogue record for this book is
available from the British Library.

Main Cover Photo - Sunset over The Twizzle, Walton on the Naze.

A contribution from the sale of this book will be made to Essex Wildlife Trust (www.essexwt.org.uk).


Typeset in 11.5pt Sabon by Troubador Publishing Ltd, Leicester, UK

Matador is an imprint of Troubador Publishing Ltd

**Mixed Sources**
Product group from well-managed
forests and other controlled sources
www.fsc.org  Cert no. TT-COC-2082
© 1996 Forest Stewardship Council

Printed by Cromwell Press Group, Trowbridge, Wiltshire

With thanks to my wife Debbie, my brother David
and my parents, for their help and support
in writing this book.

# CONTENTS

# INTRODUCTION

George Mallory attempted to climb Everest 'Because it's there'. I walked the coast of Essex 'Because I'm here'. For many years I'd harboured a desire to complete a long distance walk, but with family and work commitments, travel to traditional mountain, hill or coast walking country wasn't going to be possible. I had to look nearer to my Upminster home and although Essex isn't really noted for its scenery, it does have largely unknown coastline, probably the longest of any English county.

Hence one sunny September morning I found myself at Liverpool Street station, heading for Manningtree at the county's northern border and the start of a series of 28 walks to its boundary with Greater London. Despite living in Essex for over 40 years, my knowledge of its coast was limited and like most of the county's population, visits had been mainly to the larger towns and beaches. However as I walked towards the Thames it soon became apparent that whilst it doesn't have the high cliffs and pretty bays that traditionally define beautiful coastline, Essex has its own unique appeal.

The estuaries, creeks and salt marsh have a natural beauty, which as I was to find, is often enhanced by the hand of man. Its wildlife is plentiful and varied. Not just the birds of which Essex has internationally important populations, but huge numbers of plants, invertebrates and insects, often protected on the many nature reserves along the coast. I was to find much of interest in the county's geography, its erosion and how we are allowing the sea to reclaim sections of land. A great deal of history was found along the way, from Stone Age to World Wars, witches to ghosts, an incestuous queen to Jack the Ripper, castles to piers and churches to power stations. It is a living coast, a working coast and a holiday coast, but also a remote and in places, a wild coast. I started off just looking for somewhere convenient to walk and ended up falling in love with the coast of Essex.

When asked which county has the longest coastline, after due thought most people will answer Cornwall. Accurate figures are hard to find, but it seems generally accepted that the Cornish coast is between 250 and 320 miles. However, whilst Cornwall has two coasts, Essex has five estuaries, with many meandering inlets. Again there appears to be no precise figure, but most sources estimate between 300 and 350 miles. Essex, Cornwall and Kent all claim the longest coastline and whilst this is clearly a matter of some debate, most figures suggest that it is Essex. The key is probably where you draw the boundary between coast and river. I decided that for my walk this should be at the first fixed crossing point, which generally is around the tidal limit and ended up walking a total of 305 miles. What I can be sure is that Essex has 276 miles of sea wall, as this was stated in answer to a Parliamentary Question, although as I was to find, sometimes challenges have to be overcome to walk them

With two sons and a wife to keep happy, plus a business to run, (a glue factory in Purfleet), the easiest way to cover the coast was a series of one day walks. Each chapter covers one walk and I've tried to give enough detail on the route to be a useful guide to someone wanting to follow it, but not too many directions as to make it tedious. I often find that a lack of maps detracts from travel books, so have included a few, which I hope will set the scene. However anyone setting out to walk themselves should take one of the excellent Ordnance Survey sheets for detail. I've given an approximate mileage for each walk, which includes occasional diversions to look at places of interest, plus a few instances of doubling back when unable to get through due to unforeseen obstructions (occasionally the map wasn't right, or maybe it was my reading of it?). Some of the walks therefore could be a little shorter, but the figures are probably a reasonable guide as others too may also stray from the shortest route, by accident or design.

For environmental reasons and to prove that it is perfectly possible, my plan was to travel to and from each walk by public transport. This overcomes the problem of getting back to the car and as I was to find, although not the quickest, was the most rewarding way to travel. Rural buses and trains give far more insight into a county than simply driving through and enabled me to meet more of its people on the way. Some coverage is given to the transport, enough I hope to add interest, but I can reassure you that there are no engine numbers mentioned!

Whilst far from a definitive guide to the Essex coast, I've tried to include some information on each place of interest en route, while keeping up a narrative of the walk. I've researched information as much as reasonably possible and made every effort to ensure that all facts are accurate, but will be happy to be corrected if otherwise. Where sources gave conflicting information and unless one is overwhelming in a minority, I've either stated this or been less than definite in my wording.

Information was obtained from numerous sources, too many to mention, although I've put the occasional acknowledgement in the text. This isn't the sort of book to include lots of references, but I would like to note particular acknowledgment to Ian Yearsley for *Islands of Essex* and Tom King for *Thames Estuary Trail*, the last of which provided inspiration as well as information.

As well as historical facts, I've included some stories which while interesting, cannot always be verified. Also plenty of observations along the way, plus I hope you will forgive, some of my more

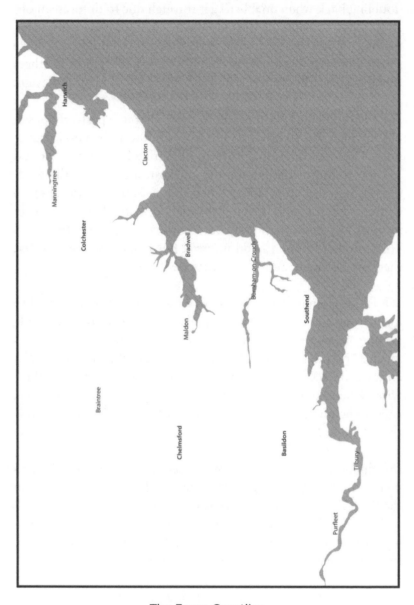

The Essex Coastline

forthright opinions. Many travel writers make up or exaggerate incidents to add interest or humour. When done well this often adds to the enjoyment, but it can have the opposite result. With a scientific rather than journalistic training, I have kept to the truth, resisting the temptation to embellish, so you can be sure that what you read of my journey is as it happened.

Travel writers seem to show little interest in Essex. Shally Hunt in *The Sea on Our Left* devoted a tiny proportion of her 350 pages to the Essex coast. Paul Theroux in *Kingdom by the Sea* skipped most of the county, taking a bus from Clacton to Southend. David St John Thomas in *Journey Through Britain* included three pages about the county as he travelled through on his way to Suffolk, but didn't actually get off the train. The Essex coast may be largely unknown, even to most of the county's inhabitants, but this to me was part of its attraction. I hope that I have been able to portray some of its charm, beauty and history and maybe encourage a few more people to seek its pleasures. There's certainly room for them.

# PART ONE

## Manningtree to Walton-on-the-Naze

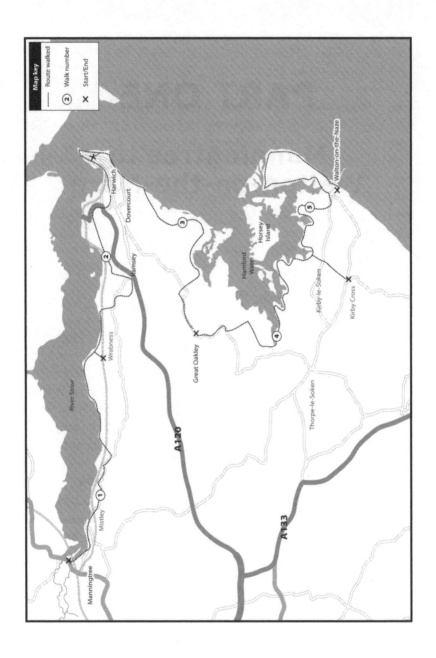

CHAPTER ONE

# MANNINGTREE to WRABNESS

(10 miles)
21st September

Is there a better way to start the day than gliding through sunlit English countryside in the restaurant car of an express train, eating a freshly cooked English breakfast and contemplating a day by the sea? Speeding through East London on the 10.00 from Liverpool Street and on to suburban, then rural Essex, I was kept well supplied with ample to sustain a day's walking. Orange juice arrived at Stratford, grapefruit as we passed Ilford, toast at Romford, a huge plate of bacon, sausage, egg, tomato and mushroom at Brentwood. More toast came at Chelmsford, followed by the bill at Colchester. At £15.95 it was probably the most expensive breakfast I'd ever purchased, but a thoroughly enjoyable start to the day.

I left the train at Manningtree. Here the River Stour forms the boundary between Essex and Suffolk and I followed the main road to the bridge which was to form the starting point of my walk. Signs at both ends indicated it to be 'The White Bridge', although all that appeared to be white was the railings on either side, the main structure being blue. At the northern end was a sign saying 'Welcome to Suffolk', although there was no such greeting for those entering Essex.

The White Bridge – Gateway to Essex

A footpath took me under the railway and along the raised bank of the Stour towards Manningtree town centre. To the left is Hogmarsh, the first of many nature reserves along the county's coast. Owned by the Essex Wildlife Trust, this typical Essex salt marsh is effectively an island, although access is possible at low tide for anyone willing to struggle through the soft mud which surrounds it. My original plan had been to visit every island en route, but having found that Essex has more than any other English county, I thought again. Learning that although you can walk to most of the islands, tides and mud often mean that this isn't easy, confirmed my decision to stick to the mainland.

Mute swan, canada goose and oyster catcher all nest in the Hogmarsh reserve and it is visited by many other estuary species. The island is threatened by erosion, which is being countered by importing dredged silt and building faggot barriers. Faggoting, the ancient technique of using bundles of brushwood to stabilise banks, is becoming more widely used again as the advantages of using natural materials are realised. The faggots slow the flow of water, trapping silt, which builds up around the branches, forming a stable barrier to erosion.

In the middle of the path, I came across a small mouse sitting impassively in the sun and taking no notice of me standing not a yard away. Concerned that he may be unwell, I waved a piece of grass under his nose and he scampered off indignantly, no doubt to tell his mates about the nasty man who interrupted his morning's sun bathing.

Manningtree claims to be the smallest town in England. Before visiting I went to the trouble of researching the relevant definitions. A town, it said, is 'an urban area with a fixed boundary that is smaller than a city'. A village is 'a community of people smaller than a town'. So that's crystal clear then! It is on grounds of its area being only 40 acres which Manningtree claims to be the smallest town, but that is apparently a matter of some dispute, depending on whether you count the area at low or high tide.

In Tudor times Manningtree was a prosperous town, profiting from trade in wool and cloth, which were loaded onto sailing barges at the quay. Its relative prosperity and coastal position, has resulted in various influences leaving a legacy of interesting and aesthetically pleasing buildings. Weavers fleeing from the Netherlands in the sixteenth century built cottages here, and the French Huguenots following in the 17th century, added further buildings reflecting another architectural style. More latterly, imposing flat fronted Georgian facades were constructed, many of which conceal Elizabethan or Tudor houses with lath and plaster walls.

The town has a small museum, inside the public library on the

High Street, but which opens only from 10.00 – 12.00 on Wednesdays and Saturdays. Today being Thursday it was closed. The main street has a selection of craft and antique shops, cafes, pubs, assorted travel agents, financial advisors and the like, but very few establishments that sold anything particularly useful. I needed only three items – a map (my 1987 Ordnance Survey map missing the small corner of Essex from Harwich to Clacton), spare camera batteries, and something for lunch. The last of these was easily obtained at a bakery opposite the library. Batteries should have been simple, but the chemist had run out and reluctantly I had to resort to the large Co-op store by the river. This had queues at each checkout, and is presumably the explanation for the paucity of useful shops on the main street. Having looked unsuccessfully in a small shop called 'Stour View', which would now be more accurately named 'Co-op View', I gave up.

Manningtree was the home of Matthew Hopkins, the seventeenth century Witch Finder General who started the great hunt for witches across England. His aim was to seek out and kill any that he found, using the traditional, if not entirely fair method of testing ladies to determine whether they were witches. The unfortunate women were 'ducked' in the river to ascertain whether they floated or sunk. Those who sunk and drowned were decreed as innocent. Those who floated were guilty, so hung, or burned at the stake.

Hopkins and his witch finders would keep suspected witches awake for days on end until they confessed, or look for evidence of marks on the body which were viewed as signs of unholy alliance with the devil. Birth marks, boils, or even just patches of dry skin were viewed as highly suspicious and Hopkins would insert a needle causing immense pain to prove his case. The possession of a third nipple (apparently not that uncommon) was regarded as proof of their satanic connections, as indeed was the more mundane ownership of a cat. Having negotiated a fee of twenty shillings for each one he exposed, Hopkins had every incentive to torture the poor ladies and try to extract a confession. By 1645 he had arrested 200 women, 68 of whom were hung or burnt at the stake. Up a side street I found the small village green where the hangings took place. Surrounded by Georgian houses, it was a pleasant spot, and not easy to imagine the scenes here three centuries previous.

My conclusion was that Manningtree is a pleasant enough town, in a lovely setting. The sort of place to spend an hour or two wandering, take in the variety of interesting buildings, a quick look in a craft shop or two, some lunch and then move on. Branding itself 'Gateway to Constable Country' is about right. Not the sort of place for a whole day out, but an ideal stop before heading the two miles up the Stour to Flatford Mill. I was however heading downstream, towards the port of Harwich.

Leaving Manningtree, the road runs close to the sea, with a wide grassy strip beside the shore, known locally as The Strand. A few elderly couples were picnicking, drinking tea, or just sitting to admire the view. With the tide up, blue sky and little boats bobbing on the water, it was a delightful scene. At Hopping Bridge, the site of witch ducking in times gone by, I came upon a large group of swans, some of the six hundred who are famous residents of this corner of the Stour estuary. I estimated that this group alone numbered around a hundred, and although graceful on the water, locals say that they are aggressive so should not be approached. Not wishing to test whether it is fact or myth that a swan can break a man's arm, I kept my distance.

To the right was Mistley Place Park, an animal rescue centre, which claims to have 2,000 rescued birds and animals. However, like the Pharisee I passed by on the other side of the road, our last visit to such an establishment resulting in us leaving with two kittens, after which our household was never the same. My wife and I have different opinions as to whether their addition has

Swans at Mistley

enhanced our quality of life, but suffice to say, that whilst agreeing to naming our previous cat 'Bog Off' (modified to Boggy once we had the children), she refused to allow me to call this pair 'For Sale' and 'Cheerio'.

As the road moves away from the sea and into the village of Mistley, I came to Mistley Towers. These two towers, about ten yards apart, are all that remains of what was once the magnificent church of St Mary the Virgin. Built in 1735, it was remodelled by the architect Robert Adam in 1771, at the commission of the wealthy local politician Richard Rigby, who wished to see a church from the windows of his mansion. Rigby had ambitious plans to turn Mistley into a spa town and a suitably grand church was required for the affluent visitors he expected to attract. His plans were however never brought to fruition. Funds ran out after he was obliged to resign his position as Paymaster of the Forces in 1784, after being unable to account for large sums of public money found in his possession.

A swan fountain in the centre of the village is the only other remaining sign of the lavish plans to develop Mistley into a spa. Behind this is Mistley Quay Workshop, a craft centre and tea room. A short road opposite led to a large village green, on one side of which is a row of small brick terraced cottages with sash windows, and on another some grander houses rendered in an assortment of pastel colours. This is part of a conservation area and is just the sort of tranquil English village scene that deserves protection.

In the centre of the village is The Mistley Thorn, a hotel built in 1723 and more recently notable for being the first pub in Essex to ban smoking. As the county's first entry into the Michelin Bib Gourmand Guide, it retains a reputation for fine food. Travellers sailing up the Stour from Harwich to Sudbury used to stop here overnight and apparently Matthew Hopkins used the former pub on this site to hold some of his witch trials. His ghost is said to have been seen here on several occasions.

Mistley was a port as far back as the 16th century, initially trading in wool, then corn, coal, timber and fish. Walking down to the dock, I was surprised to see two quite large ships berthed and that it is still an active port. It handles vessels up to 3,500 tonnes, which would often find it too costly to use the larger facilities of Harwich and Felixstowe a few miles down the estuary. A wide variety of cargos are unloaded, including sand from Cornwall, aggregates from Ireland, metals from Russia, bricks from Denmark, fertiliser, road salt and grain. With a staff of just 25, Mistley has survived by offering flexibility and service and like other inland ports, helps reduce the number of lorries on our roads. I found it quite surprising, but pleasing, that such a small port is still apparently thriving.

The village used to have an extensive malting business and although now on a much reduced scale, brewing still continues. The impressive maltings buildings on the quayside were

Mistley Towers

refurbished with help from the Prince's Regeneration Trust. In the words of the Prince of Wales, this initiative 'endeavours to release the energy of derelict and abandoned historic buildings to create places where people can live, work and enjoy themselves'. I'm sure that he would be pleased to see that this is being achieved in Mistley.

My plan was to wherever possible follow the coastline, but a sign by the dock informed that access was strictly restricted to authorised persons only, so I returned to the centre of the village. Passing the landward side of the maltings buildings, most of which have been converted to luxury apartments, and continuing past the station, I took a small road on the left. I assumed that this would lead back to the shore. This it did, but once again progress was halted by a notice, this time informing that ahead was a strictly private boat yard and was no public right of way.

Before starting the walk I had decided that my route wouldn't necessarily be constrained by the need to avoid land to which public access is denied (I might accidentally not notice the occasional private sign) and I stood considering whether to ignore the sign. My mind was however quickly made up upon seeing a second notice stating that dogs were loose. I might have been prepared to challenge a 'Trespassers will be Prosecuted' warning, but the prospect of a couple of hungry alsatians viewing me as their legitimate lunch was another matter.

Retracing my steps uphill to the main road, and finding another path on the left, I consulted my map to determine whether it was likely to lead to the shore. This is when I discovered the problem of having an out of date map. Not only was the path not shown, but neither were the houses or the school, which the shouts of young children indicated was nearby. After deciding not to chance this path, and stick to the road, an alleyway soon appeared. This time I followed it for a while. However after passing the school where children were enjoying their lunch break, I concluded that as there was no sign of a bridge over the railway cutting, this too was not heading to the sea

Steps retraced and map consulted once more, I followed the road for a mile and a half, to where a path was clearly indicated crossing the railway and heading to the shore. I had expected to walk on the sea wall for the whole way today and an uphill climb along a main road, on an increasingly hot day, was not what I had in mind. Stopping briefly and sitting under a tree for shade, I applied the sun cream which I'd only packed at the last minute and which a later look in the mirror showed, should have been put on an hour or two earlier. Invariably I get caught out by the first sunny day of the year, but didn't expect to be getting burnt in late September.

Once over the brow of the hill the walk became more pleasant and without houses or hedges, good views opened up to left and right.

A breeze provided welcome relief from the heat, and necessitated a number of smart movements to keep the hat upon my head. Once I was too slow and it sailed into the road just as a car approached. The driver stopped, but by now it had blown on to the other side and a car approached from this direction too. He kindly halted and I retrieved the said headgear, with smiles all round as we British do so well on such occasions.

Veering left, the road returns to the railway. At the site of the old Bradfield station, which closed in 1956, a level crossing leads to a grassy track to Nether Hall. I wasn't sure if there was a way through to the sea from here, so took then next path a few yards further on. This went under the railway, but as it approached the sea become rather overgrown. With vegetation spreading from both sides, it appeared that few people come this way. A sign indicated a footpath to the right along the shore, although initially in the absence of any discernable path I had to jump across mud and pools, until reaching a curved shingle beach. Dead jelly fish marked the high water line and a solitary yacht was moored in the bay. Beyond the beach was a small promontory, indicated as marsh on the map, but interspersed with narrow paths. I sat here for a while, enjoying the view, the solitude and the lunch I'd purchased back in Manningtree.

From here the path was good and ran along the shore for a mile and a half or so. This was very pleasant walking, with good views in all directions, abundant birdlife and perfect weather, yet I was the only person there to enjoy it. I recognised a group of oyster catchers with their long orange beaks, but was ashamed to admit an inability to name most of the other birds. I decided to bring binoculars and a book with me next time. Mud leaping was sometimes necessary and at one point I had to almost crawl under a willow tree, suggesting that at high tides the path may not be passable.

The impressive buildings of the Royal Hospital School stood out across the water. Originally for the sons of officers and men from the Royal Navy and Royal Marines, the school moved to its Suffolk site in 1933. Previously it was housed at Greenwich in what is now the National Maritime Museum. It was initially coeducational, but female pupils were removed in its early history, apparently due to their 'demonic influences' and it wasn't until the 1990s that girls were allowed back.

A signpost marked 'Essex Way' pointed inland and another sign indicated that this was Wrabness Nature Reserve. The site had been a naval mine depot until 1921 and Ministry of Defence activity continued until 1963, when it was passed to the Home Office. Several attempts were made to develop the land, including building a prison, but in 1992 it was purchased by the Wrabness Nature Reserve Charitable Trust, following a local appeal. Buying threatened land has always seemed to me to be the obvious way to protect it, so I was pleased to read how these 52 acres had been saved for the enjoyment of all. Soon after I visited, the Essex Wildlife Trust completed purchase of the reserve, ensuring continued protection under its most capable stewardship for future generations.

An information board tells visitors that this is an important habitat for birds, animals and plants. Nightingales and warblers breed here, and the varied plant life, including hairy buttercup, ox-eye daisy and sea aster, attracts many butterflies and moths. Particular mention was made of the cinnabar moth, the little red chap with bright red and black colouring, who we see in our gardens in early summer. Whilst it was too late in the year for the cinnabars, I did have a dance with a butterfly. A red admiral sunning itself on the path, came close to becoming an ex butterfly beneath my feet. He obviously didn't trust me to stop in time and flew directly upwards, causing me to sway and almost overbalance. Seeing this he decided to fly the other way, requiring further avoiding action as I ducked and dodged while he fluttered around my face. To any onlookers my movements must have appeared as

Stour Estuary - Wrabness

distinctly odd behaviour. Fortunately however the butterfly was
the sole witness and I don't think he'll tell.

Alongside the paved path through the reserve were numerous
blackberries, just at the ripe and ready to pick stage. I ate a few,
but suspected that most will end up as juicy meals for birds, rather
than accompanying apple in pies for human consumption.
Leaving the paved route which leads to the reserve car park, I
turned left, passing two small freshwater ponds and headed back
to the shore, where for a short distance the path followed the sea
wall.

The Essex Way then moves inland through Oakfield Wood Nature
Reserve, but preferring to remain close to the sea I took to the
beach. Walking here wasn't very easy – a choice between soft dry
sand into which every footstep sunk a couple of inches, or wet

sand, which whilst appearing the be hard, nevertheless caused each footstep to sink the same two inches. I passed an assortment of rather grand beach huts, raised on stilts above the sand, all of which appeared to be unoccupied despite the lovely weather. It was one of those days when one could truly say there wasn't a cloud in the sky. Continuing beneath cliffs to a slipway just before the next headland, I took a path which soon rejoined The Essex Way.

A sign warned that this section of coast was subject to erosion, although at 3 feet above the beach the possibility of it causing someone to fall to an untimely end appeared remote. Still I was warned, as I'm sure would have been pointed out in court should I have chosen to sue for any grievous injury caused by land disappearing beneath my feet.

Turning away from the sea at the chestnut trees of East Grove, I followed the path up the hill into Wrabness. It had been my intention to continue to Harwich, but the walk had been longer than anticipated in both distance and time. I was hot and thirsty, and to quote Bill Bryson (if he doesn't mind), 'The trick of successful walking is knowing when to stop'. Had my feet been able to express an opinion, there's no doubt they would have concurred, and the lack of a map for the route ahead was ample justification to finish here.

I arrived at Wrabness station 63 minutes before the next train, which for an hourly service is a mite unfortunate. Checking the timetable, not only had I just missed the 16.12, but the next train was the only one of the day to run slightly later (to accommodate the boat train from Harwich). Still, my map indicated a pub near the station and a large drink was definitely in order. Here I learned the second lesson as to why relying on a twenty year old map is not ideal. What appeared to have once been the pub, was now a private house, and another calling itself 'The Old Post Office' was presumably the post office indicated on the map. There was nowhere for the hungry or thirsty traveller to gain sustenance. The whole place was deserted, perhaps a sign of what happens when a village loses its services.

With time to kill, I sought out Wrabness church. This small Norman building is unusual in that its bells stand in the graveyard, having fallen to the ground in the seventeenth century. According to local legend, the reason for the bell cage being sited in the churchyard is due to satanic interference. Each time the steeple was rebuilt the Devil came in the night and blew it down, so it was decided to hang the bells at ground level. What with the witches at Manningtree, the schoolgirls at Holbrook and the bells at Wrabness, the old devil used to be pretty busy in these parts.

Scanning the map however, I was unable to find any indication of a church in the vicinity. After following Rectory Road for a while, with no sign of either a place of worship, or the vicar's abode, I gave up and returned to spend a pleasant half an hour sitting in the attractive station garden. Studying the map as I awaited my train, I noticed that some way from the station, a small cross was marked, which I recalled from Scouting days signified 'church without tower or spire'. The map's key confirmed my recollection. It does however seem a little unjust that simply for lacking a tower or steeple, the Ordnance Survey relegate the symbol of what might nevertheless be a fine building to less prominence than that of a glasshouse, triangulation pillar, windmill (with or without sails), or even a public convenience (in rural areas). Observing however that public conveniences in non rural areas don't appear to have a symbol at all, I made a note to investigate this further in some future idle moment, hopefully before I had need to use one.

No other passengers either left or joined the 16.18. This took just nine minutes back to Manningtree, from whence I had departed some five hours earlier, although I had walked almost double its direct route of 5¾ miles. My Essex Coast Walk was underway.

CHAPTER TWO

# WRABNESS to HARWICH

(11 miles)
4th October

The day didn't start well. Attempting to check my emails at a computer terminal on Liverpool Street station, I inserted a pound coin, followed the instructions and stared for several minutes at a static screen, until a message popped up saying that it was ever so sorry, but due to technical problems the machine was unable to connect me. Please come back later it advised, but I somehow doubted it would have remembered that pound it owed me. Opting against reporting the theft to a nearby pair of police officers, and reluctantly deciding that giving the machine a retaliatory, but a well deserved kick may have been viewed dimly by the said boys in blue, I headed off once more for the 10.00 to Norwich.

Having planned to sample One Railway's kippers for breakfast, I was disappointed to find that the advertised restaurant service was not available. The gentleman serving in the buffet had no idea why, and I had to make do with a rather mediocre croissant. Realising that this was unlikely to sustain me until reaching Harwich, I hurriedly left the train and purchased some lunch on the station concourse. Later I enquired of the guard, who explained that the usual electric engine had been replaced by a diesel and that it didn't have sufficient power to operate the restaurant car. I wasn't entirely convinced that cooking a couple of kippers would have caused the whole train to grind to a halt, but his cheery manner and friendly Australian accent dissuaded me from questioning his explanation.

Once again I was the sole passenger using Wrabness station. Here there is only one exit and passengers using the Harwich bound platform have to cross the tracks, making sure of course that no trains are approaching. There is a little coloured light which shows red when one's coming, but whilst I found the arrangement perfectly adequate, I was surprised that the health & safety authority allow it. A few years ago the safety authority insisted that a million pound footbridge be built to enable passengers to cross the track at the rural Welsh station of Knighton, where just four trains a day pass in each direction. At Wrabness where there are at least two passenger trains an hour plus regular freights, there is apparently no need for such a bridge.

And so to the main business of the day. Turning left out the station, crossing the railway bridge, and following the path downhill, I was soon back at the point I'd left the coast two weeks ago. The path towards Harwich runs alongside the river estuary for a mile or so, passing through the edge of East Grove and north of Stour Wood, until reaching Copperas Wood. This was just the sort of path I had been looking forward to. Sea on one side, countryside on the other, easy walking and ideal weather. It is part of the Essex Way, a long distance footpath of some 81 miles, running from Harwich to Epping. I passed a couple walking with their dog. Serious walkers with rucksacks, rather than locals taking Fido for a stroll. We exchanged pleasantries, remarking on the loveliness of the weather, as you do.

Copperas Wood is an Essex Wildlife Trust reserve, although a sign by the sea said RSPB. It is a Site of Scientific Interest with mainly hornbeam and sweet chestnut trees. The wood was severely damaged in the great storm of 1987 and some devastated sections have been left untouched for scientific study and wildlife value. Reintroduction of coppicing when the Trust bought the wood in 1980 has allowed a varied woodland flora to flourish, including red campion, yellow archangel and muscatel. Finding the latter an interesting sounding name, I looked it up on my return, learning that it is a delicate perennial with musk like scent and green flowers. Coppicing is the ancient art of cutting of trees to ground level, which leads to vigorous regrowth and a sustainable supply of timber for future generations. Trees and shrubs that are cut down this way can produce shoots that grow over 30cm in a week and a coppiced tree can live many times longer than if it had not been cut. In the past rural economies depended on coppicing, but the practice largely died out, until being revived in recent years by conservation bodies, enabling many of our woods to come alive once more. A hundred species of birds are said to visit Copperas Wood and 43 to nest here, including nightingales and all three UK species of woodpecker. The wood is home to 23 species of butterfly, including the interestingly named purple hairstreak and the only place in Essex where the white admiral butterfly is known to occur.

According to the map the path runs along the edge of the wood, but in fact it goes through the middle, crossing the railway, and coming out on the Wrabness Road. Here I turned left, following the road for half a mile, before taking the footpath on the right, heading directly away from the coast. There isn't a path by the sea for this section and although a slightly shorter option was available by road, I preferred to stay on the Essex Way, which here was an easy path running along the edge of a recently ploughed field.

I paused for lunch beside a small pond, which was virtually covered with bulrushes and holding very little water. It was one of those perfect days, with warm sunshine, a gentle breeze and cotton wool clouds that added to the scene, but none of which had the impertinence to interrupt the sun's rays. With views across fields to the village of Ramsey, its windmill and church, this was as delightful an English rural vista as one could wish for as accompaniment to lunch.

The footpath continued directly across a ploughed field, which was fine in this dry weather, but wouldn't be so easy after rain. It crossed a stile into a field divided into enclosures by temporary white fencing, each of which held a horse or two. A sign here indicated the footpath went right. Instinct however took me left and although for a short distance there was no obvious path, a sign at the next stile confirmed that this was the correct choice. It seemed that whoever is responsible for the Essex Way has decided to follow the traditional policy of road signing, and show information only at every other junction, providing a challenge to those attempting to follow the route.

A clear path heads downhill to the village of Ramsey, passing Ramsey Windmill, which is on private land, so not accessible to the public. It is a post mill, so named because the body pivots on a central post. This enables the miller to keep the sails facing the wind by swinging the whole building round by means of a large beam known as a tail pole. It's the sort of mill that Windy Miller used to run in Camberwick Green, but without the intrinsic safety hazard that meant he had to time his exit from the front door to miss the sails that swished across its entrance. This is a common Suffolk design, with a three storey roundhouse, and in fact originated at Woodbridge, being brought by boat from the Suffolk town in 1842. It last worked in 1939 and was restored by volunteers in the 1970s.

Ramsey is a pleasant village, strung out along one road, 'The Street'. Two men were whitewashing a cottage, and that was pretty well the only sign of life. There is however a pub, The Castle Inn, with tables outside, but I resisted the temptation to stop. Instead, making use of a bench thoughtfully provided on the island in the

Ramsey Windmill

road, I consulted my newly purchased map. The Essex Way appeared to continue through the village, but closer examination showed that despite no signs to this effect, it actually turned right, resuming the far side of the main A120 Harwich Road. This route took it to the easterly shore of the peninsular, however that would have missed several miles of coast. I therefore went north, taking the first of two paths which leave the road on the right hand side at the end of the village. My advice to anyone wishing to walk the Essex Way is not to rely on signage, and to take a good map. I was very glad that I had decided to terminate my last walk at Wrabness, rather than continue to Harwich without one.

Again the path ran along the edge of the field, turning right by the appropriately named White Cottage, into what the map indicated was Ray Lane and part of the 'E2 European Long Distance Route'. Putting the Essex Way to shame, this runs an impressive 4,850 kilometres from Scotland to Nice, going south from Holland after crossing the North Sea at Harwich. I assume that the sea bit isn't included in the total length. Only a couple of miles were marked on my map, and I saw no signs mentioning it, maybe explaining why it appears to be so little known. A more imaginative name might help, but no doubt it took a small army of Brussels bureaucrats many hours of meetings to come up with E2.

Other than passing a sewage works, with its characteristic aroma, the path made for pleasant walking, and I paused only to snack on the plentiful blackberries in the hedgerows. On the far side of Ramsey Creek huge lorries trundled along the A120 towards Harwich docks. Although probably no louder than the tractors working away in the fields, their noise was unwelcome. An intrusion rather than a genuine element of the rural scene.

Countryside changed to golf course on the right, and to the left an oil refinery behind a high barbed wire fence indicated that I was approaching Harwich. At least thirty large storage tanks and a maze of pipe work separated me from the main works of the refinery. Nevertheless a slight smell of petroleum was detectable in the air. A sign warned that should I choose to steal any oil I may face forfeiture of my tanker. I wondered whether this rule would apply to a more conservative thief who might just take a bucketful. I was pleased to see that the refinery had an active rail connection, with a long line of tank wagons in a siding, each one of which would otherwise had meant yet another lorry on the roads.

My pen having run out, I sought a replacement at the port of Harwich. The grandly named 'Food Villa', serving the Scandinavian bound ships, claimed to have a shop as well as a bureau de change, and café serving hot food. All I could find were a few tables, one of which was occupied by a pair of Scandinavian lorry drivers, a couple of vending machines, a deserted exchange bureau and some toilets. So that this detour was not completely wasted I made use of the latter, before moving on to the Holland ferry terminal. A walking route was thoughtfully marked, although I suspect is rarely used. The security man in a little hut watched my every step, perhaps hoping that I would relieve his boredom by straying from the designated path. The shop inside the ferry terminal was not only closed, but from the empty shell inside, appeared to have been so for some considerable time. However the café not only sold pens, but also some rather good looking chocolate cookies, so I bought one of each. The next ferry wasn't due for four hours and the place was virtually deserted.

As the best natural haven on England's east coast, and accessible at all tides, Harwich's role as a departure point for ships carrying passengers and mail to The Netherlands goes back to the sixteenth century. It is still one of the country's most important deep water ports. Harwich International, the more modern, but less appealing name given to Harwich and Parkeston Quay in 1995, was built by the Great Eastern Railway on the reclaimed marshland of Ray Island. Opening in 1883, initially with a weekly sailing to Holland, it soon became Britain's most important passenger port. A year later a service commenced to Antwerp and soon a prestigious contract to carry the Royal Mail was won.

The port was requisitioned by the military in the Second World War, when it was known as HMS Badger and during which time it received considerable bomb damage. Expansion continued after the war, with substantial modernisation taking place in the 1970s. Whilst best known for the route to Hook of Holland, three passenger ferries a week also depart for the sixteen hour trip to Ebsjerg in Sweden. A service to Cuxhaven at the mouth of the Elbe, sadly closed in 2005, removing a useful option for those wishing to travel to northern Germany without flying, now at last accepted as the most environmentally damaging way to travel.

The main port is actually 2½ miles from the town of Harwich, linked by both railway and the busy A120 road. Whilst the former was inviting, the latter was far from it, and on exiting the port complex I decided to follow a sign for the North Sea Cycle Route, a 269 mile route from Harwich to Hull. This indicated 3 miles to Old Harwich and I rightly assumed that this would make more pleasant walking than the side of a busy main road. It took me down a couple of residential side streets, across a grassy area, then alongside the A120 for a short distance, to a small retail park. The cycle route was well signposted at a series of roundabouts, the first of which had its central island covered with pebbles all painted blue. This started me thinking. What would be the more attractive; natural colour stones or ones that are painted a nice blue? I came to the conclusion that to use naturally blue stones would be best of all.

I adhered to the cycle route, although not without hesitation where it headed directly away from Harwich, and was eventually proved correct when it took me down a slope onto an old railway track. This was the original railway into the town, the line being diverted to the north when the port was built at Parkeston. With a deep cutting and a canopy of trees, it looked just the sort of location for a Crimewatch re-enactment, and I was mildly surprised to pass several young girls walking home alone from school or college. Two lads passed me on bikes, one saying a cheery hello, which quite amazed me as where I live most teenagers merely grunt.

As I had hoped, this route was far more pleasant than walking on a busy road and after about a mile it emerged at Dovercourt station. Here, where the old railway rejoined the current track, the cycle route turned right towards Dovercourt Bay and the pretty way into Harwich. Wishing to stay near the north coast, I crossed the footbridge and continued along a raised path, running on the far side of a residential street. I passed Harwich Town station, the line's terminus, although a rusty set of rails continued across the road. These stopped abruptly at the wall of Trinity House Buoy Shed. This impressive new building, which was opened in 2005, has the rather mundane job of storing and maintaining buoys. I thought it deserved a rather more glamorous purpose and certainly a name more befitting its design than 'shed'. It was built on the approach to the train ferry terminal, where wagons were shunted onto the decks of ferries bound for Zeebrugge. This closed in 1987, but the wharf with its ramp that rises and falls with the water to allow the railway to connect with the slip, is now a listed building.

From here the road runs alongside the harbour, where I was pleased to see a pair of small fishing boats, although sadly these are now more or less the total of a once thriving fishing fleet. A foot ferry service runs to Felixstowe from the Ha'Penny Pier, so called because that was the toll set for admittance when it was completed in 1854. The visitor centre on the pier was closed for the winter, so I had to make do with a plaque for information. This is on a wall facing the road, separated from the thundering lorries by about four feet of pavement. As I stepped back to read it an elderly gentleman nearby shouted a warning, concerned that I was going to keep reversing and meet a nasty end beneath the wheels of a juggernaut. Despite being fully aware of my position, I thanked him kindly, and he was able to go home thinking he'd saved a man's life. Opposite the pier is a plaque commemorating the Mayflower, which set sail from Harwich for America in 1620. Its master, Christopher Jones, was a local lad, although after marrying his second wife had moved to Rotherhithe some 17 years prior to the voyage.

Behind the harbour is Harwich Redoubt, a circular fort built in 1809 to support Landguard Fort on the opposite shore near Felixstowe. Seventy yards in diameter, it is surrounded by a deep ditch and can only be entered by one removable drawbridge. The original ten cannons were replaced by three 9 inch guns in 1872, one of which is still in place. The others are thought to be buried in the moat. The fort was abandoned in the 1920s, but taken over by the Harwich Society in 1969, thanks to whom it is now fully restored.

I was pleasantly surprised by Harwich, which maintains a flavour of its medieval seafaring past, with many well preserved old buildings. However without losing this atmosphere the town has managed to incorporate two new buildings for Trinity House, the lighthouse authority which has its headquarters here. A few yards further on is a new lifeboat station, then Navyard Wharf, a former naval yard. This is the only part of Harwich Old Town to be excluded from the conservation area. A large notice board lists ships built here from 1660 to 1826, and whilst no longer constructing navy ships, it is still an active dockyard, handling vessels up to 200 metres in length.

Along Kings Quay Street is the Electric Palace. Built in 1911 in only 18 weeks and at a cost of £1,500, this is the oldest unaltered, purpose built cinema in Britain. The first film to be shown here was 'The Battle of Trafalgar', a silent movie with live musical accompaniment and sound effects, for which the best seats cost a shilling. It closed down in 1956, partly due to the effect of being under eight feet of sea water in the Great East Coast Floods. However following almost a decade of conservation work it reopened as a community cinema in 1981.

Shortly after Naval House, the 19th century residence of the Master of the Royal Naval Dockyard, I came upon the attractive Angel Gate courtyard, surrounded by old brick houses. Continuing past Harwich Sailing Club (not to be confused with Royal Harwich Yacht Club, which moved out of the town in 1946),

I walked down to the sand and shingle beach. This is said to be one of the best places in the country for finding fossilised shark's teeth. I had a quick look, as my youngest son would have been delighted to own one, but my brief search was unsuccessful.

Above the beach is the smaller of Harwich's lighthouses, an octagonal tower 30 feet high, fittingly named the Low Lighthouse, and now the home of Harwich Maritime Museum. This opens only on summer Sunday afternoons. An earlier wooden lighthouse was painted by John Constable in 1815. The High Lighthouse, also octagonal, and built from brick, is slightly inland. Both were constructed in 1818 and designed so that ships entering the harbour could align one light above the other, in order to follow the safe channel into the harbour. This worked well until the course of the deep water channel changed and both lights became redundant. The High Lighthouse is a handsome tower and houses the National Wireless and Television Museum. I would have liked both to have seen the museum and climbed the tower, but it is open only from Easter to the end of September. A sign at the foot of the lighthouse indicated that this was the start of the Essex Way footpath, and that Epping was 81 miles distant.

On the green beside the beach is a strange contraption known as a treadmill crane. This was built in the 17th century in the nearby dockyard and operated by two men walking inside a pair of wheels, hamster style. Lacking any braking system, if a heavy load ever started to go out of control, those within the wheels faced a distinctly unpleasant spin.

With thirty minutes before my train, I had a quick walk round the town centre. I sought a snack for the journey home and hoped that the profusion of buildings of historical and aesthetic interest on the waterfront would continue inland. On the former I was wholly unsuccessful, with the few shops closed and in any case selling items with a limited market – mobile phones, bicycles, car spares etc. However on the latter I was well pleased. St Nicholas

Treadmill Crane - Harwich

church, a yellow brick gothic structure, was built in 1822, and is the largest building in the district. It was however fortunate to survive a near miss from a First World War Zeppelin bomb. The Georgian Guildhall, dating from 1769, is the only Grade One listed building in the town, and the council chambers can be viewed when open, which it wasn't today. The oldest house in Harwich is The Foresters, built in 1450, and restored after severe damage from one of the many Second World War bombing raids which targeted the town due to its naval connections and importance as a port. The Harwich Society has its base in The Foresters and must be congratulated for its role in preserving so much of the town. I had time just for the briefest of looks at The Three Cups pub, reputedly visited by Lord Nelson, before catching the 4.00 train. Harwich, I had found to be a very well conserved, likeable and interesting town. I decided to return one day with the family, but preferably in the summer, when everything would not be closed.

# CHAPTER THREE

# HARWICH to GREAT OAKLEY

(8 miles)
27th November


A sunny autumn had given way to a wild and damp start to winter, before I was able to leave the glue factory and resume walking. Checking the BBC five day weather forecast before booking the day off work, it showed a big smiley sun over Harwich. However by the night before, talk was of heavy rain, storm force winds and floods. Just light rain for the mile walk to Upminster station helped dispel my wife's doubts regarding my sanity. Her view was that one of sound mind would not venture onto deserted coasts in such weather.

Today I got my kippers for breakfast. One Railway's menu promised 'Whole wood smoked Lowestoft kippers, grilled to perfection and topped with butter' and quite superb they were. By Manningtree the proverbial cats and dogs were falling from the sky, so I passed the half hour wait with a drink that allowed me access to the warm and dry buffet. Privately run, this is more of a pub than a buffet and a real asset to the station.

This was to be my last journey on the 'Mayflower Line', as the Harwich branch is now branded. As usual I sat on the left hand side, which affords fine views across the Stour Estuary. By

Harwich the rain had relented a little, so suitably protected with waterproof, leggings and hat, I made my way past the High Lighthouse and once more to the shore. A container ship was turning slowly, ready to head out into the North Sea and some unknown destination beyond. A long breakwater, built by the Victorians in an attempt to stop shifting sands from silting up the port, marks the end of the Stour Estuary and start of the sea proper. It was also the point of a sharp change in direction of my walk. So far I had been heading due east, but from here the predominant bearing was south west. As it was marking a minor milestone on the journey, I felt I should walk to the end, but with wind blowing and rain failing, was not that disappointed to find a sign warning of danger. It was a nice polite sign too, not a 'Keep Off' instruction, but a more gentle request, 'For your own safety please keep off breakwater'. As it had asked so nicely, I obeyed.

Six miles out into the North Sea, and visible from here on a clear

North Sea - Harwich

day, lies an unlikely, but fascinating tale of British eccentricity and defiance. Roughs Tower was one of a series of sea forts built to repel German air raids in the Second World War, but subsequently abandoned by the military. On 2nd September 1967, Paddy Roy Bates, a former British Army Major, occupied the fort, settling with his family and proclaiming it as his own state, the Principality of Sealand. Bestowing upon himself the title of Prince Roy of Sealand and that of Princess to his wife, Bates and others who have declared loyalty to Sealand have occupied it ever since.

In 1968 the British navy were sent to regain the fort, but retreated after warning shots were fired from Sealand, in response to what they considered to be an incursion into their territorial waters. Still being an English citizen, Bates was summoned to appear at Chelmsford Crown Court, but the judge ruled that the court could not hear his case as it had no jurisdiction outside British national territory. This was not only a victory for Prince Roy, but provided recognition that Sealand was not a part of the United Kingdom. As it was not claimed by any other nation, the Judge's ruling effectively upheld Sealand's declaration as a new Sovereign State.

On 1st October 1987 Britain extended its territorial waters from 3 to 12 nautical miles, which would have brought the fort back into British jurisdiction, had it not been for Prince Roy the previous day also extending Sealand's own territorial limit to 12 nautical miles. As no treaty had been signed between Britain and Sealand, the normal international convention of dividing the area between two countries down the middle can be assumed. The British Government therefore has no more rights to claim Sealand, than does Prince Roy to the Port of Harwich.

In an even more bizarre turn of events, in 1978 Sealand went to war. A group of Dutchmen visited the Principality, apparently to discuss business on behalf of a German businessman. However, whilst Prince Roy was away in England, they kidnapped his son and took Sealand by force. Roy assembled a party of his own men and recaptured the island, holding the attackers as prisoners of war. The Dutch government petitioned for their release, which Roy granted under the Geneva Convention on the grounds that the war was over. The German he however held onto, as he had accepted a Sealand passport, so was considered guilty of treason. The German government sent a diplomat to negotiate for the release of their citizen, who Prince Roy eventually allowed to leave, and there have been no further attempts to oust him, although shots were fired again in 1990 when a ship strayed too close to the old fort.

Sealand was founded on the principle that any group of people dissatisfied with what they consider as the oppressive laws of existing nation states, may declare independence in any place not claimed to be under the jurisdiction of another sovereign entity. Its de facto recognition by other nations appears to have proved the validity of this aim, and despite a serious fire in 2006, Sealand continues to thrive, now hosting blossoming offshore internet businesses.

Passing beneath Beacon Hill, on which remain a number of watch towers and gun emplacements dating from 1870 to the Second World War, I soon reached Dovercourt. Adjacent to Harwich, but notably more lively, there has been a settlement here since prehistoric times and the town is mentioned in the Domesday Book. Halfway along the long promenade I turned into the town, where there is a small but busy shopping centre. Of interest is Kingsway Hall, a grade two listed building, built in 1874 in Italian style, and still used as a centre for arts, music and drama.

In the mid eighteenth century, John Bagshaw the MP for Harwich, and wealthy East India merchant, had ambitious plans to develop Dovercourt. It was to be a new town with terraces and gardens to rival Brighton. He was however bankrupted by the venture and only Orwell Terrace was completed. This line of impressive white buildings, with listed status, considerably enhances the character of the town. Cliff Gardens, between Marine Parade and beach are another legacy of Bagshaw's design and contribute to what is a little changed and pleasant sea front.

Continuing along the promenade, I reached the two Dovercourt lighthouses, the tallest at the top of the beach and the other at the end of a short rocky breakwater. Like those at Harwich, these were a pair of 'leading lights', which ships could position one above the other to steer a safe course to harbour. Built by Trinity House in 1863, they superseded the Harwich pair, which had been made redundant by changes in the harbour entrance channel. The cast iron structures, containing powerful gas lamps, were originally mounted on movable bases so they could be re-aligned as the channel moved. The lights were used until 1917, when the harbour entrance was buoyed, but remain as impressive and well preserved iron structures. A sign on the tallest indicated that they had been restored in 1983 with help of grant aid and generous public support. Ironically the one thing now looking in need of restoration was this very sign, which was barely legible from lack of paint.

By now the rain had stopped and dog walkers started to appear on the previously deserted promenade. A long line of beach huts, painted in an array of colours, and behind them a recreational area with sports pitches, boating lake and swimming pool, marked the end of the town. Close by used to be Warner's Holiday Camp, which became 'Maplins' for filming the exterior scenes for the 1980s BBC sitcom 'Hi-de-Hi'. The camp, which had accommodated 850 holiday makers, and had been used as a military base in World War Two, was demolished soon after filming and is now a housing estate.

Turning right, the path continuing alongside the shore is the Essex Way, with views across Pennyhole Bay to Walton-on-the-Naze. There is a campaign to establish an official naturist beach in this area. However checking their website, some 10 months after

Lower Lighthouse - Dovercourt

launching just one person had registered his support, so I suspect that anyone wishing to bare all will still have to do so on a purely unofficial basis.

With more shelter here, there were noticeably more birds, and I soon spotted a curlew busily poking about by the sea. This is Europe's largest wading bird and easily recognisable by its long down-curved bill, which it uses to probe mud for its favourite foods of worms, shellfish, crabs and shrimps. It breeds in spring and early summer, preferring damp upland pastures and moorlands, but winters on the coast. Here it feeds on exposed mudflats and sand, moving to salt marsh and nearby fields at high tide. There is concern at reducing numbers due to changes in agricultural practice, but Hamford Water makes an ideal habitat.

Upper Lighthouse - Dovercourt

The Essex Way follows the high sea wall, inland of the salt marsh around South Hall Creek. Paved as far as the entrance to a caravan park, it then became quite muddy. A drier path ran below the sea wall and in the interest of more rapid progress I took this option for a while. A lone coot patrolled the fresh water channel running alongside, which shielded from the wind and sea, was dead still and silent.

Hamford Water is a large basin, extending four miles inland and largely filled with islands, tidal creeks, sand, mudflats and salt marsh. It could be described as a 'riverless estuary', being fed by just three small brooks and is sometimes referred to as the 'Walton Backwaters'. The creeks and islands were the setting for Arthur Ransome's book Secret Water. This quiet and remote area is managed by English Nature and the Essex Wildlife Trust. It is of international importance for its populations of waders and wildfowl that feed here in winter and of national importance for its resident breeding birds. Its wide range of habitats and plants support large numbers of invertebrates. The basin is home to an impressive list of wintering birds populations, including avocet, teal, shelduck, dark-bellied brent geese, black-tailed godwit, ringed and grey plover and redshank. As one of the last remaining areas of its type worldwide, Hamford Water is a hugely important site and attracts much interest from birdwatchers and conservationists.

The area supports one of Britain's rarest coastal plants, sea hogs fennel, which highlights an excellent example of the interdependence of species and the potential catastrophic effect upon them from global warming. A large and attractive plant, growing up to five feet tall, with feathery leaves and yellow flowers, sea hogs fennel is the exclusive foodplant of the Fisher's estuarine moth. This attractive moth, quite large and pale orange-brown in colour, is entirely reliant on the sea hogs fennel, where its caterpillars live, remaining hidden until they emerge in September as adult moths. The only UK populations are around Hamford Water, and there is concern that rising sea levels will force out the sea hogs fennel, which whilst growing in coastal areas, is not salt water tolerant. To safeguard both the sea hogs fennel and the Fisher's estuarine moth, Essex Biodiversity Project are working with Essex Wildlife Trust to encourage it to grow on higher land, away from the rising sea. There must be thousands of similar examples across the world, many on a far larger scale and not all with the good fortune to have environmentalists working to preserve them. Each time we jump in our cars for an unnecessary journey, turn up the heating, or leave a light on, we are contributing to the eventual demise of so many species, be they humble moths or noble polar bears.

The Essex Way heads off inland to Little Oakley, but I continued on the sea wall, now heading once more towards the shore. The sun came out for a few minutes, highlighting the pristine whiteness of a swan against the dark waters of the channel to my right. I stopped for lunch, sitting on the thick carpet of shells at the top of Irlam's Beach. The Naze was now only a couple of miles across the water, but such is the size and irregularity of Hamford Water, it would take a walk of at least five times this length to reach it.

I walked along the beach, exploring what appeared to be the remains of some sort of jetty, and upon returning was somewhat surprised to find a gentleman relieving himself against the sea wall. After averting my gaze to allow him to finish without embarrassment, I climbed back up to the path, where his wife, who strangely was carrying two large shopping bags, asked me if they could get back this way. Having ascertained that back meant returning to Harwich, and wondering why the question if they had come this way, I explained that it was not possible to do so by way of the beach. Warning of the mud and creek barring their way, I carefully described the route along the sea wall. We parted in opposite directions, me on the sea wall path, and them on the beach, going just the way I had told them not to. There were no news reports that night of a pair of lost shoppers being gobbled up by Essex mud, so I assume they got back safely.

The wall now ran alongside the sea. This stretch being high and concrete, was not attractive, but easier to walk on. At the end of the section the defences had recently been fortified with extra rocks and concrete blocks, the work having left the banks muddy and bereft of grass. I was soon to find out the reason for this reinforcement.

The sea wall once again took the long route inland of a large area of salt marsh. With a myriad of tiny islands interspersed with a maze of channels, this looked on the map like a pair of lungs, the blue channels acting as bronchioles. The right hand lung was attached to the shore. The left, the other side of Dugmore Creek, was made up of Pewit and New Islands. A sign indicated that land was owned and managed by Little Oakley and District Wildfowlers Association, which is responsible for 1,000 acres of the northern shore of Hamford Water. The notice was somewhat confused, asking people to keep to footpaths, to beware of strong currents and deep mud, then adding a more definite 'Keep Off'. Some of the mud looked the sort that could easily swallow a person up and I needed no persuasion to keep away.

Although there had been no more rain, the wet grass had made the bottoms of my jeans wet and the dampness was now approaching my knees. My feet were uncomfortable and soaked, not helped by inadequate footwear. Several years of living at the back of the cupboard had for some unexplained reason caused my walking boots to shrink, so it had been necessary to choose between ill fitting boots and two pairs of trainers. Neither of these was at that nice comfortable, mid life stage. One was past their best, with worn soles, and the other not quite run in to maximum comfort. I had selected the latter, but today had confirmed the need for some new boots, which my good wife had already promised for Christmas.

After about a mile the path came to a small slipway, with a rather rickety raised wooden walkway heading out into the creek. A seat had been provided by the local wildfowlers in memory of Albert Allcock, and I was glad to make use of it for a few minutes. Continuing past an area of mud charmingly named 'Bulls Ooze', I met a couple walking in the opposite direction. The gentleman told me that I would be able to go no further than a fence some 100 yards ahead and should turn back. Enquiring as to why, he said that it was 'Hush hush', but seemed distinctly unwilling to give further information. He added however that the recent sea defence strengthening I had seen was to prevent the water getting in, and poisoning the North Sea. Naturally my curiosity meant that turning back was not an option, so I continued to the fence, which signs made it very clear that one should not pass. This was not your usual Keep Off or Trespassers Will Be Prosecuted:

## YOU ARE APPROACHING A RESTRICTED AREA

This is not a public right of way or footpath.
You are strongly advised to return the way
you came as trespassers caught anywhere
in this area will be prosecuted under the
Explosives Act of 1875 and 1923

It would clearly have been unwise to continue and even my desire to make a defiant quick hop over the fence and back was thwarted by many strands of barbed wire. Consulting the map I realised that this was a major blow to my plan for the day, which had been to follow the coast as far as Thorpe le Soken. The only option was to turn right, taking a muddy track heading directly away from the sea.

On the path I met an elderly man walking his dog, and enquired of him as to whether he knew why one could not continue along the sea wall. His simple, but unhelpful response was 'Oh yes'. The locals certainly seemed reluctant to let strangers know more of the hidden secret, but I pressed him further. Eventually, maybe realising that despite my camera and note book, I was probably harmless, he elicited that it was an old explosive factory, and still used for storage. Its location, on marshes and a mile from the nearest house, must be ideal. The map shows a number of small buildings, widely spaced so that an explosion in one would not spread to others. The manufacturing process used mercury and there was concern from local fisherman that proposed developments at Harwich Container Port could lead to sea water washing contaminated soil into Hamford Water, affecting the shell fish that are commercially fished there. The port development was given approval in early 2006, so this may have precipitated the recent sea defence work I had seen a mile or so east.

The path took me to the B1414 main road, coming out opposite Little Oakley Hall, a pleasant old house, set back from the road.

A few yards on I turned right, up the drive to the old St Mary's Church, now a private house and painted a rather incongruous pink. A path runs from here along field boundaries, coming out at Great Oakley Hall, where I rejoined the road, soon entering the village of Great Oakley. Although there is relatively new housing on the outskirts, the village centre retains character, with some interesting looking old cottages, a small shop and an attractive looking pub, The Maybush, which is reputedly haunted by a marbles player. A chapel opposite the war memorial had recently been sold, this being the second church in the village no longer used for its original purpose, suggesting a decline of interest in the Good Lord in these parts.

An hourly bus service links Great Oakley with Harwich to the north and Clacton to the south, the bus stopping at the war memorial. Those waiting have to stand, with no seat being provided, something which the local community or council would do well to put right. As is the way with country buses, it soon dived off the main road to serve the villages of Beaumont and Thorpe Green, where no passengers boarded or alighted, before stopping in Thorpe-le-Soken. With forty minutes before the train, I got off in the village, where the driver lectured a group of schoolboys as to the behaviour expected of them before allowing them to board.

Thorpe-le-Soken is a busy village, with interesting stories surrounding two former residents, both of which are outlined in Stan Jarvis's book *Hidden Essex*.

The first concerns a Sir William Gull, born in 1816, the son of John Gull a barge owner in the village. William began his career as a school master in Lewes. His ability was noticed by a Benjamin Harrison, the treasurer of Guy's Hospital, who found him employment at the hospital. Here he became a lecturer and learned physician, being elected as Professor of Physiology in the Royal Institution in 1847. Gull attended to Edward Prince of

Wales during an attack of typhoid in 1871, and was created a baronet for the skill and care he had shown in saving him from what in the days before antibiotics, was frequently a fatal disease. Gull was buried in Thorpe-le-Soken in 1890, however local legend has it that the coffin resting in the churchyard contains nothing but stones to weight it. It is suggested that Sir William was in fact still alive, but locked away in an asylum, under the name of Mason. The reason – that he was Jack the Ripper. Five years after the 'burial' a story appeared in the Chicago Sunday Times-Herald saying that Jack the Ripper had been tracked down by a medium Robert James Lees and found to be a distinguished West-End physician, who was certified insane. The story said that a fake funeral had been held and the physician put in an asylum under the name Thomas Mason.

Some credence was given to there at least being a connection, by an article in *The Criminologist* by Dr Thomas Stowell in 1970. He suggested that Prince Albert Victor, grandson of Queen Victoria, was the Ripper, dismissing the official report of his death from pneumonia, and saying instead that he died of syphilis. This he concluded had driven Albert mad, in which state of mind he carried out the five Jack the Ripper murders. Stowell named private accounts written by Sir William Gull as his source of information. Shortly after his article had been published, Stowell however wrote a letter to *The Times* withdrawing his allegations against the Prince. Just one day after the letter was published Thomas Stowell mysteriously died and further investigation was thwarted when his papers were burned by his family. Whether Gull resides in Thorpe-le-Soken, or whether there were dodgy goings on to protect a deranged Prince, could perhaps be resolved by digging up his coffin, however to this day it remains untouched.

The second tale is one of romance, and concerns a pretty young lady by the name of Kitty Canham. She was born at the nearby Beaumont Hall in 1720, the daughter of a well-to-do local farmer. A stunning young woman, her parents were delighted when she married the Reverend Alexander Gough, the newly appointed vicar of Thorpe-le-Soken. However, bored with life in the vicarage and unhappy in her marriage, Kitty ran off to London, telling no one of her intentions. Here, through remarkably good fortune, she fell into good company and was introduced to Lord Dalmeny, son of the Earl of Rosebury. The two fell in love and entered into a blissfully happy marriage, Kitty having omitted to mention that she was already married to the vicar. Her lifestyle could not have been more different, and the couple spent a four year honeymoon travelling around Europe. Tragically, aged only thirty two, she became ill whist in Verona. Realising that she was soon to die, Kitty confessed her bigamy in a scrawled note which read 'I am the wife of the Reverend Alexander Gough, vicar of Thorpe-le-Soken in Essex. My last request is to be buried at Thorpe'. Such was her new husband's devotion, he granted her wish, having her body embalmed and packed in a special case, which he accompanied on the voyage back to England. Her burial was said to be most poignant, with both husbands consoling each other standing side by side at the graveside in St Mary's church, united in their grief for the pretty Kitty Canham.

CHAPTER FOUR

# GREAT OAKLEY
# to KIRBY-le-SOKEN

(9 miles)
11th December

Sitting in the warm comfort of the train as it pulled out of Colchester, I can admit to a degree of smugness as I looked at people running for cover from torrential rain and wind. Arriving at Thorpe-le-Soken station, to just light drizzle, and with 35 minutes until the bus, I decided to walk into the village and pick it up there. Two minutes down the road, the wind blew up from nowhere and the heavens opened. Not ordinary rain, this was stair rod stuff. The sort that bounces up a couple of inches as it hits the ground. For ten minutes I sheltered as best as I could behind a tree, but bereft of leaves, it offered limited protection. With a slight abatement, I hurried back to the station and waited out of the rain. Now I was wet through and most frustratingly the drenching had been avoidable.

With a disappointing lack of transport integration, the bus doesn't come into the station yard, so you have to wait by the roadside, where neither a seat nor shelter is provided. Aware that buses running ahead of schedule is far from unknown, I walked the 200 yards down to the stop in good time. The small amount of water that may have evaporated from my clothing since the downpour was soon replenished by continuing steady rain. After a while I was joined by a gentleman with a large umbrella. No words were exchanged and we studiously gazed in different directions, lest eye contact should lead to a moment of British awkwardness regarding the possible sharing of the umbrella. His presence at least provided reassurance that a bus should be on its way and five minutes after the due time a purple and white single decker came splashing under the railway bridge.

The run to Great Oakley takes 15 minutes, but with my coat spread out over the seat and trousers drying by the heater (still on my legs I hasten to add), this was one of the rare occasions when you want the bus to halt at every stop and the driver to pull over to count his money (as they invariably do when you're in a rush). Alas drying time today was limited to the timetabled 15 minutes, after which I was only marginally less wet and the weather unchanged.

Alighting opposite the war memorial, I spied the locally hostelry, The Maybush. Thoughts of a warm and dry country pub, hopefully with a blazing fire, a bowl of chips and maybe a home made pie, drew me closer. Perhaps I could have a convivial chat with a genial host. He might even tell me the secrets of the explosive factory. The decision was made. The vision lasted just as long as it took me to walk through the door. It was dark and cold. The hearth was empty. I was the only customer and my enquiry of the landlord as to whether he was serving food was met with a gruff 'not doing food today'. I settled for a quick drink and he settled for continuing to read The Sun. I left after ten minutes.

With light rain still falling I turned left from The Maybush, heading down the narrow lane, then right at a T junction into Pesthouse Lane. This is a 'protected lane', an Essex County Council designation to preserve the traditional character of historic lanes. It is one of three in the surrounds of Great Oakley.

After a short distance I took a footpath which heads left across a grassy field. Three large horses, wrapped up in their winter coats, looked up, surprised to see a human visitor. Crossing a stile, the map shows the path heading across the middle of the next field. However with plenty of mud, but no sign of path, I decided the easiest option was to return to the road and take the long way round.

Continuing along Pesthouse Lane, I turned left at Workhouse Corner, where a 1777 parliamentary report recorded that up to 20 inmates could be accommodated in a workhouse providing shelter and employment of sorts for the poor. A few yards further on my map showed the letters 'Ws' printed in blue, but in another of Ordnance Survey's mysteries, the key showed no explanation as to its designation. Also to remain a mystery was the name 'Cabbage Row' shown on the map to the east of the road. Opposite this a footpath headed into another muddy field, so once again I took the long way by road, although this was not unpleasant with open countryside and glimpses of the distant sea. Ignoring a further footpath which headed straight into a ploughed field, I followed the road down a gentle hill and round a 90 degree bend at Moze Cross.

This is about as close as the road goes to what the map calls 'Great Oakley Works', the mysterious chemical plant that was the reason for this long detour inland. It is situated on Bramble Island, an area of reclaimed marshland protruding into Hamford Water, although with water on only three sides, it is not actually an island at all. The factory was built in 1898 by the High Explosive Company Ltd, who supplied explosives to the Ministry of Defence. In 1905 it was acquired by Exchem, whose company name makes any involvement with explosives less obvious. In fact I found it impossible to find out whether there is still a connection with explosives on this site.

Bramble Island is the base for Exchem Organics, the company's chemical division, which manufactures fine chemicals and fuel additives, but does not deal with explosives. However Exchem PLC has another division, Exchem Explosives, supplying products to the quarrying, mining and demolition industries. Indeed, should you ever want someone to help you blow things up, Exchem Explosives claims to be 'The perfect partner to fulfil all your explosives and blasting requirements'. This division of the company is based in Derbyshire, so is there still any connection with Bramble Island? Exchem's website would suggest not, but if so why the barbed wire fences and warnings to trespassers of dire consequences under the Explosives Acts?

Just beyond Moze Cross a concrete track leaves the road, heading south across open farmland, past New Moze Hall, eventually turning sharp right and stopping abruptly near a small wood. With no path, I squelched my way round the edge of the field bordering the end of the wood, where I came across a disturbing sight. In several small chicken wire cages were wild birds, crows and magpies, obviously unhappy at their confinement and flapping frantically as I approached. The smaller cage held a magpie, with barely room to open its wings, and from the roof hung a long dead and partly eaten rabbit. On the ground next to the cage were several more rabbit carcasses, all hollowed out, presumably having been eaten by birds. Another cage contained two crows and a magpie, with more room than the first, but again looking distressed to be confined. I had no idea why these birds were in cages, but it certainly didn't look like a practice that should be happening and the remote location, a mile from any road and half a mile from the nearest farm, increased my suspicion.

The next day I called the RSPCA. The local inspector phoned me back, asking for exact directions so she could visit. She believed that they were probably larsen traps, which are a legal method used by farmers and gamekeepers to trap birds. Provided they were properly licensed and checked every day, she said there was nothing the RSPCA could do to stop them. Birds are attracted to the cages, either by food or by the presence of another bird, which reassures them that it must be safe, but when they land, a false floor opens, trapping them. Naively I asked what the farmers did when they caught them, to which of course the answer was, kill them. This too is legal provided it is done humanely and not in the view of other birds. Now I wished I'd let the poor birds out and was quite upset to think of their fate when the farmer returned.

The traps are only permitted for the capture of corvids, the family of birds including magpies, crows, jays, jackdaws and rooks, however birds of prey are often also caught. Many instances of cruelty, with birds left to starve, or harm themselves whilst desperately trying to escape, have been recorded. In Denmark where the traps were invented, they are considered inhumane and banned. There is an organisation 'Against Corvid Traps' that campaigns for their abolition. I hope that they are successful.

Leaving these poor birds, but at that time not knowing of the fate that awaited them, I walked along the edge of the next field. The map showed a path here, but none existed. In the corner was a large grassy mound. Obviously man-made, there was no indication of what this was, and neither the map or my research provided any information. From here a path headed to Lower Barn Farm, which houses a number of small workshops, one of which claims to manufacture East Anglia's finest kitchen furniture. At Quay Farm, a more traditional agricultural establishment, a short and very muddy path led through a gap in the hedge to the long disused Beaumont Quay and at last the sea. It had taken me an hour and ten minutes from Great Oakley and adding the last part of my previous walk, the Bramble Island detour meant a couple of hours away from the coast.

Lying in the mud is the wreck of an old wooden barge. The Rose, originally a 42 tonne Thames sailing barge, was launched in 1880, and plied the coast for fifty years before conversion to a lighter (a towed barge with no sail or engine). It has lain here, slowly decaying, since the 1960s. Beaumont Quay, which was built in 1832 using stones taken from the old London Bridge, saw flourishing trade in the 19th century, once boasting a 600 tonne coal store, a large granary, lime kiln and its own stables. The granary was demolished as unsafe in the 1960s, but the well preserved limekiln remains. This is the most westerly point of Hamford Water, and the head of Beaumont Cut, a man-made channel constructed to allow heavily laden barges sufficient depth of water to reach to quay.

As I walked eastwards along the sea wall a heron took flight, soaring gracefully then landing at a spot fifty yards further on. As I approached, once more it took off, again soaring round once, and landing a similar distance ahead. After repeating the exercise for a third time, it finally got bored with the game and settled in the channel by the sea wall.

I passed an elderly gentleman with two small dogs. His 'good afternoon', in response to my 'good morning', reminded me that lunch was long overdue. At Landermere Quay a wooden seat overlooking the small stony beach made an ideal spot to eat my sandwiches. With a yacht moored in the small bay, and the tide right up, this was a beautiful and peaceful place. Although no one else was around, I felt guilty when my phone disturbed the tranquillity, a friend calling to tell me the surprise news that West Ham had sacked their manager.

Landermere Quay is said to have been a popular location for smugglers, who used to shelter their boats at the nearby Skippers Island, returning to dock at the quay under cover of darkness to avoid the customs men. The quay was purchased in 1781 by Richard Rigby, the Lord of the Manor who we came across earlier in Mistley, with his plans to turn this into a spa town. He improved the facilities, building a row of cottages and an inn called the Kings Head. This was subsequently purchased by a George Munnings,

Landermere Quay

the commander of the local customs cutter Repulse, and much feared by the smugglers. Ironically, the Kings Head lost its licence in 1913, due to having become a notorious smuggler's haunt. The attractive line of cottages Rigby built are still inhabited. One of them, Gull Cottage, was once home to the Sir William Gull, the physician with alleged Jack the Ripper connections, who may or may not lie in his grave at Thorpe-le-Soken.

The path continues atop the sea wall, distinct, although rougher and less well trodden than the section nearer to Harwich. The view towards to Skippers Island, across dark pools and small islets, reminded me of the peat bogs of Rannoch Moor and the far north of Scotland. Although no more than a couple of miles from habitation, the area had the sense of remoteness, where not only did I see no one, but it would have been surprising to have done so. It having rained all morning, and passing no one all afternoon, I was probably the only person to walk this path today.

There is a 500 metre walking route to the mile long Skippers Island, although this is only passable at low tide. Before visiting permission needs to be obtained from Essex Wildlife Trust, who own the island. Livestock used to be driven across the causeway, but it is now no more than a path, and today with the tide high, much of this was covered. Trees grow on the higher parts of the island, and there is some rough pasture. The lower land, which used to support grazing, has reverted to salt marsh following breaches in the sea wall.

Oystercatcher and shelduck are among the sea birds who breed on the island, as do species of warbler and a recent colonist, the nightingale. Many species of wader and duck can be seen, as can brent geese who winter here, travelling from the arctic tundra where they breed. A large flock of these swam close to the shore, babbling characteristically, but appearing otherwise unconcerned at my presence. Although an estimated 120,000 spend winter in the UK, mainly on the south and east coasts, because the majority are found at just a few sites, it is afforded amber conservation status. This denotes that there is some concern, but that the species is not currently globally threatened or in severe decline.

Sea hogs fennel grows on Skippers Island, as do a number of other interestingly named localised species, including adder's-tongue fern, parsley water-dropwort, lax-flowered sea-lavender and dyer's greenweed. These help support a varied insect population, also with charming names, such as the essex skipper butterfly, featured ranunculus and roxy wave moths, and short-winged conehead bush-crickets. Common seals frequently visit the island, which is carefully managed to encourage devolvement of salt marsh and prevent scrub from encroaching onto rough grassland.

Passing Honey Island, another spot favoured by seals, around 70 of which are thought to live in Hamford Water, the sea wall turns sharp right. It then heads south, around the large inlet of Kirby Creek. With farmland to the right and the deserted creeks of Hamford Water to the left, the views must have changed little for many years. The only building close to the sea is Marsh House, and its old wooden barn, alongside which was parked a red and white helicopter, a rare sign that we were in the 21$^{st}$ century.

A small stream, Marsh House Ditch, which runs into the sea nearby, was the site of a potentially serious pollution incident in November 2005. A local oyster farmer noticed high levels of e-coli in the shellfish and investigating, found what appeared to be sewage in the stream. He tracked this back to the Anglian Water pumping station half a mile inland at Malting Lane. The Environment Agency were alerted and their tests showed levels of contamination likely to be harmful to aquatic invertebrates. To put these into perspective, a typically clean river will have a Biochemical Oxygen Demand (BOD – a measure of biodegradable substances which remove oxygen from water) of less than 3mg/litre and crude sewage would have a BOD between 250 and 400 mg/l. The level in the sample taken was 354 mg/l. The ensuing clean up, requiring polluted water to be pumped from ditches and contaminated sediment dredged out, took 18 days and cost Anglian Water £100,000. Investigation showed the cause of pollution to be the failure of a pump, compounded by the automatic alarm failing to activate. Anglian Water pleaded guilty to causing poisonous, noxious or polluting matter to enter controlled waters and were fined the sum of £12,000 under the 1991 Water Resources Act. It was agreed that had it not been for the diligent action of the oyster farmer the incident could have been far more serious, showing how easily man's action, deliberate or accidental, can damage this unique area of Britain.

The light was beginning to fail as I reached Kirby Quay, a truly enchanting spot. The large Quay House was originally a granary, standing alongside the quay where barges tied up, transporting coal, grain, sand, fertiliser and fish until the mid 19th century, when the railway took over. Like Beaumont and Landermere, not all cargoes landing at Kirby Quay were strictly legitimate and boats creeping in at the dead of night made smugglers large profits on goods ranging from coffin nails to playing cards.

A channel extends slightly inland, and across a small wooden bridge is a thatched cottage. In the stillness, with dusk approaching, the quay with its converted granary, yacht moored alongside and little cottage, made for what must be one of the most beautiful and atmospheric little corners of Essex. A true gem, yet hardly known or visited. If Kirby Quay were in Devon or Cornwall, it would be high on the tourist trail. Even if care was taken not to spoil the actual site, visitors and their cars, gift shops, cafes and ice cream vans would change its character. I'm very glad that Kirby Quay is hidden away in a remote and unspoilt Essex backwater, to be found and enjoyed by the few who venture this way.

I felt that there was probably just enough light for one more short stretch along the coast, and consulting my map found that the path continued beside the quay. A sign indicated that this was the case, but unfortunately it pointed straight across the water at the mouth of the channel. Presumably this footpath can only be used at low tide. A short distance along Quay Lane I discovered an opening into a field, from which it looked possible to reach the coast. Here I stopped to consider whether in rapidly dwindling light it was sensible to venture back to the deserted coast path. Whilst keen to continue, my good wife had specifically warned me against such action and I didn't wish to be one of those people who prompt the rescue services to use words such as 'foolhardy' or 'reckless'. Reluctantly I headed inland to the village of Kirby-le-Soken.

The village name goes back to the Norman conquest, Soke, a

Saxon word signifying an area which had been afforded special privileges. Thorpe-le-Soken, Kirby-le-Soken and Walton-le-Soken (now Walton-on-the-Naze), comprised what was known as the Liberty of the Sokens, part of an area owned by St Paul's Cathedral. Kirby was the most important of the three villages, holding a Court Leet of the Liberty in July each year, when property transactions were recorded. Parish registers record an unusual custom, unique to the Soken villages, where by way of gratitude for conducting a burial service, the vicar was entitled to the 'best upper garment' of the deceased. With death rates far higher three hundred years ago, the vicars of these parishes must have been well dressed men.

The village has two pubs, The Red Lion and The Ship Inn. A sign outside the latter offered steak and kidney pie at £5.50 and through the window its welcoming light lit up wooden boards offering a host of wholesome dinners. What a contrast to Great Oakley's Maybush. Maybe that is a pub for locals whilst The Ship aims to attract visitors.

Walking up the hill to Kirby Cross station, many houses displayed outdoor Christmas lights, a fairly recent practice, which like so many of the changes to our society, emanated in the USA. I suppose a few tasteful lights is OK, but the waste of resources and energy that goes into the huge displays which some people now choose to erect, seemingly to outdo their neighbours, strikes me as almost obscene. People even drive around specifically to visit certain roads, now famous for these displays of tackiness, adding their own bit to energy consumption, $CO_2$ emissions and onset of global warming. One day the sea will breach the wall at Kirby-le-Soken. Is it too much to hope that the house with a particularly excessive selection of bells, stars, holly, Santas and illuminated palm trees on its walls, roof and garden, will be the first to flood?

# CHAPTER FIVE

# KIRBY-le-SOKEN
# to WALTON-ON-THE-NAZE

(11 miles)
20th December

On hearing an announcement on Romford station that the Clacton train was running late, I enquired in the office as to whether the Walton-on-the-Naze connection would be held at Thorpe-le-Soken. The answer was, yes it's only an hourly service, so should wait. Arriving at Thorpe-le-Soken 14 minutes late, there was however no Walton train opposite. As about fifteen of us stood hopefully on the platform, a man appeared from the booking office and directed us to the waiting room, advising that the next train was not for another 45 minutes. Apparently the decisions are made in London and while he would have liked to have held the connection, or to have organised a replacement bus, local staff are no longer permitted to use their initiative. Responding to my comment that I would write a letter to One Railway, he assured me that they would take no notice. He'd worked there for forty years and said they don't listen to him.

After initial minor mutterings of discontent, the other passengers settled themselves silently in the waiting room, resigned to the delay. I completed my token protest to the booking clerk, a complaint he had clearly heard many times before, then walked into the village to determine if there was a bus to Kirby-le-Soken. There is. It runs at 8 minutes past every other hour. This was however the hour it wasn't running. After a quick look at the impressive St Michael's Church, and wander round the frosty paths of its large wooded churchyard, I returned to the station. Here I found a notice explaining that Walton connections are held for up to 12 minutes, meaning that as the indicator showed that the next Clacton train was running 13 minutes late, slavish adherence to the policy would soon deposit another group of dissatisfied passengers on Thorpe-le-Soken station. A degree of flexibility would mean a better service, but unfortunately all too often to train companies it seems that maintaining punctuality targets are more important than making sure their customers are happy. Maybe they should put the man from the booking office in charge.

I walked from Kirby Cross to the Kirby Quay, which with sunshine breaking through the mist, frost on the ground and the inland pool covered with ice, looked even more enchanting than when I had left it a week ago. The tide was again high, but this time just low enough to allow me to cross on the footpath, which was about an inch above the water. Great care was required on the icy surface, as the consequences of a slip into the ice covered water to the right did not bear contemplation.

A reasonable path runs north along the sea wall towards Peter's Point, where it turns east towards Walton. I saw more birds along this section than any previous, recognising curlew, oystercatcher, heron, sandpiper and shelduck. Had I have remembered my little book I would have been able to add more to the list. A huge flock of brent geese, five hundred at the very least, took off from a field, circled twice over the sea, then having stretched their wings sufficiently, returned once more to the grass.

Opposite, across The Wade, is Horsey Island, the largest and only inhabited island in Hamford Water. The causeway, unimaginatively named Island Road, was largely under water, although the jetty on the shore still stood high and dry. This was the state of tide when the island is accessible from the mainland by neither boat nor foot. In previous centuries sheep were swum to and from the Horsey, although one wonders why they just didn't wait for the tide to fall. Some farming continues on the island, but its main importance is now for its wildlife. It is a national nature reserve and important habitat for many seabirds.

Horsey Island is one of a number of experimental sites on the Essex coast in which sediment dredged from Harwich Harbour has been deposited in an attempt to reverse salt marsh erosion. In 1998 20,000 cubic metres of mud was sprayed from a dredger on a spring tide, with sunken barges placed to reduce wave attack, allowing the tide to disperse the sediment. After 9 months considerable salt marsh growth had occurred, and the process was repeated in 2001, raising the height in order to encourage plant growth. The experiment appears to have been successful, but ongoing monitoring is required. Horsey Island provides protection against wave action for much of Hamford Water and if it were to further erode away the whole nature of these fragile backwaters could be changed.

The map shows the footpath turning inland along Island Lane to Kirby-le-Soken, but although none was marked, a reasonable path continued along the sea wall. Beyond Rigdon's Lane, another track heading inland, it became less clear. On several occasions I had to hop over the fence to continue on the seaward side of the wall. After the small bay of Coles Creek is Titchmarsh Marina, ahead of which a large bank of bare earth blocked the way. The only way forward was to climb this, which left a couple of inches of very sticky mud on my trainers. The top was little better, with recently germinated shoots of grass poking through soft earth, which was perfectly flattened and obviously not yet intended for walkers' feet. Again there was little option but to proceed,

Kirby Quay

although now in full view of the marina buildings, I was relieved not to be greeted at the end by an irate groundsman. The earthworks formed one side of a huge new dock, deeply excavated, but not yet opened to the sea.

A blue tankard on the map indicated a pub on the site, and I had planned to stop here for lunch. It however turned out to be an upmarket affair, the Harbour Lights Restaurant and I didn't feel that the yachting fraternity would take too kindly to a scruffy walker joining them. Especially one who would be depositing upon the carpets generous amounts of mud collected from their own new lawns.

With no path shown from here to Walton, rather than picking my way through the marina, I followed Cole Lane inland. A car pulled up next to me and the driver asked if I would like a lift. He didn't appear offended by my refusal on the grounds that I was walking the whole Essex coast, so did not wish to cheat, although I wasn't sure if his smile was one of respect or sympathy. The map shows a path heading off towards Walton by some crumbling farm buildings, but after walking through wet grass to the end of the first field, beyond which no through route appeared apparent, I returned to the road. The exercise had at least served to wash the remaining mud from my trainers, but in return soak my trousers to the knees. Slightly annoyed at myself for this unnecessary diversion, I stayed on the lane and turning left at the end, followed the main road the mile or so into Walton-on-the-Naze.

First priority was lunch. Although the guide had promised that every third business was a café, this being mid afternoon in late December, most were closed. To be more precise, only one was open, The Round Table, where a bacon sandwich and excellent bowl of chips was well received. The only other diners were a grandmother and her granddaughter, who had also travelled by train for a day by the sea. Their conversation provided some amusement, with the rather posh older lady trying to impress the girl with her knowledge of young people's music, identifying Slade as their Merry Christmas played. The girl couldn't have been born when Slade were around and whilst she was charming to her grandmother, was probably glad not to be in her home town with any of her friends listening.

Walton is a typical seaside town, having grown extensively with arrival of the railway. There has been a settlement here since Saxon times, and the discovery of many flints suggest that the area supported a large Stone Age population. Although not settling here, the Romans are thought to have used the calcium rich clay for building the walls of Colchester. The town's heyday was during the Victorian era, when large numbers of visitors arrived for day trips, or to stay in the imposing new hotels. The most impressive of these, Marine Terrace, was built by Peter Bruff, the civil engineer responsible for bringing the railway to the town in 1867. He also built the pier, South Terrace (which was destroyed by bombing in World War Two) and Clifton Baths. This became the Pier Hotel, for which my trawl for information turned up the following gem of a review: 'The Pier Hotel – what an absolute shithole full of all the Walton low life!! Filthy pub, toilets even worse floors covered in urine, light fittings hanging off the wall. Was once a nice old fashioned family pub with friendly staff. Not a good advert for Walton.'

Bruff had plans for a tramway linking Walton with Frinton, but other projects took him away and he sold his interests in 1897. The town however continued to grow, with the pier being lengthened and bathing machines installed. After the First World War two cinemas were built and a large boating lake replaced the old tide mill. It remained a thriving resort until the outbreak of World War Two. Then the holiday trade ceased, the pier had to be partly demolished to prevent German landing, and some of the town was destroyed by bombing. After the war people had little money for holidays, and soon with the advent of foreign packages, most preferred to go abroad. Although some tourists returned to Walton, by the 1960s it was usually for day trips or to stay in caravan parks, rather than the hotels and guest houses, most of which eventually closed.

Lunch at The Round Table marked only the halfway point in the day's walk. Circumnavigation of The Naze, the peninsula to the north of the Walton, was to be the second stage. I walked through the town, passing a school just as the children came out excitedly wishing one another a happy Christmas, through the deserted coach park and joined the main road by a caravan park. A sign pointing along a rough roadway past a scrap yard indicated access to the sea wall. I followed a couple in wellingtons, who I assumed were fellow walkers, but they disappeared into a compound in which a fairground was laid up for winter. The path reached the sea at a small quay from where wildlife boat trips run in summer months. As I headed north the sun was setting to my left, over the stretch of water known as The Twizzle. After pausing to take a few photos, I realised that it would soon be dark and that I was just setting out onto several miles of desolate and deserted sea wall. Quickening my step, I reckoned I could just reach the less isolated cliffs of The Naze before it was dark.

The map shows the path ending after a few hundred yards, but as it continued onwards I ignored the sign marking the end of the right of way. To the left was Walton Channel and beyond it Hedge-end Island, a low lying marshy area, which is thought to have been connected to Horsey Island until separated in 1897 by the 'Black Monday Floods' which affected the whole Essex coast. To the right was Walton Hall Marshes, which with no obvious routes through them and a number of channels to cross, meant that were the sea wall path to end, I would have to turn back the way I'd come. Conscious that the light was now fading and that there were still nearly two miles of sea wall to negotiate, I gave my wife a quick call. Not however letting on that it was getting dark, for fear that she would worry, but more so of the admonishment that I would receive. I just let her know where I was, a precaution just in case some accident should befall me. With the temperature around zero and the ground still frozen, a night in the open would not have been advisable.

Walking really quite quickly now, I turned sharp right at the top of the headland, the path following Cormorant Creek towards the open sea. Fog had now come down and the lights of Harwich were only just visible on the far side of the bay. The roar of an unseen Sea Cat ferry reverberated across the sea as I headed rapidly onward. A large wooden cross loomed out of the fog. I had no idea what this signified, but hoped it didn't mark the point of demise of a rambler who may have misjudged nightfall and got lost on the salt marsh. The footpath is shown continuing down to the beach and into Walton, but a sign warns of dangerous mud, telling people to stay close to the base of the cliff. Further on other signs warned of the edge of the cliff eroding, giving nature the choice of either falling rocks or glutinous mud with which to hurl its wrath upon any unfortunate walker.

With it now almost dark, I was relieved to reach a paved track which runs to the foot of The Naze, between a lagoon and the John Weston Essex Wildlife Trust reserve. This was named after a leading Essex naturalist, who was warden here until his death in 1984. The reserve consists of rough grassland and thickets of bramble and blackthorn, plus four shallow ponds, three of them man-made to encourage wildlife. Reed warblers have colonised these and other nesting birds include lapwing, sedge and redshank. It is also an important landing point for migrating birds, such as firecrest, barred warbler and red backed shrike. Whilst limited in my recognition skills, I am normally aware of the existence of most British birds, but the red backed shrike was new to me. Slightly larger than a house sparrow, they used to be fairly common, but as a result of loss of habitat, changes in agricultural practice and most needlessly, egg collection, it now rarely breeds in the UK. Good numbers however still stop by on their migration routes, first in early summer, then returning in early autumn. They eat insects, small birds and mammals, which rather than consuming immediately, they take back to a larder, where the unfortunate prey is impaled on a thorn or twig.

Another selection of intriguingly named plants grows here, including slender thistle, parsley water-dropwort, pepper saxifrage, fenugreek and bush grass. Fenugreek has a multitude of uses, its leaves as a herb and its seeds as a spice, often used in the preparation of curries. It has a variety of medicinal uses, ranging from an aid to digestion, treating lung congestion, reducing inflammation and fighting infection. Nursing mothers apparently use it to increase milk production and it is also said to increase breast size. Now I'm always a little sceptical of herbs which purport to cure so many unrelated ills, but have to confess considerable doubt as to the validity of last of these claims. Surely if it were true someone would already be selling it to those ladies who may feel dissatisfied with what the Good Lord dealt them in the mammary department. Maybe an enterprising farmer could plant a field of fenugreek and make his fortune selling the harvest as a natural alternative to the silicone implant, suitably marketed of course with appropriate before and after pictures.

A maze of paths head to the top of The Naze, which mostly being beneath trees and scrub were very dark, making it impossible to pick out the muddy areas. I slid and slipped my way onwards, staying on paths heading upwards, knowing that this must eventually lead to the top. I could have made good use of the echo sounding capabilities of the bat who flew a couple of feet from my nose. The open grassy area at the top was a little lighter and here I came across a small stone plaque inscribed with Psalm 93, verse 4 'Mightier than the thunder of the great waters, mightier than the breakers of the sea – the Lord on high is mighty'.

The Naze Tower stands high at the end of the greensward. This 85 foot octagonal brick built tower was erected in 1721 by Trinity House as a navigational marker for the port of Harwich, a duty which it still performs today. Known locally as The Landmark, the tower was opened to the public for the first time in 2004. In summer months for the fee of £2, visitors can climb the spiral staircase and enjoy the extensive views from the observation platform at the top. Needless to say, those arriving after dark on a cold winter's evening are not afforded such opportunity.

With no sea wall protecting it, The Naze, which is formed of Red Crag and London Clay, is eroding rapidly. The tower currently stands some way back from the cliff edge, however at the current rate, within 50 years it will have toppled into the sea, joining on the beach an upturned Second World War pillbox, which tumbled over the cliff some years ago. Efforts are being made to stem the erosion, and these attract many school fieldtrips to study the effect of groynes, sea wall and riprap (rocks laid to dissipate the energy of waves). A local pressure group, The Naze Protection Society, campaigns for more coastal protection, but in such a sensitive area, with conflicting interests of nature conservancy and geological protection, a long term solution acceptable to all is difficult to find. Some say that nature should be allowed to take its course, while others want a sea wall to preserve the cliffs.

Erosion of the cliff face uncovers many fossils, which can found lying on the beach, especially after storms. The two million year old Red Crag contains the remains of shells from creatures whose descendants now live in the Pacific Ocean, to which the sea here was once connected via the Bering Straight. The London Clay beneath was deposited fifty million years ago as a sea bed. Preserved in this are fossils of crabs, lobsters, turtles and sharks teeth, indicating that The Naze was then part of a tropical sea. The Naze has produced some of the best bird fossils found anywhere in the world, making it a site of international importance. Over 600 species have been found, including the phorusrhacos, a ferocious cockerel sized bird, with a fierce hooked beak, that evolved to become an eight foot flightless carnivore. It is thought that this concentration of bird fossils may have been due to volcanic activity or a meteorite explosion which caused intense heat and wholesale mortality. Thin layers of volcanic ash, possibly originating from Scotland, can be seen in the clay to support this theory.

It is possible to walk the two miles into Walton along the beach, but in the dark I followed the road downhill, past the Coastguard Station, to the promenade. I was pleased to see that Bruff's Marine Terrace has recently been refurbished as part of the town's efforts at regeneration, and now once more stands as an impressive example of Victorian seaside development.

Judging walking times for unfamiliar routes can be difficult, but as far back as The Naze I felt that the quarter to five train was just catchable. Making rapid progress along the promenade, with frequent glances at my watch, quickening pace further as I headed up the hill to the station and even breaking into a jog for the last few yards, my timing was perfect. I arrived with a minute to spare. The platform however was deserted. Examination of the timetable showed that whilst trains leave Walton all day at 45 minutes passed the hour, this one goes at 43. I had missed it by a minute. I think I might have said bother.

Left with the best part of an hour to wander round Walton in the dark I headed down to the pier. Although this claims to be the second longest in Britain, it is actually third behind Southend and Southport. The original pier, a wooden jetty solely for landing of goods and passengers, was built in 1830 and was one of the first to be constructed in England. Walton had become a popular destination for visitors travelling on steamers from London to Great Yarmouth, so following severe storm damage a new and longer pier was opened in 1895. Originally 244 metres long, successive extensions took its length to 793 metres, and to assist passengers reach the pier head, an electric tramway was installed. This was replaced with a diesel locomotive hauled train in 1948, which ran until the 1970s. The head of the pier is a popular spot for sea anglers, and the shore end houses an extensive collection of amusements and rides, which despite the absence of any customers, remained open on this cold and dark evening. I spent a few minutes feeding loose change into a variety of slot machines, pressing nudge and hold buttons that blatantly ignored my instructions, before leaving with empty pockets and not the pleasure of even a single win.

The next train left 5 minutes late. They don't hold London connections at Thorpe-le-Soken, so allowed the fast train to depart one minute before mine arrived. I therefore missed the last train from Romford to Upminster and for the want of this one minute had to travel via London, arriving home 1½ hours late. Needless to say I wrote a letter.

# PART TWO

## Walton-on-the-Naze to Peldon Rose

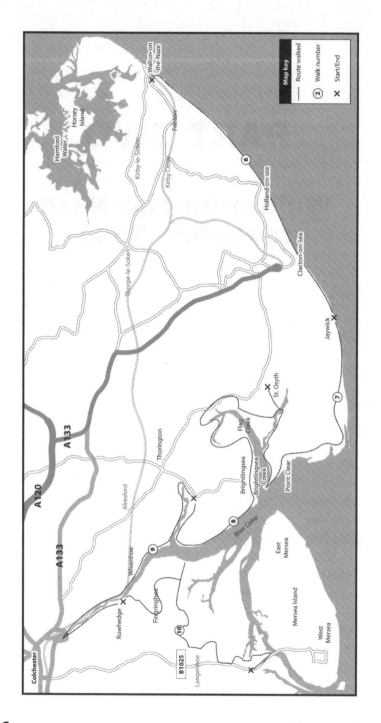

CHAPTER SIX

# WALTON-ON-THE-NAZE to JAYWICK

(10 miles)
21st January

When Bill Bryson said that the trick of successful walking is knowing when to stop, he could have added 'and when not to start'. This was one of those days. Leaving Walton station I was greeted by fierce winds and horizontal freezing rain. Walking down the hill this blew directly into my face, as if someone was firing little arrows at my unprotected skin. More than once I questioned why in such weather I had chosen to leave a warm and cosy house for the wild and deserted coast.

I stopped in the shelter of the pier entrance to don waterproof leggings, before setting forth along the narrow promenade. To the right, hundreds of wooden beach huts, four or five deep, line the shore. To the left, huge waves roared in from the North Sea. I was to see no one else on the path for the next 5 miles. My only company were sanderling, unperturbed by the wind as they scampered across the beach, seeking morsels from beneath the sand.

The good news was that the wind was now directly behind,

propelling me towards Clacton, and blowing the rain only onto my back. The bad news was that my leggings were six inches too long, meaning that I either had to pull them up after every step, or allow them to slide uncomfortably under my shoes. I looked like a penguin and felt not much warmer.

Then my phone rang with news from work that was not good. Like any factory we have occasional spills, but being glue, our products aren't the easiest to clean up. This time however it wasn't just a bit of glue on the floor – it was two tonnes and it was my fault! There's a tap on the bottom of each mixer for taking samples and I had been forever asking the operators to leave a container underneath to catch the drips. As a reminder when popping in at the weekend to check all was well, I'd hung a bucket over the pipe. Unfortunately the mixer's vibrations caused this to slide along the pipe onto the tap's handle. Its weight must have opened the tap a little, allowing the bucket to gradually fill and its increasing weight to fully open the tap. It would have drained slowly, but with no one in the building for almost 24 hours, the entire contents of the mixer were emptied out onto the floor. £2,500 worth of glue wasted. A three day clean up was required, pumping it into containers for disposal and scraping dried sticky adhesive off the floor, but the culprit was out here on the wild coast of Essex. My guilt was only lessened by knowing than none of those cleaning up would have wished to swap places and be walking along a deserted sea wall in a rain storm.

Frinton-on-Sea adjoins Walton, but walking alongside the sea, it is easy to miss. A greensward above the cliff separates the town from the beach, and although there are a number of paths, none indicated that they led to the town. Guessing correctly, I took the second, continuing high up on the grass and then along the main street, Connaught Avenue.

Until late Victorian times Frinton was just a tiny hamlet of less than thirty inhabitants, with a few cottages, several farms and a church Then in the late 19<sup>th</sup> century the area was purchased by a developer, who succeeded in his aim to build an exclusive seaside town in which the wealthy could holiday. Aristocracy and even royalty used to stay here. The 1919 guide to the town explains that it is the ideal summer retreat for 'jaded and worried people from the thick air and hurry of the crowded towns, who are anxiously on the alert to discover peaceful little spots, not too far away to involve tedious journeys, and yet close to the reviving sea.'

Frinton is still is famed for its exclusivity and conservative nature and was reputedly the last town in England without a pub. Although drink was available at a number of hotels and clubs, many residents considered that a public house would be the first step along the road to ruin, and mounted a strong campaign when Eamonn Ryan, a rich entrepreneur, proposed opening a pub in the town. After a three year battle the council granted permission and the Lock & Barrel, a name chosen by a local competition, finally opened in the High Street in September 2000. Shepherd Neame, the brewers who managed the pub, sell a beer called Spitfire and arranged a flypast by a Spitfire aircraft at the first opening time. The pub was packed, but the Secretary of the Residents Association famously stated that this was 'the worst day in Frinton since the Luftwaffe beat up the town in 1944', a remark which found its way into the Times Book of Quotations.

The town's conservative residents had already lost a battle in 1992, with the opening of the first fish and chip shop. Using a pun in that way of chip shops and hairdressers, 'Young's Other Plaice' hardly looked as if was bringing disrepute on the town. Stepping inside I was greeted by a young man, obviously delighted to have a customer and eager to give me his very best service. I got up to order at the counter, but was quickly ushered back, so he could do things properly and take it at my table. Once seated, I was permitted to submit my simple request for cod and chips. I was however helpfully directed towards the lunchtime special, of cod and chips with a cup of tea, at a lower price than the standard menu without the tea. He seemed a little disappointed that I preferred a cold drink, so couldn't take advantage of this deal, but as he was so keen to follow convention, I resisted complicating matters by asking for the lunchtime special without tea. The freshly fried cod was excellent, as I told the young man when he came to check all was well and again when he appeared to relieve me of my plate the moment it was empty. For reasons of time and capacity I reluctantly declined the inviting selection of deserts; treacle sponge, chocolate pudding, jam roly poly and the schoolboys' favourite, spotted dick. Presenting the bill, the young man was very keen to explain that he had charged me for the lunchtime special despite my refusal of the tea, for which of course I thanked him profusely. He said that he looked forward to seeing me again, but I didn't like to admit that I was merely passing through, however I shall use this opportunity to recommend his fine food and impeccable service.

At the foot of Connaught Road I came across St Mary's Church, the smallest complete church in Essex and the only ancient building in Frinton. It was built in the 13th century, but with thick nave walls normally associated with Norman buildings. Temporary extensions were added as the town grew in the 1890s. These were removed and the building restored as it had been when a new church, St Mary Magdalene, was constructed in 1928. St Mary's still holds services every Sunday and after regaining its licence in 2000, is also used for weddings. Unusually for a town church, the doors are left open and visitors are welcome. Recent entries in the visitors book provided apt words of description; 'quaint', 'beautiful', 'delightful', 'inviting' and 'peaceful', saving me the trouble of finding my own.

I returned to the mile long sandy beach, which lined with hundreds of Edwardian beach huts, is said to be geared to families looking for a quiet day out. Naturally there are no funfairs, amusements or rides, or even anywhere to buy food or drink, the town priding itself on permitting no ice cream sellers by the beach.

St Mary's Church Frinton

This helps keep it clean and litter free, for which the beach has been awarded a yellow flag.

Frinton is described as a time capsule and a true escape from the modern world, although it didn't appear to be as exclusive as I had expected. Two tall blocks of flats overlooking the sea rather spoil its Victorian character and I was surprised to see the Star of India restaurant at the foot of the main street. Neither was the town full of elderly people. Maybe it did go to pot once the chip shop opened.

I set off once more on the sea wall, passing Frinton Golf Club where two solitary players braved the elements. In 2008 the town's more liberal influences reached even this most traditional of institutions. Much to the displeasure of some of the club's 600 members, a 113 year old rule that players must wear knee length socks with shorts was relaxed. Short socks are now permitted, although a strict dress code still applies. Shorts must be tailored, shirts have collars and no denim or tracksuits are allowed on the course or in the clubhouse. It seems that Frinton is becoming less famous for the exclusivity of the town, but instead for its residents who object to a chip shops, pubs, or sight of men's legs.

The tide was high as I continued along the sea wall towards Clacton and in several places waves were breaking over the wall. Good timing and a quick dash were necessary to avoid a soaking. One section of the path was separated from the raging sea by a wall only a foot high and with the wind blowing a gale I kept well away from the edge. I was happy for it to assist me towards Clacton, but had it taken me to Belgium I would have been late for tea.

After the golf course, the only other remaining length of undeveloped land between Walton and Clacton is the 100 acres of Holland Haven Country Park. This grazing marsh, with hides for bird watching, was the proposed landfall point for power

Rough sea near Frinton

cables to an offshore wind farm development on the nearby Gunfleet Sands. A drilling rig was to be sited in the disused quarry, but concern was raised about great crested newts and common lizards living in this area. Whilst it is protected due to declining numbers from habitat loss, the newt seems to have an uncanny knack of being found at every site where developments are opposed. Maybe some enterprising protester is running round the country with a bucket of the little fellows to let loose just before the surveyors arrive. The wind farm wasn't built so the newts remain undisturbed.

A tall radar tower looks out to sea, one of twelve that watch over the 26,000 ships passing through the Thames Estuary each year. The tower is unmanned, but linked to the Port Control Centre in London by microwave radio. Behind this is Holland Haven Nature Reserve.

By the path I came across a large rock, with a metal plaque cryptically inscribed:

## AW PROJECT CLEANWATER

### For Cleaner Beaches at Holland and Clacton

**The Lady on the Bike grew and presented an Oak tree to Anglian Water in tunnelling achieved with 100% safety while building a 2.1 metre diameter sewer from Holland Haven to Anglefield Clacton in 1997**

This commemorates a seven mile tunnel, built by Anglian Water in world record time, to take sewage from Clacton to the treatment works at Holland Haven. Prior to its construction the town's Victorian sewers were often unable to cope during periods of rain, meaning that raw sewage used to overflow onto the beach. I could see no oak tree and the role of the cycling lady is left to the reader to speculate.

At Holland-on-Sea waves crashing over the sea wall forced me to walk on the upper promenade. Until the 1920s this was a small village known as Little Holland, but while it retains its own identity, housing development has now joined it to Clacton. Although the sea on my left was wild, I missed the solitude and nature of Hamford Water. Walking in built up areas isn't the same. All of today's walk was on concrete, and the soles of my feet were aching.

At Clacton I found a café for a drink and more importantly a sit down in the warm. The waitress bought me a toasted tea cake, apologising that they only had two settings, underdone and burnt. I didn't like to point out that she had managed to achieve both, the bottom being black and the top barely brown. On leaving the café and finding that the rain has restarted, it was tempting to catch an early train home. However after walking a few yards towards the station, I stood firm and I opted instead to explore Clacton, before returning to the sea.

Clacton has been popular as a watering place since Victorian times. Its climate is drier and warmer than most of Britain, and the unspoilt south facing sandy beaches of the Tendring Peninsula (Walton, Frinton and Clacton) are marketed as the Sunshine Coast. With a population of 53,000 Clacton is larger and brasher than its two neighbours. It was the first place I'd walked through that was self-sufficient, in that its residents don't generally travel elsewhere for shopping and amenities. The lower half of the town is dominated by amusement arcades, with their neon lights and irritating jingles, but on a cold January afternoon, virtually no customers. The centre however appeared to have the usual selection of chain stores and burger bars, not much in the way of interesting architecture and little to suggest its proximity to the sea.

Like Walton, Clacton grew up in the latter part of the 19th century, although has a history far beyond this. The beach is in fact one of the oldest known sites of human habitation in the UK, a 400,000 year old spearhead having been found in the cliffs along Marine

Parade. At this time Britain was joined to Europe and the Thames flowed here. Bones of woolly mammoths, lions, elephants and giant oxen have been found, telling us some of the former residents who used to drink from the river.

There is evidence of a Stone Age settlement and pottery has been found dating back to the Neolithic Period. Celtic farmers worked the land around 100BC and their gold coins have been found on the beach. Romans, who were based at Colchester, also lived in the area and a number of their urns were found when the Grand Hotel was built in 1897. The town's name came from Saxon times and a leader by the name of Clacc; 'Claccinga-ton' meaning Clacc's people. A record from around 1,000 years ago shows that the village of 'Claccingtune' was required to provide two men towards a ship's crew. In the Domesday Book of 1086 it is recorded that 'Clachintuna' was populated by 45 tenant farmers and 50 small holders.

Other than a spot of smuggling and plundering the occasional ship wreck, for centuries farming remained the main way of life. Mechanisation however led to loss of jobs, low wages and much unrest. This reached a head on 7th December 1830, when a crowd of farm workers surged into the village with the intention of visiting local farms and smashing their machinery. It took a force of 1,000 farmers and local gentry to quell several days of rioting.

Although as far back as 1824 the owner of the Ship Inn was advertising a bathing machine available for hire, development was slow due to a trust that prevented prospective purchasers from buying land. This expired in 1864, when Peter Bruff, the railway engineer who also developed much of Walton, bought up much of the area. In 1886 he was granted powers to extend his railway, build a pier and to turn Clacton into a seaside resort.

The pier opened in 1871 and an exclusive arrangement with The Woolwich Steam Packet Company brought visitors in their droves.

Clacton Pier

In 1890 arrivals by boat totalled 71,922, and the opening of the railway brought even more day trippers, with 327,451 paying to go on the pier in 1893. Hotels, pubs, shops and houses were being put up at a great rate and Clacton Urban District Council was formed to take control of the development. However, the day trippers arriving on cheap trains from East London were not the kind of visitor Peter Bruff wanted. To attract the more discerning and more to the point affluent visitors, he built theatres and operetta houses, and organised open air concerts. Well known acts were booked and Stanley Holloway once performed at the West Cliff Theatre, which still puts on an old style summer show.

With the railway bringing visitors from London and the Midlands, fewer paddle steamers called, the loss of business causing the pier to go into liquidation. However an Ernest Kingsman took it over and spent £200,000 adding a host of attractions; three theatres, a dance hall, zoo, funfair, restaurant, casino and even an open air swimming pool. Butlins opened in 1937 and the town remained a vibrant resort until the outbreak of war.

Victoria Road Clacton was the scene of England's first civilian casualties of the Second World War. On the night of 30th April 1940 a German Heinkel 111 H-4 bomber was about to lay parachute mines in the North Sea, when it ran into thick fog. The crew apparently became disorientated and on crossing the coast just before midnight, came under attack from anti-aircraft batteries at Bawdsey, Felixtowe and Harwich. Although it may not have received a direct hit, the exploding shells caused considerable damage to the plane's controls. The pilot began circling over Clacton and dropped red flares. These may have been as a warning, or because it was searching for a landing place, but losing height the plane clipped chimneys before crashing into the home of Frederick and Dorothy Gill. For a few moments there was a deathly silence, then one of the mines exploded with a huge blast. The home was flattened and the charred remains of the four crew were found next to their aircraft. A search of the rubble was started and eventually 19 year old William Gill was pulled out, badly injured but alive. Sadly his parents were less fortunate and along with the German airmen, they were buried in Burrs Road Cemetery. The couple's unmarked grave was found in 1994 and a Commonwealth War Graves Commission headstone erected, which was dedicated on the 59th anniversary of their death.

Although still popular for holidays in the late 40s and 50s, the town never regained its pre-war position and decline set in as more and more people chose to travel abroad. Now it is very much a resort catering for the day tripper, with most of those choosing to stay longer being either the more elderly who stay out of season, or families holidaying in the many nearby caravan parks.

Having walked back down the main street, I turned right at the pier, passing the recently restored Marine Gardens. These were originally laid out in 1924, each of the five having its own theme. The first is the War Memorial Garden, with formal hedges and in the summer a display of bedding plants. Next is the Rose Garden, enclosed by low stone walls, then the 1920s Garden, originally called the Sunken Garden. The Mediterranean Garden contains mature shrubs and plants which thrive in this warm spot and the Sensory Garden those with interesting odour or touch. Nice enough on a cold January day, in summer these must be a pleasant refuge from the brashness of the gaudy amusements.

Walking along the low promenade, three times I had to go down to the beach to skirt round big diggers scooping up sand deposited by storms the previous week. These had been England's strongest winds for 17 years and I was glad that a last minute change in domestic circumstances meant it had been necessary to postpone the walk, which I had originally planned for that day. Although as with all the walks, I had intended to go ahead regardless of the weather, today's winds of maybe 30 miles per hour were quite enough, and last week they'd reached almost 100.

Opposite a small breakwater is the first of Clacton's two Martello Towers, this one being converted to a restaurant. With England under threat from invasion by the French at the start of the 19th century, Prime Minister William Pitt decided to build these circular towers, each with cannon on its roof. The name Martello, and the basis of the design, came from a circular stone tower built at Mortella Point in Corsica, which in 1794 the Royal Navy had experienced great difficulty in capturing. Seventy four were built along the south coast and a further twenty nine to the east in Essex and Suffolk. Each tower cost between £2,000 and £5,000 to construct, and whilst this seemed good value in 1803 when Napoleon's troops were camped at Boulogne poised to invade, by the time they were completed Nelson had won at Trafalgar, and there was much criticism of the expenditure.

Soon after the impressive new lifeboat station, the built up area ended at Clacton golf course. The beach too became more rugged, with an area of sand dunes, the first I had seen so far. Approaching Jaywick I passed a lady walking two small dogs. There was no need for words, our respective facial expressions communicating to the other the folly of walking in such weather.

It had been my intention to walk a further four miles to Point Clear, but once again a late start due to One Railway failing to hold the Walton connection, meant that darkness would soon be arriving. This time I was told the real reason why they won't hold the connection. The Government imposes large fines for late trains, so in order to avoid these the operators opt to leave passengers behind. What a way to run a railway. Hence I stopped at Jaywick, which has good bus service and had to wait only a few minutes for short ride back to Clacton station.

# CHAPTER SEVEN

# JAYWICK to ST OSYTH

(11 miles)
31st January

A bus tour around the residential streets of Clacton took me back to the interesting little town of Jaywick. The settlement's history goes back to when the North Sea was dry land and retreating ice had left a pocket of water, which was used by prehistoric man. In Saxon times, Jaywick was called Clakyngewyk (I can't pronounce it either!) meaning 'dairy farm of the people of Clacc'. The small farming community was changed almost overnight in 1928, when Frank Stedman, a London based businessman, bought the land for £7,500. His plan was to build a seaside holiday village and he quickly erected 2,000 chalets to house visitors. Within three years Jaywick had become a town, with its own shops, buses, amusements and lifeboat. There was even a mile long miniature steam railway, which ran from the furthest estate to the sea, for which in 1936 the return fare was sixpence.

The 1931 Clacton directory listed only six permanent dwellings in Jaywick, however much to the Council's displeasure many of the chalets were already being used unofficially as homes. As time went on the rule that none of the timber chalets could be occupied permanently fell quietly into disuse and private sector landlords

**80**                                          **ESSEX COAST WALK**

bought up the properties to rent as homes. Over the years the chalets became more outdated and in need of both repair and renovation. The housing is now some of the poorest in Europe and the town's infrastructure has been neglected for years. In spite of, or maybe because of this, a strong sense of community has evolved and most of its residents have no wish to live elsewhere.

As I walked along the sea wall it was easy to see why Jaywick had been so badly hit by the 1953 floods. With just a four foot wall to protect them, the wooden chalets that had been built for holiday use didn't stand a chance. Many were lifted and overturned, while some just floated away. Of the 700 people living there, 37 were drowned.

A few of the sea front chalets had been burnt out or lay derelict, but most are lived in, the occupiers having made varying efforts to make them homely. Running perpendicular to the sea are a series of unmade up roads, which with their ramshackle chalets looked more like something from the Third World than the prosperous South East of England. It has been called 'Soweto-on-Sea' and I could see why Clacton's residents call it a shanty town. I'd never seen a place like Jaywick, but it has character and I liked it.

When the chalets end, the caravans begin – thousands of them in the Martello Beach Holiday Park. Here there is even less protection and much damage was caused by the 1987 hurricane. Another Martello Tower stands near the entrance to the park, this one being used to house a new art project. There's a short section of open land before the small village of Seawick and another caravan park, Seawick Holiday Village.

At St Osyth beach a path runs close to the shore and had I been so inclined I could have followed this to St Osyth Naturist Beach. Having no desire to bare all in public, I was unaware both of its existence (it is not signposted), and of the unofficial rules which govern its use. There are apparently three distinct areas. The first is for straight naturists, presumably where those people content simply to discard their clothes, hang out, so to speak. The second is for men only and frequented by gays, most of whom are said to behave respectably, but a few of the more lonely ones apparently engage in certain indecent activities that should not be performed in public. The third is the sand dunes, where couples pitch tents and the advice is to leave by 5pm if you're not into 'swinging'.

The path to the beach is a dead end, with no way across a small creek, so I stayed on the sea wall. This runs inland from an attractive area of salt marsh, with many little channels and pools. Here I spotted a tall white bird standing at the edge of a shallow pond. I thought it was an egret and a look in the excellent Birdwatcher's Pocket Guide, which my son had given me for Christmas, confirmed that it indeed was. I was chuffed to see what is a relatively rare bird and furthermore to have recognised it. The little egret is a small heron, living mainly along coasts and estuaries, where it is an active hunter for fish. Not native to the UK, it was first seen here in numbers in 1989 and started breeding on Brownsea Island in Dorset in 1996. A count by the Southend RSPB group found 483 little egrets living in Essex and I had seen one of the 20 recorded around St Osyth.

Lee-over-Sands, the next settlement, is linked to civilisation by an unadopted road. With a few scattered houses it reminded me of the sort of outpost you might find in Norway or Iceland. All sorts of odd discarded items surrounded some of the houses, which is something I've noticed at other remote settlements. Is it because they don't want to part with anything, or because they think no one will see the mess?

Opposite an unusual looking wooden building is the entrance to the 652 acre Colne Point Nature Reserve. One of Essex Wildlife Trust's major reserves, this consists of a long shingle ridge, enclosing an area of salt marsh through which Ray Creek flows. It is the best developed spit on the Essex coast and the development of its shingle structure is of much interest to those who study the origins and evolution of landforms. The reserve is rich in plants, including the rare sea barley, curved hard-grass, dune fescue, sea heath and rock sea-lavender. A wide range of marine invertebrates live in the mudflats and shingle pools of the inter-tidal areas, and provide food for large numbers of wading birds. Colne Point is on a major migration route for finches, skylarks, chats and pipits, which in turn attract birds of prey as they pass through. The reserve is also important for its insect population, with good numbers of beetles, moths and spiders, plus a selection of solitary bees and wasps who make their nests in the sand. Visitors are advised to wear waterproof boots and be prepared to wade, as parts of the reserve often flood at high tide, including around the footbridge which is the only access.

From Lee-over-Sands the sea wall runs inland of an extensive area of salt marsh. There were good views across Brightlingsea Reach to Mersea Island, and in the far distance the twin hulks of Bradwell Power station could be seen for the first time; clearly visible, but many miles of walking ahead.

The map shows the footpath ending just past a sewage works, but although a path from here headed inland, a small sign indicated that it also continued along the sea wall. I followed this towards the village of Point Clear, where it ended abruptly in a thicket of bramble bushes. With the other path now a mile behind me, and no wish to retrace my steps, I climbed down the bank onto the rough grassy area below. Avoiding the patches of mud, I clambered over big tufts of grass, until reaching a sign stating 'Private Ray Creek Holdings'. The sign was old and rusty. Old enough to cast doubt as to whether it still applies, so I continued, exercising my right to roam.

A couple of hundred yards further on and just beyond a low, but ramshackle fence, was a small landing area, with a few boats pulled up on the hard. Two signs here, one on a post and one on the side of a shed requested 'Shore Nesting Birds. Please Keep Away'. Now birds don't tend to nest in January and clearly the boat users crossed the area, so once again I ignored the sign and carried on.

The next fence was more serious. Rusty barbed wire, although again not in the best condition. Here the sign warned:

STOP

NO ENTRY

ADDER AREA

I'm no expert on adders, but I do know they like dry places, yet here it was wet. And why should they choose to live in this spot, behind a barbed wire fence, but not along the rest of the shore? This was suspicious. I stopped to consider for a while. It was now even further back to the path over the clumpy grass. I hopped over a low bit of the fence and carried on. Walking here was easier as there was an area of cut grass, sloping down from the gardens of houses that back onto the shore. These were seriously posh houses, with huge gardens, and gates leading out onto the shoreline. It was most kind of them to cut an area for me to walk away from the adders. Then I reached an insurmountable obstacle – a chain link fence, six foot high and running right down into the mud below the low tide line. Again I stopped to review the options. Inspecting the mud I decided it was too soft to risk walking round the fence. I seriously thought of legging it through one of the large back gardens, but then spotted a lady watching. She stood in her garden, looking at me as if to say, take one more step and I'll let the adders loose. Grudgingly I turned back. It had all gone so well until now. Trains on time, bus arriving just as I reached the stop, beautiful sunshine, unseasonable warmth. Now I had to trudge back across rough ground and make a long detour, just because a few residents of Point Clear didn't want people walking between their nice houses and the sea.

Another look at the bramble thicket revealed a tall fence in the middle of it and absolutely no way through. Reluctantly I set out to retrace my steps to the sewage works, but then with great delight, after just ten yards I found the way through. There was another path below the sea wall. This ran through a gap in the hedge, on a little wooden bridge over the ditch, along the edge of a field and into the village. It was well hidden and not marked on the map, so just a little sign might have helped. The sea wall path ending in the brambles was well trodden and I can't have been the only person to come to this dead end.

The road led into Point Clear, where my wish to walk close to the sea was once again thwarted. At a left fork were no less than five signs indicating that Beacon Heights Private Estate was indeed private. It was a no through road and only residents were permitted. These were the big houses that backed onto the sea. The ones whose owners put up signs about snakes to keep people away. As I stood once again considering defiance, a Jaguar drove into the estate, the driver looking at me as if I had no right to be even near this exclusive little world. As he drove off, probably to release the adders, I noticed the personalised number plate, the height of pointless self indulgence.

When walking past a village shop which advertises fresh cakes daily, one feels compelled to enter. My choice was a large chocolate cornflake cake, but I was given the only one of the three on the counter with no smarties on top. Turning left onto the main road through the village, I said good afternoon to a lady walking her dog, but received just a blank look in return. Point Clear was the first place I'd been through that I didn't like. Others may look down on Jaywick, but shanty town or not, I much preferred it.

A footpath left the road and headed towards the sea. On the left a tall metal gate, with barbed wire above it, blocked the way to the forbidden foreshore. Another high chain link fence, this time going right out into the deepest mud, meant that even if I had avoided the owners of Ray Creek, the nesting birds, the barbed wire, the threatening lady, the mud and the adders, I would still have been unable to get through.

At Rose Cottage, a little old cottage with a large ship's bell standing outside, I was finally able to get down onto the beach. In the afternoon sunshine, the gently curving Point Clear Bay was most pleasant. A sign had warned of soft mud, but with the tide at its mid point this remained covered, allowing me to walk next to the sea, with the waves gently lapping onto the sand. Just across the water was Sandy Point, the end of Colne Point Nature Reserve. This small raised sandy area appeared at first to be an island and it was only on consulting the map that I realised it was the tip of the long promontory.

I returned to the sea wall at the end of the beach and soon found yet more chalets. Most were shut up and obviously holiday homes, but a few appeared to be permanent residencies. The path ran to the front, a sign at the start saying 'Private Estate, No Cycling', It wasn't clear as to whether walking was permitted, so I gave myself the benefit of the doubt and carried on. The path soon curved round, turning back almost 180 degrees as it rounded St Osyth Stone Point. This marked the end of a long stretch of open sea from The Naze to Point Clear, but it was now time to head inland once more. In summer a ferry runs from here to Mersea Island, but unless I was to wait until April, I had to negotiate the many ins and outs of the Colne Estuary.

The path continued in front of chalets, passing yet another Martello Tower, this one housing a war museum. From here it headed east along Brightlingsea Creek towards St Osyth. The town of Brightlingsea was only few hundred yards over the water, but it was to be a fifteen mile walk to get there. There is a ferry in summer, the service restarting in July 2004 after a two year gap when the ferryman retired. The new boat was purpose built and continues a long tradition, the first ferry being recorded here in 1699.

For some miles I'd been hearing mysterious distant rumbling sounds and their source was now evident. At the wharf opposite, two blue cranes were digging at a huge mountain of scrap metal and loading it onto a ship. Every so often their excavations caused an avalanche, with the tumbling metal making a loud roar that echoed across the water.

To the right of the sea wall, behind a long freshwater channel, was another huge area of static caravans. I have no idea how many caravans there are between Walton and Brightlingsea, but I can tell you that it is a lot. Apparently in summer the population of St Osyth rises from 4,000 to 20,000. To the left was a strip of salt marsh and beyond this, in the middle of the creek, Cindery Island. Here are many oyster pits, relics of a once thriving industry on this coast. Another smaller and unnamed island lies downstream of Cindery. Until around 200 years ago the two used to be joined, but they were separated by tides flowing from St Osyth creek, apparently assisted by the owner of St Osyth Priory cutting away part of the island to allow easier access for his yacht. Another tiny outcrop of land, Pincushion Island, lies at the mouth of St Osyth Creek, its rounded shape explaining the unusual name.

I followed St Osyth Creek for a couple of miles, the high sea wall gradually changing to a riverside path and eventually ending at a small harbour. Here several surprisingly large boats were moored, which must only be able to reach the sea on the highest tide. A road crosses a causeway between the harbour and the still waters of Mill Dam Lake. As I stopped to take a photo a flock of a dozen swans swam up to me, following close behind until I reached the edge of the lake. Doubtless they were hoping for a snack, but I had nothing to give them.

St Osyth had a mill for many centuries. The first was recorded in the Domesday book, although its exact location is unknown and there had been a tidal mill by the creek since at least the 15$^{th}$ century. The last was built around 1730 and was a well known local landmark. When it closed in 1930, the owner, a George Simmet, still endeavoured to make a living from the premises. Initially he opened a tea room, however this attracted little custom. He tried hiring out rowing boats on the lake and employed a man with a speed boat, but visitors were few and the villagers weren't interested. His next venture was fish farming and he stocked the pond with flounders. Crowds used to watch the harvesting, for which he used the simple method of opening the culvert at low tide, blocking it with a net and waiting for the water level to fall. Once the flounders were, well, floundering, on the bed of the lake, it was a simple matter to scoop them up into crates. When the pond froze one cold 1930s winter, the enterprising Mr Simmet charged locals to skate on the lake, although with no way of preventing access, few bothered to pay. In the war, with beaches closed, a few more visitors were attracted to the lake, but not enough for George's enterprises to make a profit. There had been much debate as to whether the mill should be restored, but the decision was finally made by the forces of nature. On January 26th 1962 a gale lifted the roof, depositing it onto the road. A Mr M. Norfolk of Jetty Road, St Osyth was driving towards the village in the early morning, when he suddenly found the timbers blocking the road. It was reported in the Clacton Gazette that he swerved but was unable to avoid a crash.

From the lake it was just under a mile up a gentle hill and into the centre of St Osyth. This interesting village is dominated by the Priory and its 383 acres of land. The large gatehouse is the most impressive of the 112 buildings in the parish listed for their historical or special architectural interest. Although it used to be open to the public, following a change of ownership visitors are only allowed into the priory on one day each year. There is much local concern that the owners are more interested in developing the site for financial gain, than in allowing public access to these beautiful buildings and grounds.

St Osyth is reportedly the driest recorded place in the UK, with an annual rainfall of just 513mm per year, low enough to classify it as a desert by some definitions. The village was originally called Chich, the Saxon word for bend, because the first settlement was by a bend in the creek, but this later became Chich St. Osyth. The original part was eventually dropped, but the story behind the new name is far more interesting.

Osyth was the daughter of Frithewald, King of the East Saxons. He founded a nunnery in the settlement of Chich and having raised her in the Christian faith, made Osyth the prioress. In the autumn of AD 653 a party of Danish raiders came ashore and broke into the nunnery, intent, as was their wont, on rape and pillage. Osyth shielded her nuns, standing up to the Danish chief and rejecting his demand that they deny their faith. Enraged, the chief immediately ordered one of his men to behead the young lady. According to legend, Osyth then bent down, picked up her head and carried it to the church, where she indicated with her bloodstained hand the place that she should be buried. Meanwhile, at the point where she had fallen a new spring of the purest water had suddenly issued forth from the ground. For her martyrdom in dying for her faith and protecting her nuns, Osyth was canonised and the village named after her. On one day each year her ghost is said to appear, carrying her head as she walks along the priory walls.

As I sat reading the map while waiting for a bus back to Clacton, a lady joined me, enquiring as to whether I was lost. Once we'd cleared up the misunderstanding that I wouldn't be visiting Bournemouth, as it was only the Essex coast I was walking, we had an enlightening conversation. She used to live in St Osyth, but it isn't the place it was, because she doesn't know everyone there anymore. She now lives in Clacton, which has become a terrible place where parents swear at their children and young people get arrested in the street. She'd move away if it wasn't for her mother you know. Jaywick is worse. Full of drugs and worse, whatever worse may be? Then we moved on to housing. When someone says

I'm not racist but, it's like when a football club chairman gives his manager a vote of confidence. You know what's coming. And so it did. She'd seen a programme where Asians had bought up all the houses in an area – 'well it's not right is it?' Like many people of her generation, she clearly didn't think that her attitude was prejudiced, but what was considered acceptable 30 years ago is now thankfully looked on differently. I was glad that the timely arrival of the bus prevented the need for me to answer.

# CHAPTER EIGHT

# ST OSYTH to
# BRIGHTLINGSEA HALL

(14 miles)
26th February

Do the friendliest bus drivers get chosen for the country routes, or is it the rural driving that makes them so pleasant? The driver of the 78 from Clacton had a cheery word for each of his passengers, most of whom were obviously regulars, and was interested to know where I was walking. As I alighted at St Osyth Quay he wished me a good day and urged me to take care. I hoped that this was just a friendly goodbye and not a warning of hazards to be met en route.

A footpath path runs through the boat yards on the north side of St Osyth Creek, but disappointingly there's no access to the next three miles of sea wall. The path turns away from the water after a few hundred yards, making a gentle rise across a grassy field. Here views opened up towards Brightlingsea on the left and St Osyth Priory on the right.

After a short distance I reached Howlands Marsh, a rather remote Essex Wildlife Trust reserve. This is one of the few coastal grazing marshes still surviving in Essex and consists mainly of low lying hummocky grassland, split up by dykes and salt water inlets. Natural depressions in the grassland are evidence of former creeks, which dried up when the sea wall was built. Another selection of curiously named plants grow here: spiny restharrow, glaucous bulrush, slender hare's-ear, lady's bedstraw, sea clubrush, and knotted parsley. I sat in the observation hide for a few minutes, glad to be out of the wind, but the reed warblers, buntings, curlew, dunlins and redshanks who frequent the reserve must have seen me go in, as not one showed its face.

There's another hide by the creek, but I continued on the main path. This runs alongside the access track to Wellwich Wharf and quarry, before turning right through the edge of a wood. Here a long line of logs had thoughtfully been laid to allow walkers to cross a patch of water. However, the water was obviously deeper than usual and as I found when stepping on the first log, they were floating. To attempt to cross would undoubtedly have led to a cartoon style episode, with rotating logs, flailing limbs and a big splash. Squeezing through undergrowth seemed a more sensible option. The path runs up to the B1027 Brightlingsea Road, just before which a sign warned 'Danger Archery in Progress', although of course it wasn't. I did wonder if there's much you can do if a stray arrow approaches. Is there time to duck?

For the next mile there was no alternative but to follow the road to the top of Hollybush Hill. Passing yet another caravan park, then the local refuse dump (or Civic Amenity Site as the sign rather grandly described it), I came to a nice looking pub, The Flag Inn. It had just started to rain and after a minute's contemplation the temptation of warmth and food drew me inside. The lady behind the bar had to check with the kitchen, but yes they were doing bar meals. The menu however consisted of just half a dozen sandwiches, two of which weren't available and no hot snacks. I fancied a pie or toasted sandwich. She offered the alternative of a three course roast lunch in the restaurant, but whilst appealing, I reluctantly declined for reasons of time and unsuitable attire – too much mud!

A footpath leaves the road after the short terrace of Hill Cottages, running through the edge of a small the wood. It comes out where the Bentley Brook runs into the head of the creek. The map shows the letters 'NTL' at this point, which the key informed was 'Normal Tidal Limit'. Looking closer I found that this is shown on almost every river and stream that enters the sea, but in my many hours of studying Ordnance Survey maps I'd never noticed it before. I walked along the sea wall for almost a mile to the corner opposite Eastmarsh Point where the creek splits. The map is confusing, as the seaward end is denoted as Brightlingsea Creek, but further inland it becomes Flag Creek, although once this divides neither fork seems to be named.

One of the problems with walking in the winter is finding somewhere dry and sheltered to sit and eat lunch. Hence the attraction of the pub. However, by now the rain had stopped and although the ground was wet, I found a position on a large concrete block by the water's edge. The only problem was that across the creek the Flag Inn was just visible and whilst my ham roll was nice enough, I had to try not to think of the roast lamb that I'd declined half an hour earlier.

The head of the creek was a further mile or so along the sea wall. From here the path continued into Brightlingsea, but I had hoped to follow the opposite bank of the creek for the four miles to the town. However no path was marked on the map, and although I could walk a few yards, barbed wire soon blocked the way. I returned to the footpath, which took me past Marsh Farm House, with its extensive lawns leading down to an attractive lake.

After passing high above an old flooded gravel pit, the path came out at Red Barn Road. Turning immediately left, I followed a lane towards East End Green. Just after the houses ended I passed a lady walking a puppy, but she completely ignored my cheery 'Good Afternoon'. When walking in the countryside it is convention to say a friendly word of greeting, but in towns of course one only speaks to people you know. It would appear rude to ignore a walker on a footpath, but odd to speak to the same person if passing them in a town. A lane on the edge of a town is a grey area. I thought it merited a word, but the lady obviously didn't.

I stayed on the lane, turning right at the crossroads, as the alternative footpath was extremely muddy. A short path on the left ran alongside an old farmhouse and to the shore. This too was very muddy and at one point I had to cling to a fence, working my way along the slightly drier bank. A path continued onto the marsh towards disused oyster beds, but a sign advised that this was a dead end and liable to regular tidal flooding. Instead I turned right, walking for a mile or so along the sea wall into Brightlingsea. Here I a saw an egret, meaning that unless it was the same one at St Osyth beach, I'd now seen 10% of the local population.

A small shipyard before the wharf meant that the path moved inland, running along the edge of a ploughed field. This was the muddiest section yet encountered. For a while I managed to avoid the worst of it by squeezing into the hedge, but once this was blocked by thick brambles, had no option but to splash through the mud. I was glad not to be wearing trainers, my new walking boots now at last comfortably worn in.

I followed the road round the back of the wharf, where the cranes were still noisily loading scrap metal and to the main waterfront of Brightlingsea. A small plaque indicated that the Town Hard had been given by Wm Bannell in 1898. I sat here for a while, looking across the creek to Point Clear. In summer this must be a busy place with boats coming and going, but today there was no action whatsoever. It was time to turn the map over, the first side which I'd followed since Wrabness, ending here at Brightlingsea. I surveyed the reverse, which runs as for as Tollesbury and after the requisite dozen attempts, finally managed to refold it.

The sea front was dominated and to be honest spoiled, by a large building site, The Waterside Marina. Some expensive looking apartments were nearing completion and although I'm sure it will look good one day, it didn't enhance my view of the town.

Brightlingsea's traditional industries of oyster fishing (which went back to Roman times) and shipbuilding, have greatly declined. It is now largely a dormitory town for Colchester and a popular retirement destination. Although it has a small beach, the town is more of a yachting centre than seaside resort. Colne Yacht Club has its club house next to the Hard and caters mainly for cruising members, with an active cruiser racing fleet. Brightlingsea Sailing Club runs an active competitive sailing programme and has produced many champions at international and Olympic level. The North London Sailing Association runs residential sailing courses for young people. It is based in an unusual old building close to the Hard, which dating from 1780, was once the Old Custom House and before that the Port Wreckhouse.

Here's a favourite quiz question and the cause of many a dispute. Name the Cinque Ports? Everyone knows that cinque is five, but there always seem to be more towns claiming such status. If the question is name the original cinque ports, the answer is that there indeed were five; Hastings, Sandwich, Dover, Romney and Hythe. However the harbour at Hastings silted up, so Rye and Winchelsea were appointed 'Limbs of Hastings' to assist in its duties of providing ships and men to the Monarch. In the 14th century these were granted full member status, bringing the number of Cinque Ports to seven. Another thirty Limb Ports were appointed, including Brightlingsea, as a limb of Sandwich. The town proudly holds on to this ceremonial connection and is the only community outside Kent and Sussex to retain a link to the Confederation of

Cinque Ports. Each year on 'Choosing Day', the first Monday in December, an ancient ceremony takes place at All Saints Church, when a Deputy is elected from a Guild of Freeman. He is the Mayor of Sandwich's representative and in the past would have been responsible for maintaining law and order in the town. Each July the Deputy is confirmed into office in an historic ceremony at Sandwich Guildhall and every June the Mayor of Sandwich visits Brightlingsea, with a colourful procession running through the town.

Brightlingsea's activities as a small port came to national attention in the mid 1990s, due to its role in the controversial export of live animals for slaughter. In January 1995 strength of public opinion had led to a general refusal by major port operators to export live animals for slaughter in Europe. Most people believed that they would be more humanely slaughtered close to their farms of origin, without the stress of a long journey. Even more so that young calves should not be transported to France to be reared in the cruel veal crates, already banned in the UK. With the major ports closed to this unpopular trade, exporters looked for other routes and a number of tiny ports were selected, including Brightlingsea.

There had already been demonstrations at Dover and when the first lorries rolled into Brightlingsea on Monday January 16th, their paths were blocked by hundreds of people sitting in the road. These included a disabled man who slid off his wheelchair in front of them. The lorries turned back. The next day the weather was so bad that the boat didn't arrive, but on Wednesday the lorries were back. Again Brightlingsea residents sat in the road, but this time they had to contend with a massive police presence. Officers in riot gear with helmets, thigh armour, forearm protectors and wielding long batons, waded into the demonstrators as they sat peacefully in the road. TV news footage of riot police attacking passive protestors, including women, children and pensioners, caused widespread shock. People could not believe that the police could treat ordinary people like the worst football hooligans. The East Anglian Daily Times showed a huge front page photograph of a riot policeman apparently stamping on children and pensioners. The Today newspaper carried the headline 'Like a Lamb to the Slaughter. Brutal Police out of Control at Port Protest'.

On Thursday Brightlingsea citizens again stood in the road, the protests now bolstered by many others who travelled to the town to try to stop the exports. Again the police battered them and many went home nursing bruises, but with even greater resolve. By Friday night there were 2,500 people waiting for the lorries and 65 vans of riot police. Lorry movements were banned in the town after 11.00pm, but the police chose to ignore this and escorted the trucks through late in the night.

The 'Battle of Brightlingsea' as the press dubbed it, continued. Hundreds were arrested, including doctors, teachers and children as young as 13. A crèche was set up by the campaigners, Brightlingsea Against Live Exports, but a number of mothers were arrested, amid claims that they had been deliberately targeted by police. Protesters, particularly activists from outside the town, tried different tactics. They walked very slowly in front of trucks, but could only delay them. They formed human chains, linking their arms inside pipes, but the police eventually broke them. Locals parked their cars in the road, but they were towed away. On one day they planned to set up a tripod made from scaffold poles, with a protester hanging from it and others chained to the poles, but the equipment mysteriously disappeared from its hiding place, amid suggestions of phone taps and bugs.

The protests continued, not just for days and weeks, but for nine months. Every single day until 27th October 1995, when it was announced that there would be no more shipments of live animals through Brightlingsea. The wharf owner had been convicted of threatening behaviour, one of the exporters had pulled out as a result of the protests and the other eventually went bankrupt. During the 9 months, 150 convoys had passed through the town, 250,000 animals had been exported (52 of which died during the journey), 598 people had been arrested (421 from the local area), over 1,000 complaints had been made against police and the cost of policing the protest estimated to have reached £4 million. The protesters however had won, the live exports were stopped and the town could now return to normality.

The centre of Brightlingsea is half a mile back from the shore, along straight residential streets. Unusually most of the small detached houses were of different designs. I paused at a crossroads and a man told me I looked lost. He directed me to the town centre, adding 'such as it is' and to a café where I stopped for toasted tea cakes.

The town centre is indeed a modest affair – a few shops, a church (St James), but with one particularly outstanding building, Jacob's Hall. At 600 years old, this is said to be the oldest timber-framed building in England, although the Figgs building in Berkhamsted makes the same claim. It has a long and varied history, being altered and extended many times, notably in the 15th century by some rich shipping merchants named Beriffe. They had a ceiling of beautifully carved oak built into the hall and enriched and enlarged the house, which even then was of considerable importance. Changes in the 19th century were however far less beneficial. The house was split into seven lets, the front plastered over and a shop selling the unlikely combination of boots and sweets, erected between the wings. In fact Jacobs as originally built, was unrecognisable both inside and out. Around 1923 the house was accidentally 'discovered' and restoration began. The shop was pulled down and most of plastering removed, with everything possible done to preserve the building as a perfect example of early English architecture.

Walking along Station Road, the site of the long closed railway terminus (it burnt down in 1968), I returned to the sea. At a boating lake a mother and young boy were feeding bread to the ducks, although a flock of black headed gulls were gobbling most of it. I was pleased to find that there is an open air swimming pool on the sea front, as nowadays these are quite uncommon, many having fallen victim to local authority cost cutting. Understandably I suppose, as they rely on good weather, but on warm sunny days swimming outdoors is a far greater pleasure than in a steamy and echoey covered pool.

A paved promenade lined with colourful beach huts runs to Westmarsh Point, where Brightlingsea Creek joins the Colne Estuary. By the Colne is one of Brightlingsea's best known landmarks, Bateman's Tower. This is a folly built in 1883 by John Bateman as a recuperation area for his daughter who was suffering from consumption. The roof was dismantled during the Second World War so that the tower could be used as an observation post for the Royal Auxiliary Observer Corps, but reinstated in its original form in 2005 thanks to Heritage Lottery support. It is used by local yacht clubs for administration of sailing races in the Colne estuary and open to the public on race days.

The next 3½ miles were very easy walking along the old Wivenhoe to Brightlingsea railway. This used to run along the bank of the Colne and with the sun now starting to show, made a very pleasant walk. Known as the Crab & Winkle line, the railway closed under the Beeching Plan in 1964. I'm told that I travelled on it not long before closure, when the steam trains had been replaced by a diesel railcar, but aged only two sadly I hold no recollection. It must have been a scenic ride and it's a shame that it wasn't taken over by preservationists. Had it survived another ten years I'm sure it would have, but unfortunately the idea of turning lines into tourist attractions arrived just too late for many branches.

The path passes through Brightlingsea Nature Reserve, a grazing marsh managed by English Nature and home to an abundance of wildlife. The sheltered Colne Estuary provides a rich larder for both resident and migrant birds. It is designated as a Ramsar site under the Convention of Wetlands of International Importance. Criteria supporting this status include its population of dark-bellied brent geese, common redshank and black-tailed gobwit, 12 species of nationally rare plants and 38 species of endangered invertebrates.

Across the Colne the views are firstly of Pyefleet Channel and Mersea Island, then to Langenhoe and Fingringhoe Marshes, which are M.O.D. firing ranges and closed to public access. The many signs on the far bank presumably warn yachtsmen not to land. The two marshes are separated by South Geedon Creek, at the mouth of which can be seen Rat Island, another Essex Wildlife Trust Reserve. This 33 acre marshland is the site of the county's largest colony of black headed gulls, over 4,000 pairs being counted there in the mid 1980s. The estuary's plentiful supply of fish and invertebrates support such numbers, although as I saw in Brightlingsea, they are just as happy stealing bread intended for ducks.

I made good progress along this straight, level and mercifully dry path, before stopping for a brief rest at Aldboro Point. Upstream I could just see the town of Wivenhoe, however the direct route onwards was blocked by Alresford Creek. The railway had crossed this on a steel girder swing bridge, but that was dismantled for scrap after the line's closure. The track bed approaching the bridge is quite overgrown, but I pushed past bushes to see where it used to stand. Stone pillars remain at either end and on the opposite bank is the tin shed which was used by the pilot man who opened the swinging centre span of the bridge. His cottage was nearby, although this has now gone. There is a campaign to build a new footbridge for walkers and cyclists, which would allow the whole course of the railway to be followed without need for the long detour around the creek.

I returned to the main path and the point where the map shows it crossing the Alresford Creek at a ford. This I had read is just passable with wellingtons at low tide, but now the water was clearly too deep. Surprisingly there were no signs to warn the adventurous walker, or to absolve the relevant authority of legal responsibility should any meet an untimely end in the creek.

A finger signpost indicated a footpath along the near bank, which I followed for a few hundred yards, until it faded away, eventually stopping at the inevitable barbed wire fence. Maybe I should have taken note that the path was not shown on the map, but one thing that I had learned by now, was that you can rely on neither signposts nor maps as to whether a path really exists.

Back at the ford, I found what looked like a path running behind the sea wall, but not wanting another false start, elected instead to follow the track running away from the creek. After about a mile this becomes a made-up lane serving a gravel extraction complex, after which peace was regularly shattered as a succession of lorries trundled by.

The lane passes the edge of Thicks Wood, the scene of a very sad and sobering story. Dr Alasdair Crockett, a professor at Essex University and one of the country's top experts on modern life, was reported missing in September 2006. A former research fellow at Nuffield College, Dr Crockett had taken up a senior part-time post with the prestigious Institute for Social and Economic Research, a think-tank that monitors life in modern Britain. A talented and successful man, his life changed as result of a single bite from a tiny insect, from which he contracted Lyme disease.

The micro-organism borrelia burghdor feri is transmitted by wood ticks, blood sucking parasites who normally live on deer, but will also bite humans. The common symptoms of headaches, fever, drowsiness and muscle pains can usually be treated successfully with antibiotics, but if not diagnosed early it can affect the central nervous system. This causes a variety of non-specific, but often major and long term symptoms, including mental disorders. Dr Crockett was badly affected by the illness. Although he fought it bravely and tried a number of treatments to alleviate the symptoms, he knew there was no cure. He suffered severe anxiety and following a land, sea and air search, two days after he went missing Dr Crockett's body was found in Thicks Wood. No longer able to suffer the debilitating effects of the disease, the professor had taken his own life. Aged just 38, he left a wife and two young children.

Lyme disease and its potentially serious effects appear to be little known, but the most common victims are ramblers, usually in forest or heath areas. Dr Crockett's family have appealed for greater awareness of the need for the prevention of tick bites, and of the importance in recognising symptoms so that early diagnosis and treatment may be made.

Sensible precautions include wearing long sleeves, tucking trousers into socks, using insect repellent and inspecting skin for ticks. If a tick is found it should be removed by gently gripping as close to the skin as possible, preferably using fine tweezers or a tick removal device. Although they are only about the size of a poppy seed, it is important to check thoroughly, as the risk of infection is very low if the tick is removed quickly.

Whilst most tick bites don't require medical treatment, the advice is to visit your doctor if you experience symptoms, or notice a red spot, which gradually grows bigger, often with a pale area in the middle. These are called erythema migrans and can appear at any time from 3 to 30 days after biting. Only 20% of those infected actually remember being bitten, so it is important to be aware of the possibility of having caught Lyme disease if you have been in a place where ticks could live, even if you are not aware of being bitten.

The lane continued past another area of woodland, Gravesend, before coming out at the top of the hill opposite the outstanding All Saints church of Brightlingsea Hall. Built around 1250, with the 97 foot tower added in the late 15th century, the church is visible for miles around and used as a navigation aid by shipping. The tower is said to be one of the best in East Anglia. It was built in three stages and contains a minstrels gallery, ringing room holding the frame of the peal of tubular bells, and bell chamber which houses the two remaining bells.

In 2004 controversy hit All Saints when the vicar closed the churchyard to further burials. It contained 1,600 marked graves and he said there was no more room. With the adjacent parish church of St Osyth 12 miles away by road, although only 3 minutes by boat, residents of Brightlingsea were enraged. Some tried to get the vicar, Reverend Richard Selenius, removed from his post. The episode made the national press and a question was even asked in the House of Commons. The vicar however maintained that there was simply no space for further graves. Despite his decision being upheld by a local court, the campaign continued and after allegedly being abused and threatened, Reverend Selenius resigned in April 2005. Finding space for graves is becoming a problem for many churches, but one hopes that others can resolve the problem with greater decorum than the parishioners of Brightlingsea.

With the railway long closed, Brightlingsea is served by a half hourly bus service to Colchester. Boarding the double decker outside the church, I doubled the number of passengers, the other being a teenage girl who chatted to the driver all the way. It's amazing how bus drivers seem quite content to disregard the 'Please do not distract the driver while the vehicle is in motion' rule, when an attractive young lady is on board. Alighting at Wivenhoe with half an hour before the train, I bought possibly the worst pie and chips I'd ever had. The pie was well beyond the cardboard stage, the bottom having been baked to the consistency of plywood. I wasn't sure whether the many hours it had obviously been kept hot would have killed the salmonella, or encouraged them to breed. Not wishing to take the risk I put it in the bin.

CHAPTER NINE

# BRIGHTLINGSEA HALL
# to ROWHEDGE

(10 miles)
14th March

This morning my seven year old son told me he didn't think he'd make it to be an adult. The reason – global warming. They'd had a talk about the environment at school and the lady told them that rising sea levels would cause London to flood, so he quite expected to drown. Of course we explained that it wouldn't happen for a long time and not at all if everyone starts to care for the planet, however on the train to Wivenhoe I read a worrying article in The Telegraph. The latest satellite data showed the Arctic sea ice reducing by 8.6% per decade and some computer models predict an ice-free Arctic by 2050. An area five times the size of Wales is being lost each year; (why do we measure rain forest and ice cap decline in units of the area of Wales?).

Whilst I could reassure my son that it was still a relatively slow process and that we must all do what we can to halt it, unless there is a huge change in the way man chooses to live, the world that our children inhabit will be very different to the one we know now. Not only do we have global warming and pollution to contend with, but fossil fuels are running out. This fact seems to be almost forgotten, but meanwhile we continue to use up oil reserves driving our cars and gas making electricity; living for the moment and not considering that one day these precious resources will run out. We will have to learn to live without petrol driven cars, but one day the oil from which so many crucial chemicals and materials are manufactured will be gone. We must change our whole attitude to the environment and resources. For starters, instead of automatically jumping in the car, we must consider whether a journey can be accomplished on foot, bike, train or bus.

To this end, I was pleased, although have to admit slightly surprised, that the first eight walks had been achieved with relatively little difficulty from public transport. Barring those missed connections at Thorpe le Soken, every train and bus had been on time, and I'd been able to travel to and from some quite remote parts of coast with relative ease. My contribution to global warming was negligible and by patronising rural transport I was helping to ensure it continues to run.

Leaving the Brightlingsea bus at All Saints church, I walked back towards Thorrington. A fairly new paved path, separated from the road by a hedge and with views across Alresford Creek, made an easy walk, on what used to be a dangerous stretch for pedestrians. After about a mile a footpath on the left leads to Thorrington Tide Mill. This impressive and picturesque building is hidden away, just a few yards from the main road. Built in 1831, the timber framed mill is in remarkably good condition and still grinds occasionally. It is one of just a handful of tide mills still in working order in the UK. The mill is owned by Essex County Council, who restored the machinery, and is opened once a month on their behalf by the Brightlingsea Society. Walking across the causeway in the warm sunshine I could see fish rising in the otherwise still lake. With the attractive mill, old cottages behind, and views back to the church, this was a truly charming spot. Another little known Essex gem that would attract plenty of tourists if it were in a different area of the country.

The path continues along the bank of Alresford Creek, although if preferred a more direct route can be taken across fields. The tide was up and in the spring sunshine the creek looked so much better than some of the expanses of mud that I'd walked alongside on dull winter days. There seemed to be more birds about and I paused for a while to watch a pair of shelduck pottering about on the water.

By the ford, opposite where I had left the creek on the last walk, I got talking to a local man. We started of course with the weather, concurring that it was extremely warm for mid-March and expressing our disbelieve that it was supposed to snow in a couple of days. We agreed that the forecasters probably use a crystal ball. He told me that 25 years ago the ford was passable at low tide, but that changes in the water flow (he thought partly due to a treatment works) had moved the mud. Although near to the bank the base is gravel, towards the middle of the creek there is soft mud 4 to 5 foot deep. There have been many rescues of people stuck and the only way to cross now is the rather undignified method of dragging yourself along lying on a board.

As we talked a party of 15 or so walkers, all in their 'senior years', came down the lane from Alresford. These were the first serious walkers I'd seen since Wrabness, but with the winter almost over, I guessed the coast paths would no longer be quite so deserted. I left them chatting quietly amongst themselves as they wandered around by the water.

Just beyond the ford is an interesting piece of industrial archaeology. A couple of hundred yards from the creek is Alresford Quarry and from here to the river there used to run an ingenious system for carrying sand. Full buckets suspended from a cable ran down to the wharf, where on rounding a wheel, they

Industrial Archaeology Alresford Quarry

tipped, dropping their load into barges waiting below. Whilst clearly not used for some time, the structures remain, as a rusting, but interesting relic. Several towers with wheels fixed above stood on the slope and the more complex contraption at the wharf end appeared largely intact. All that was missing was the cable and buckets. The quarry is still active, although sadly now using lorries rather than boats.

At the head of the creek is Alresford Lodge, set back from the water with fine views across the Colne. This was built on the site of a Roman villa, which was uncovered in 1884. Initially a section of mosaic pavement was found, which prompted excavations that yielded pottery, glass, coins, a spearhead and axe. Eventually a corridor some 100 yards long, a room containing 20 square feet of mosaic and part of a hypocaust central heating system were unearthed, showing that this was a significant villa. Unfortunately, in an act of Victorian recklessness, the site was not preserved and a house built over it.

By the way, I make no apologies for using mixed imperial and metric units, as this is one of the idiosyncrasies of the current English language. Like most people I say miles, so that's what I've written. Being of the generation who were bought up on yards, it feels right to use these rather than metres when describing the walk, but in this context 'a few yards' or 'a few metres' is pretty much the same. When describing locations or buildings I've stayed with whatever units the source quoted. Conversion results in either loss of accuracy if staying with round numbers, or what can be worse, a precise conversion of a rounded number (say 100 yards to 91 metres), implying a greater degree of accuracy than may be correct.

I was now back on the bank of the River Colne, where the path again follows the old Brightlingsea railway. Small trees and shrubs have grown up since the line closed, and it was hard to imagine that little steam trains used to puff down here. For a short section a narrower path ran closer to the water, by a small area of salt marsh. Here I found a sheltered spot with a view towards Wivenhoe to eat my lunch. The sound of gentle breeze and birds singing was punctuated by occasional bangs from the artillery ranges over the river, then the muffled chatter of the walkers as they passed by on the main path.

The railway line leaves the shore a mile short of Wivenhoe, but it remains easy walking along the sea wall. Just before the town is the Colne Barrier, built in 1994 to protect Wivenhoe, Rowhedge and Colchester from tidal inundation. It has been used far more often than expected due to more regular surge tides, but has performed its task admirably, and as a result development of the Colne's floodplain has taken place. Whilst functional, it's a shame that unlike the Thames Barrier, this concrete and steel structure has no architectural merit. In fact it is quite ugly.

Upstream is Wivenhoe Sailing Club, which runs regular dingy races using unique Wivenhoe One design. These craft were designed in 1935 by the local doctor, Walter Radcliffe, especially for the prevailing conditions on the Colne. Of the 19 built, 16 are still kept locally, most of which still race.

I had to walk round a Bryant Homes building site before coming to the town's attractive and historic waterside. This is very much a mixture of old houses and modern developments. At the end of the first terrace is the Ferry House, which was home to the ferryman until the service to Fingringhoe and Rowhedge ceased in 1952. An important link between the communities, the ferry was used by workers from the far side, who then caught the train to travel into Colchester, and in the opposite direction by the local doctor to visit his patients. In recent years a new service, operated by volunteers, has started running two hours either side of high tide on summer weekends, providing a useful link for walkers.

Quay House on the corner of Rose Lane is an early 19th century three storey building of yellowish grey bricks. John Harvey, a renowned yacht builder lived here in the 1860s and his son, John Martin Harvey was born here in 1863. He became famous as one of the last great actor managers, who ran theatres and played lead roles, his greatest triumph being the portrayal in 1899 of Sydney Carlton in The Only Way, based on Charles Dickens' A Tale of Two Cities. He was knighted for his success in the theatre and in 1989 to mark Essex Heritage Year, the County Council fixed a plaque to the house in his memory.

At the Rose and Crown, a mid-nineteenth century building on the quay, I caught up with the walkers, some sitting at tables outside the awaiting their lunch, and others on nearby public seats eating bags of chips. There's been a pub on this site since the 18th century, when smuggling was rife, and many houses near the quay had hidden storage spaces between rooms for concealing illicit goods of tobacco, silks and brandy.

A few yards further along the quay is the Nottage Institute, the River Colne's Nautical Academy, with a maritime museum open to visitors on summer Sundays. The academy was founded in 1896, using a trust fund left by Captain Charles Nottage, an army officer and keen yachtsman. Before his death aged just 42, Nottage had instructed that his legacy be used to set up an institute so that 'Colnesiders could improve themselves in navigation primarily, or make up their skills generally'. For over a century it has been training professional seamen, fisherman and amateur yachtsmen and women in the skills of navigation and seamanship.

The next section of quay is mainly newly developed, with modern houses looking out across the Colne and an attractive paved walkway along the shore. Wivenhoe seems to have successfully married old and new, providing an attractive environment to live, but without losing the atmosphere of the historic buildings along the quay.

Impressed with Wivenhoe, I continued on the path that follows the bank of the Colne. To the right was Wivenhoe Nature reserve and over the river the attractive frontage of Rowhedge, where drinkers sat in the sun outside The Anchor. With the afternoon sun providing welcome, but most unseasonable warmth, I found a secluded spot and changed my jeans for shorts. With this their first airing of the year, I was quite shocked to the whiteness of my legs, which I have to admit, like those of most men, are never the most agreeable of sights.

At the edge of Wivenhoe Wood the path joins up with the

Wivenhoe

Wivenhoe Trail, a walk and cycleway, which was established by the Borough Council in the early 1990s. The path runs between the river and railway line and links the town with Colchester. It was surprisingly busy with walkers, cyclists and the odd runner, which I assumed was due to a combination of warm weather and proximity to towns. It certainly made a change from the miles of deserted paths I'd covered until today. Many of those I passed looked like students from Essex University, whose 1960s grey concrete towers stood in the distance.

Approaching Hythe, a suburb of Colchester, the far bank of the river becomes industrialised, with a long line of mainly disused warehouses. In what could have been a scene from The Bill, a lone motorcyclist clad entirely in black with a dark visor over his face, appeared in front of one the abandoned buildings. I watched for a minute as he waited motionless by the river, but no gun was drawn, no drugs deal took place, and he soon sped off along the deserted wharf.

Where the Salary Brook meets the Colne a cormorant sat on top of a pole, relieving himself of copious amounts of poo as I passed. I wished my son had been here to laugh. My map was dated 2000 and showed none of the new developments on the east bank. A modern and impressive campus has been built along the quay, much in keeping with the university's excellent standing, and in contrast to both the old grey towers and its sixties reputation as a hotbed of student activism.

I stopped at the Quay Café, situated amongst the student buildings but open to all, and sitting in the sun, enjoyed a slice of chocolate cake. Crystal ball or not, the forecast was right and two days later snow did fall in the South East, yet today I was sitting outside at a café table in shorts and T-shirt.

Further building development meant I had to walk away from the river for a short distance, before taking the road bridge, the first crossing of the Colne. This completed the first major section of walk, the area bounded by the Stour and Colne estuaries. At a rough calculation about a third of the distance was done.

King Edwards Quay on the west bank has been a port area for Colchester since the mid 12th century, although until 1701 large boats could only navigate the river on the highest of spring tides, so goods had to offloaded onto smaller vessels at Wivenhoe or Rowhedge. In 1698 an Act had provided for the widening, deepening, and straightening of the river, the work to be paid for by tolls to be collected by the Mayor for 21 years. However despite many attempts at improvement, navigation remained difficult. In 1880 Colchester traders complained that some ships took up to an extraordinary 7 days to get from Wivenhoe to the Hythe, but by 1883 the commissioners had bought a steam dredger and four years later a vessel as big as 325 tons reached the port.

Despite the difficulties, from the Middle Ages, both coastal and continental trade from the Hythe was important. By 1637 there was a weekly service to London, and with steam replacing sail in the 1830s, the journey time was reduced to just 7 hours. In 1892 3,000 vessels, mainly Thames sailing barges, used the dock and it remained a busy port into the latter part of the 20th century. In 1984 at total of 2,501 ships, carrying 1 million tons of cargo docked at Hythe, Wivenhoe or Rowhedge, although the number at Hythe was rapidly reducing as companies used larger ships, which couldn't reach the upper quays. From 1980 to 1985 the number docking at Hythe fell from around 1,200 to 500, but now it is no longer regularly dredged and after usage dropped to a mere handful of vessels, the port officially closed in May 2001.

A couple of interesting boats were moored alongside the quay. The T.S. Colne Light is an old lightship, launched at Dartmouth in 1954 and now a base for the Colchester Sea Cadet unit. The Fertile, a 58 tonne Thames sailing barge, runs trips down the Colne in summer months. Built in 1935 and rescued from a Medway scrap yard in 1984, the vessel is included in the National Register of Historic Ships.

From the quay I made my way through an industrial estate, then back to the river by the disused warehouses. It was unclear where the path ran, and only at the end of the buildings did I realise that you were supposed to go between them and not along the river bank. The way I'd taken required walking along a narrow section between a fence and the river, with a not inconsiderable drop to soft mud below. This was OK where I could stay close to the fence, but in several places vegetation necessitated going right to the edge. With the momentum of a fall from height, one slip here could have left me with perhaps just my head poking out of the mud below. Needless to say I took it very carefully, but it's not the route I'd recommend!

A grassy path along the river bank then runs the couple of miles to Rowhedge. I preferred this to the made up path on the other side, and it was far less busy, with just one young couple passing me. To the right of the path are Hythe Lagoons and Marshes, which support a variety of plants, many of them rare, and with the usual array of curious names: mouse-eared hawkweed, knotted bur-parsley, spiny rest-harrow, bird's foot trefoil, hairy buttercup, and creeping bent, being just a few. The water courses range from fresh water to almost fully saline, providing varying habitat for a wide range of flora and fauna. Small mammals abound, and barn owls and kestrels can often be seen hunting over the marshes. The nationally scarce roesel's bush-cricket is abundant, as are various species of dragonfly, damselfly and butterfly.

Rowhedge has a nautical history going back 2,000 years, when the Romans established a supply base here, the Emperor Claudius landing in AD43. Now I must admit to a degree of scepticism when I read that he brought with him a number of elephants, but research from various sources has confirmed it to be true. When the Romans arrived, Colchester, or Camvlodvnvm as it was then, was the most important Iron Age settlement in Britain and an obvious target for the invaders. In an early equivalent to Mr Bush's 'shock and awe' tactic, Claudius brought the elephants, who acted both as beasts of burden and to scare the enemy. It must have been truly terrifying for the ancient Britons to meet the invaders riding on these huge animals, the like of which they'd never come across, and they could hardly be blamed for legging it.

From Roman times until comparatively recently, Rowhedge acted as an out-port for Colchester, unloading those vessels too large to make it further up the river. By the Middle Ages construction and repair activities were well established, and for several hundred years a wide variety of trading ships, fishing craft, warships and all sorts of specialised vessels, including even the odd submarine, were built or repaired here. However by the end of the 20th century commercial traffic had so declined that continuance as a port was no longer viable, and on 14th April 1999 the M.V. Ruhrort of Duisburg brought the last cargo up the Colne to Rowhedge Quay. So almost 2,000 years after the Roman troops of the 20th Valeria

Legion landed their cargoes of food, wine and of course elephants, the river fell silent. Apart from a small number of inshore fishing craft the only maritime activity to enliven the scene is now virtually entirely leisure based. A small marina has been built, helping to maintain marine activity in and around the village and in 2006 a new floating pontoon improved access to the water, particularly for the Wivenhoe ferry.

For the past few years a mysterious happening has been occurring regularly in Rowhedge – the unexplained appearance of push bikes in the river. Always in the same spot by Lion Quay, usually in good condition and obviously still used, the bikes just turn up, lying in the mud. No one knows who they belonged to, or how they got there, but a local councillor usually fishes them out, only for another to appear before long. Someone must know the explanation, but to the residents of Rowhedge it remains a mystery.

I walked the length of the waterfront, from the marina to the small industrial area at the downstream end. On the small green area next to the Anchor pub, is an unusual metal sundial, commemorating the opening of the Pearsons Quay in September 1976, by the Montreal Olympic yachting gold medallist Reg White. Beyond this a row of cottages back onto the river, with several signs indicating that access to the waterfront is private. Hence it is necessary to follow the road for the short distance to the warehouses that mark the end of Rowhedge village.

I would have liked to have walked further, but this was one of the days where I was to be constrained by public transport. There is a very creditable half hourly bus from Rowhedge to Colchester, but beyond here little in the way of regular transport until reaching Mersey Island. So having completed what was an easy and enjoyable day's walk, made all the more pleasant by the unseasonably warm weather, I wandered into the village to find the bus stop.

My meanderings took me past three interesting churches. The main village church of St Lawrence was built in 1838 and has an unusual hexagonal shape. The attractive brick built former primitive Methodist church, was designed by S. Wilson Webb in 1913. The Mariners' chapel in Chapel Street was built in 1851 and now houses Rowhedge Christian Fellowship. This describes itself as a 'Bible believing church', something one would consider pretty fundamental to the Christian faith. I presume they mean that their interpretation of the bible is more literal than some other churches.

The village was deserted, and without an apparent centre there was no indication where the bus would stop. I kept wandering, looking for someone to ask, but the only sign of life was a ginger cat called Boddington, who ambled up to me, meowing for attention. As I stroked the happy feline a young chap passed by, but it transpired that he too was not local and also lost. However he thought that he knew where the bus went, but fortunately just as we set off in what was completely the wrong direction, another gentleman appeared and was able to assist us both.

Arriving almost immediately, the bus took 40 minutes to Colchester station, for a fare of £1.70, contrasting with the 10 minute ride from Wivenhoe to Brightlingsea Hall at £2.50. It was Comic Relief day and in Colchester town centre the bus filled with school children wearing strange items of attire. Their conversation made interesting listening, with the girl behind me, who could have been no more than 13, asking the lad in the next seat if he thought her best assets were her boobs or bum. Maybe my memory has failed me, but I don't recall having such conversations with young ladies at such an age. His answer, predictably, was boobs.

CHAPTER TEN

# ROWHEDGE to PELDON ROSE

(12 miles)
19th April

I have come to the conclusion that rural buses are run for the benefit of the young and the old, neither of whom actually have to pay. Presumably most of those in between own a car and choose to drive, but quite rightly subsidise the services through their taxes. With my fellow passengers on the 10.28 to Rowhedge all being well over 60, I was the only one purchasing a ticket, but the bus was quite busy and clearly a vital service to those using it to shop or visit friends.

The tide was down, but the waterfront at Rowhedge and the views across to Wivenhoe, were still most attractive on this most sunny of mornings. A day when the only blemishes in a totally blue sky, were vapour trails of jet planes, flying miles overhead to unknown destinations. At the end of the village the path runs between warehouses and the river, although a notice attached to a telegraph pole advised that it was temporarily closed. As this was dated June 2004, I assumed that the bridge repair to which it referred had been completed, and continued on my way.

The Roman River, a small tributary of the Colne, meant a detour further inland, but the path alongside its meanderings made an enjoyable walk in the sunshine. I caught up a gentleman walking two dogs, although as I approached he picked up the smaller one. He told me it was a chihuahua and had a tendency to run off when strangers approached. We walked together for a while before, on learning I was heading for Mersea, he told me to go on, as my pace was double his.

At the end of the tidal section is Fingringhoe Mill, which was built in the 16th century as a tide mill, but converted to steam in the 1800s. It was active until the mid 1990s, producing flaked maize, but has now been converted to private residencies. From here I made a short detour up the hill to St Andrews church. This most attractive building has a 12th century nave, and a 14th century tower faced in narrow bands of flint and stone rubble. Turning back along Abberton Road I could have taken a footpath to the right, heading dead straight through a field of bright yellow rape, but with my aim to stay as close as possible to the shore, I continued into the small village of High Park Corner.

Here the road splits into three, with the left fork running down to where the old ferry crossed to Wivenhoe and the middle road to the Ballast Quay, where gravel is still loaded onto barges. However as there isn't a path along this section of the Colne's banks, I took the right fork that runs parallel with the river. At Lower Brickhouse Farm road turned to track as it passed by more gravel pit workings. Several tracks ran to left and right, but the many signs indicating private areas and danger from quarry workings, kept me on the correct route. Another nice path along the edge of fields led to Fingringhoe Wick, a major Essex Wildlife Trust reserve, its importance and interesting history meriting a reasonably detailed description.

Half a million years ago sea levels were 100 metres lower than now. England was joined to continental Europe and the Thames flowed passed Colchester, joining what we now know as the Medway near

Fingringhoe Mill

Clacton, before crossing the North Sea plain to join the immense Rhine river. Over thousands of years wide flood plains were created, into which the waters deposited vast amounts of silt and gravel. Although most of Essex was just beyond the ice sheet, successive ice ages and their torrents of melt waters added further layers of silt, sand and gravel. Known in this area as East Essex Gravels, these deposits still underlie much of the north east of the county, hence the many gravel pits around the Colne estuary.

It was only when the last of the Devensian ice melted, as recently as 14,000 years ago, that the land started to settle into its current shape. Subsequent changes were largely man made. Woodland of birch, pine, alder and hazel, which provided home to reindeer, brown bear, lynx, moose and woolly mammoth, was gradually felled by man as he changed from hunter to farmer. A hand axe found at Fingringhoe, dating from somewhere between 15,000 and 50,000 years ago, provides evidence of Palaeolithic (Old Stone Age) activity. Several more recent Neolithic (New Stone Age) flint axes have been found in quarries nearby. Around 4,000 years old, these belonged to our first farmers, the people who stated the process of woodland clearance.

The Romans farmed at Fingringhoe, the Essex climate then as now, ideal for arable crops. Ships exporting the harvests around the empire brought back the black rat and house mouse, accidentally introducing them into England. Scores of artefacts have been unearthed, ranging from brooches, coins, and spoons, to pottery, a sickle and a metal cooking pot of the type issued to Roman army legionaries.

The Manor of Fingringhoe was included in the lands of West Mersey Priory, which in 1046 were granted by Edward the Confessor to the Abbey of St Ouen in France. Farming continued through medieval times, and what had become Wick Farm was recorded on the first map of the area produced in 1751. By 1812 this was a part of the 800 acre Manor of Fingringhoe, and it continued as largely arable land for another hundred years. Then in 1921 the farm was sold to a gravel extraction company, which was to change its face once more.

Unlike today's efficient extraction techniques, quarrying was haphazard, with holes dug wherever the gravel was easiest to access and spoil piled in any convenient spot. This hotchpotch of trenches, holes, gullies and humps formed the basis of the landscape that is 'The Wick' today. For 40 years gravel was extracted, moved around by conveyor belt, washed, sorted and sent down chutes into trucks on the small railway which ran to the end of the jetty. Here barges took it around the country, mainly for building use. In eight years in the 1950s 250,000 cubic yards of gravel were shipped to construct the Isle of Grain oil refinery in the Thames estuary.

In 1959 the pit closed and the barren landscape was put up for sale. The Ministry of Defence sought to purchase it to expand their existing training ranges, but there was local opposition. Fortunately the newly formed Essex Naturalists' Trust saw its potential as a nature reserve, with varied habitat, plenty of fresh water and on the banks of a major estuary. With the support of local people, apparently to the extent of guaranteeing the bank loan, the Trust completed purchase from Brightlingsea Aggregates in 1961.

The task of transforming an industrial wasteland into an attractive area for people to enjoy and in which wildlife would thrive, was immense. Working to a management plan to maintain biodiversity, a plan that remains relevant and extremely successful to this day, volunteers set about making the reserve safe and suitable for visitors. Scrap metal had to be removed, physical hazards made safe and the sandy beach cleared. The old jetty was converted into a walkway and a bird hide built at the end. The jetty had long been a hazard to shipping and although a hurricane lamp was hung on the end, one foggy night a ship ran into it. The damaged section was blown up by a naval team from HMS Ganges and now a red light is powered by a solar panel. Nature soon started to take over the old man-made features, with barren sand becoming gorse heathland, dry gravel forming areas of grassland and ponds filling with water plants and insects. Numerous species of mammals, birds, invertebrates and wild flowers made their homes in the varied habitats and increasing numbers of visitors came to the reserve.

Initially only Trust members were permitted, but by 1970 public visitors, paying an entrance of three shillings, outnumbered them by three to one. It was decided that Sundays should be for Trust members only. They were asked to park facing the river, with membership stickers in the rear window, so the warden could use binoculars from his cottage to check no one had gate-crashed. To dissuade passing yachtsmen from landing, a sign was erected on the beach, however some misread the large board saying 'Essex Naturalists Trust', perhaps to be disappointed on moving in for a closer look. Naturism was less well known then, but the change of name to 'Wildlife Trust' eventually overcame such confusion.

Left to its own devices, scrub and woodland would eventually take over the area, reducing the range of habitats and hence the species present. By the 1980s most of the original gravel pit features had gone and the Trust took the decision to intervene, re-creating conditions that were abundant in 1961. Scrub was removed, ponds dug out and ground scraped to leave bare earth to be colonised once more by wild flowers and insects.

This policy of biodiversity has proved extremely successful, with surveys recording surprising numbers of species.

Twenty four mammals are thought to be present – brown hare, brown rat, house mouse, harvest mouse, wood mouse, yellow-neck mouse, rabbit, mole, field vole, bank vole, water vole, common shrew, pigmy shrew, water shrew, stoat, weasel, badger, fox, grey squirrel, hedgehog, muntjac, brown long eared bat, pipistrelle bat and on the shore, common seal.

The bird population has changed through the years as the habitats have altered, but has always been large in both numbers and variety. Whilst yellowhammer, linnet and reed warbler have been lost, growth of woodland attracted sparrow hawk, magpie and carrion crow. Nightingales breed in thickets and pochard, tufted duck, dabchick, ruddy duck and mute swan nest on the lake. Blackcap, whitethroat, lesser whitethroat, reed warbler, garden warbler and chiffchaff are among other regular breeders, and marsh harriers can be seen swooping over reeds seeking out moorhens and coots.

Amongst the reptiles and amphibians living on the reserve are great crested newts, smooth newts, common toads, common lizards, slow worms, grass snakes and a thriving adder population, who can often be seen basking in the sunshine. Strangely frogs are rarely found. The ponds provide home to an incredible 160 invertebrate species, including 65 aquatic beetles and nymphs, and the larvae of assorted dragonflies, damsel flies and mosquito. Of the nearly 600 species of bees, wasp and ants living in Britain, over 130 have been recorded at The Wick, including 19 that are listed as Nationally Scarce and 3 Nationally Threatened. The varied habitats attract a wealth of lepidoptera with 28 types of butterfly and an astounding 716 moths recorded here. Nine of the UK's 27 species of crickets and grasshoppers have been found on the reserve, as have 104 species of spider. Fingringhoe's flora is equally diverse, with around 350 species recorded in a 1982 survey. Interestingly this is the same number as were recorded in 1962, but the changing conditions meant that the two lists were very different. The number of fungi varies according to weather conditions but can easily exceed 100 in a damp year.

A compete list of all the flora and fauna species recorded in the reserve from 1961 to 2004 totals around 2,400 a truly remarkable figure and testament to the superb work of the Essex Wildlife Trust, its wardens and many volunteers. With modern agricultural practices, urban spread and climate change, such nature reserves are in increasingly important oasis for wildlife. Without them the diversity of our wildlife and the very existence of many species would be at greater risk, and we all owe a debt to those who work so hard to protect it.

I spent a most enjoyable couple of hours walking round the reserve, following a nature trail down to the river, looking in all the bird hides (from one of which I saw another of my egret friends) and wandering round the ponds. Near to the beach I saw the wreck of 'Fly' a ballast barge which worked on the Colne. One of three vessels built at Appledore in Devon in 1899, Fly was the only one to survive their maiden voyage, her sister barges 'Bee' and 'Ant' sinking off Dover in a storm which struck the trio on their way to Essex.

The Visitor Centre, which first opened in 1975 and has since been considerably extended, contains excellent interpretation displays and facilities for visiting school groups. Huge picture windows look out across the marshes and a spiral staircase leads to an observation dome with views around the reserve. From the well stocked shop I purchased the former warden Laurie Forsyth's excellent book 'Island of Wildlife', from which I have obtained much information on the reserve. The Wick is a beautiful place and a credit to the Essex Wildlife Trust.

From Fingringhoe to the river's mouth, it isn't possible to walk along the west bank of the Colne. Firstly it is marshland (Geedon Saltings, Langenoe and Fingringhoe Marshes) and secondly it's an army firing range. I had instead carefully planned a route along the footpaths which run along the boundary of the range, coming out near Mersea Island. The path leaves the road at South Green,

Wreck of The Fly - Fingringhoe

half a mile from Fingringhoe Wick, and although a sign warned that one should not pass the line of red boards if a red flag is flying (as it was), I assumed that this meant walking onto the range, not the footpath on its perimeter. However, after a few hundred yards a sign instructed that one should go no further if the gate was closed (which it was). This not being the sort of warning one would ignore, I returned to the road, until another path departed to the right after South Green Farm. Once more however my way was barred by a gate and dire warnings as to the consequence of passing it. Yet another sign warned of the risk of touching any 'military debris', with the blunt statement 'it may explode and kill you'. A not so distant burst of machine gun fire served to reinforce the warnings and once again it was retracing steps time.

The nice walk through fields that I had planned was not going to be possible and the only alternative was three times the length by road. I cursed the army. Yes, they need to train somewhere, but wouldn't it be a simple matter just to point their guns across the marshes, allowing walkers continued access to the footpaths?

South Green Road headed in exactly the opposite direction to Mersea, although as road walking goes it couldn't have been much better – a typical Essex lane, running between fields, with no hedges and very little traffic. Abberton Road was busier, but not unpleasant, and just before its end I took a small lane to the left. Approaching was a group of twenty or so squaddies, running in formation with two sergeants at the front. I stopped to let them pass, then waited as one straggler, encouraged by another officer, followed about 50 yards behind. I didn't envy them one bit running in the bright sunshine, on what was now a very warm day, particularly the poor chap at the back, who certainly wasn't sharing my enjoyment of an afternoon in the countryside.

A paved track runs to Crouch End House and on to Langenhoe Rectory. Here it goes around a small wood, but a footpath was signed through the middle. The wood was a mass of bluebells, out early this year with such a warm spring, and I stopped for a few minutes to enjoy the flowers and take a few photos.

Photography was a sore point, as the day before I'd accidentally deleted all the photos from walks seven and eight. My usual camera is a Minolta SLR, the old fashioned type that uses film, but to get pictures for publication I'd been using my wife's digital. I'm sure digital has many advantages, but I still prefer film and with this you can't inadvertently erase all the images. It is also my opinion that the quality of photo is often be better, not for technical reasons, but because when each exposure has a cost one tends to spend more time composing the shot. Digital cameras can lead to quantity not quality approach. Neither do I approve of altering images on a computer. That's cheating. The photos chosen for this book were all taken as I walked the coast. They haven't been enhanced and with the weather often dull, may not be of perfect quality, but I hope they portray the sites and atmosphere that I experienced.

At Langenhoe Hall I linked up with the path I'd originally intended to use, and from here followed a short lane to the main B1025 Mersea Road. This was busy and after half a mile of squeezing into the hedge at each passing vehicle, I was glad to leave it. A path on the left ran across a grassy field along a low embankment, presumably an old sea defence, to the higher banks of the sea wall. Bordering salt marsh and Pyefleet Channel, it appeared little used, with the grass being less trodden than almost any point on the walk to date. Nevertheless, away from the road, it was an enjoyable walk for the mile back to the B1025 and Mersea Island.

With a population of 6,500 and an area of about seven square miles, Mersea is Britain's most easterly inhabited island. It is the 7th largest island in England and the 8th highest in population. Like most Essex islands, you don't always need a boat to reach Mersea, a man-made causeway, The Strood, linking it to the coast. This is

Pier – Fingringhoe Wick

covered only at the highest tides, at which times an ambulance is often stationed on the island to provide medical assistance in case of emergency. Having heard many mentions of The Strood on Essex Radio weather and tide forecasts, I was interested to see it for myself. The first crossing was constructed by the Romans and the current causeway dates back to around AD700. When I arrived the surface was wet, but the water had receded either side of the fenced road and it had been passable for a while. I walked a short distance towards the island and whilst I would have liked to explore further, decided that I should stick to the unwritten rule of the walk (stay as close to the shore as possible, but don't walk around the islands) and maybe save the island exploration for a future project.

Mersea is made up of two very different halves. East Mersea is largely rural, being mainly agricultural, with houses dotted about and an extensive country park. All but around 300 of the island's population live at West Mersea. This is a residential and commercial area, with active yachting and fishing and seaside attractions. It has become a popular holiday and day trip destination, with its fair share of the ubiquitous Essex caravan.

The island's history goes back to prehistoric times, with Neolithic axes and Bronze Age beakers having been found. The Romans came here in numbers, with traces of mosaic pavements, villas and burial tombs remaining, as well as over 25 Red Hills, the remnants of operations to extract salt by evaporation of sea water. A Roman soldier, visible only from the waist up, is said to haunt The Strood and occasionally to be seen marching on the road to the mainland.

The Romans introduced oyster fishing, which has remained an important industry on the island for 2,000 years. The oyster fishery is officially opened on the first Friday of September each year. The Mayor of Colchester, the Town Clerk, and the Town Sergeant, all in their full civic regalia, are taken on an oyster dredger into Pyefleet Channel. A flotilla of small boats carrying invited guests follows and oaths are sworn, pledging devotion to the monarch. The Mayor dredges and consumes the first oyster of the season, then proceeds with his guests to an oyster lunch, which celebrates the opening of the fishery. In another ceremony, originating in the 14th century, he hosts a grand Oyster Feast on the last Friday in October, inviting local people who are involved in various good works.

The mainland to the west of The Strood is owned by the National Trust, but managed as another nature reserve by the Essex Wildlife Trust. Closest to the road is Bonner's Saltings and beyond this the slightly raised area of Ray Island. Its mix of scrub, grassland and saltings provides home to a wide variety of wildlife, with significant breeding populations of redshank, shelduck and oyster catcher. Large numbers of waders and wildfowl over-winter here, with flocks of up to 2,000 brent geese, fattening up before retuning to Siberia.

There's a path onto the reserve, (although it floods at high tide), but not around the shore, so it was another detour inland and back to the busy B1025 towards Peldon. Here the increasing wind led to another hat in road incident. This time I was wearing a large sun hat, with a particularly broad and firm rim. A couple of gusts had tugged at it, but been thwarted by my quick action in grabbing the hat as it lifted, however the third time I was too slow. It landed just behind me, but then rolled on its rim in a perfectly straight line along the edge of the road, with me following a few feet behind. The hat continued for a remarkable distance, at a pace just too fast to catch, before slowing and inevitably falling to the right and into the path of an oncoming car. The last time this happened the driver had smiled understandingly. This driver looked at me as if I was mad!

I reached The Peldon Rose, a most attractive 15th century coaching inn, 15 minutes before the bus was due. Just time for a very welcome drink and to enquire as to where the bus stops. The answer was that I should stand on the green, but look both ways, as alternate buses to Colchester took different routes. It appeared right on time, coming up the hill from Mersea and dropped me in Colchester town centre half an hour later. I'd decided to get something to eat here, which turned out to be a good move, as wires down near Chelmsford meant a very slow journey home. That made it 4 out of 20 train journeys that had been delayed, however so far, and much to my surprise, the buses had maintained a 100% punctuality record.

# PART THREE

## Peldon Rose to
## St Lawrence

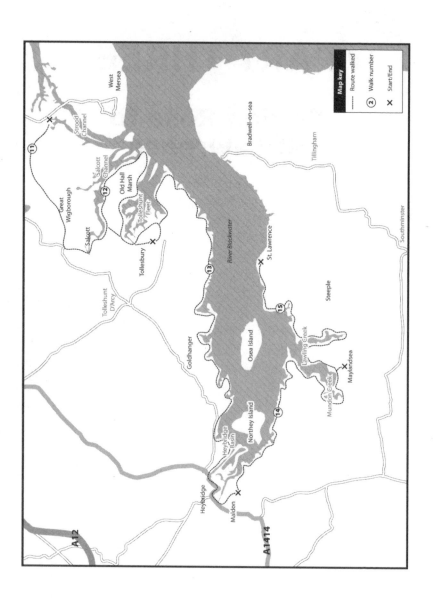

**Map key**

⎯⎯ Route walked

② Walk number

✕ Start/End

West Mersea

Strood Channel

⑪

Great Wigborough

Salcott Channel

⑫

Salcott

Old Hall Marsh

Tolleshunt Fleet

Tollesbury

Tolleshunt D'Arcy

⑬

River Blackwater

St. Lawrence

⑮

Osea Island

Steeple

Goldhanger

Lawling Creek

Mundon Creek

Maylandsea

⑭

Northey Island

Heybridge Basin

Heybridge

Maldon

A12

A1414

Bradwell-on-sea

Tillingham

Southminster

# CHAPTER ELEVEN

# PELDON ROSE to TOLLESBURY

(11 miles)
22nd May

When the Victorians built the railway from London to Norwich they bypassed the town of Colchester, putting the station a couple of miles away at the foot of a hill. Little could they have realised the inconvenience this would be causing the best part of two hundred years later. Most buses to Mersea start at the bus station in the town centre, so I had to wait for the shuttle train that runs every half hour linking Colchester North and Town stations. Once again it wasn't until three hours after leaving home that I could start walking. This however was to be the last journey to the eastern end of the county, so from now on, in theory at least, travelling times should be shorter.

Alighting at Peldon Rose I walked for a short distance along the road towards Peldon, then took a track on the left, which heads down to the shore. There's no path marked on this stretch, but I'd hoped to be able to walk on the sea wall, however the track turned out to be just a driveway to a private house. The only way to the shore was through their garden, which I considered for a few minutes. However after exploring the possibilities of skirting round the hedges, and seeing a fence across the sea wall, I opted to take the simpler route by road. This meant missing a few miles of coastline around Feldy Marshes, but even had I negotiated the garden and fence, it was quite likely the route would be blocked further on. Before starting out I had envisaged that for most of the coast I'd have been walking along sea walls. With access denied for various reasons, there was however more inland and road walking than expected, although this too was usually enjoyable.

The village of Peldon is spread out around a triangle of roads, with the church of St Mary the Virgin at the northern corner. Notices all around the village advertised a festival weekend, with a whole selection of events – an Antiques Roadshow, art exhibition, crafts, beer tent and the church tower open. All in all a most British of affairs. The Peldon Plough is a classic example of Essex white painted weatherboard construction and has a reputation for serving fine local fish. As I passed the chef was sitting outside drinking tea and I was very tempted to call in. However although I was already quite hot, it didn't seem right to pause so soon, so I made do with a swig from my water bottle.

At the triangular green at the end of the village I stopped to consult my map, exchanging greetings with an elderly man cycling very slowly on his way to post a letter. To break up the road walking and get closer to the sea, I chose to take the slightly longer route through Copthall Grove. A path was shown on the left just past Harvey's Farm, which I followed for a short distance until it reached a large field. Here the way forward was unclear and as I wandered around looking for a way through, a gentleman appeared in the grounds of his house. Accompanied by four black labradors, he asked if I was lost or looking for something. I showed him the map and the path I was looking for. He advised that this was a bridleway, only to be used with permission and that the farmer got very upset if people walked along it. With visions of shotguns being wielded, I heeded his warning and returned to the road.

Little Wigborough, a mile further on, consists of just a scattering of houses and a couple of farms. It rather strangely possessed quite a sizeable wooden bus shelter, although examination of the timetable showed that just a single bus calls here each day. Great Wigborough is another spread out village and the road passed through only the outskirts, which meant that I missed the 14th century St Stephens church. Situated on a slight hill, this had been visible for some miles and there been more time I would have liked to look inside. This and the very small 750 year old church of St Nicholas at Copt Hall, Little Wigborough, are supported by The Friends of Wigborough, a charity dedicated to raising funds for their maintenance. With a population of just 50 and like so many English villages, Little Wigborough couldn't sustain its church without charitable help. I wholly concur with Dr Simon Thurley, Chief Executive of English Heritage, that 'The parish churches of England are some of the most sparkling jewels in the precious crown that is our historic environment'. We owe a debt to those dedicated people who help to ensure that our churches are maintained as places of worship, to be used and appreciated now, and by future generations.

On a September night in 1916 the area around Great Wigborough saw some quite remarkable events. The war in France was at stalemate and the Germans had started using Zeppelins to bomb England. Great Yarmouth had received the first attack in January 1915 and the Essex towns of Harwich, Southend, Braintree and Maldon were all targeted. The airships were difficult to shoot down and it wasn't until 2nd September 1916 that the first one was destroyed in Hertfordshire. The next successes were on the night of the 23rd/24th September, when two more were brought down, this time over the Essex countryside.

Super Zeppelin L33, 650 feet long and 75 feet in diameter, was returning from its first mission where it had caused the deaths of several Londoners, when it was hit by an anti-aircraft shell. The damaged Zeppelin turned over the Essex countryside and above

Chelmsford was attacked by a squadron of night fighters from Hainault Farm Aerodrome. The airship's captain Alois Bocker ordered guns and equipment to be jettisoned, but still losing height, soon realised he wouldn't be able to make the journey back across the North Sea. It eventually crashed near New Hall Cottages, Little Wigborough, where Bocker decided to burn the Zeppelin. First and with commendable thoughtfulness, he knocked on the doors of the cottages to warn the residents of his intentions. However, terrified, they refused to open their doors, so the Captain proceeded to set fire to his craft. He then gathered his crew together and marched them down the lane towards Peldon.

A local policeman, Special Constable Edgar Nicholas, had seen the fire and was cycling down the lane towards it. Surprised to meet a body of men marching along a lane at that hour of the morning, he dismounted and torch in hand asked Bocker whether he had seen a Zeppelin crash. The Captain, in perfect English asked how many miles it was to Colchester. Nicholas replied that it was about six and was thanked for his assistance. The Constable however had detected the foreign accent, so followed the men as they marched. At Peldon he met two other Special Constables and the three men escorted the Germans to the Post Office, where they found the local constable PC Charles Smith. He took charge of the situation, formally arrested the men and politely refused their request to use the telephone. The police officers then escorted the prisoners to Mersea Island, where they were handed over to the military.

The next day PC Smith was rewarded for his 'coolness and judgement' by promotion to sergeant and from then until he died in 1977, was known as 'Zepp' Smith. Such was the public relief at the destruction of the Zeppelin that an appeal was made and the money raised used to buy an inscribed pocket watch for each of the police officers involved. The one presented to Edgar Nicholas now resides in the Essex Police museum at Chelmsford.

At nearby Great Wigborough a baby daughter was born to a Mr and Mrs Clark at about the same time as the L33 was set alight. At the suggestion of the attending doctor, Dr Salter from Tolleshunt D'Arcy, the baby was christened Zeppelina.

Shortly after Great Wigborough is Abbotts Hall, the headquarters of the Essex Wildlife Trust, a 700 acre working arable farm and nature reserve. I had hoped to meet the warden here, but forgot to bring his phone number to make arrangements and he had to leave for a meeting at Fingringhoe just as I arrived. However, I spent an enjoyable and interesting couple of hours wandering round on my own.

Abbotts Hall became a site of international interest, when on the morning of 4th November 2002 the largest coastal realignment project ever undertaken in Europe reached a crucial stage. Breaches were cut in the sea wall and at high tide the sea swept through, converting over 200 acres of arable farmland into salt marsh.

The scheme was part of a nationwide initiative to restore the UK's rapidly declining coastal wetlands. Around 100 hectares of salt marsh are lost every year in South and East England alone, and a global loss of up to 50% is predicted for the next century. In the last 25 years we have lost 40% of Essex salt marsh, an internationally important wildlife habitat. The idea behind coastal realignment is that a natural coastline which can grow and adapt is the most sustainable defence against rising sea levels. It will be increasingly difficult to bolster traditional sea defences, but the newly formed salt marsh and lagoons absorb the waves' energy, providing an effective barrier to the incoming tide.

The breaching was carefully timed to precede the October spring tides, allowing each tide to bring in huge numbers of seeds from the existing marsh outside the wall. By midsummer, fields that had grown barley the previous year and which still bore its stubble, were carpeted with thousands of new salt marsh seedlings. The dominant plant species of marsh samphire, sea blit and lesser sea spurrey soon colonised the developing marsh and marine creatures moved in. Shore crabs, shrimps, common jellyfish and lugworms found their way in through the breaches, along with small fish; herring, common goby, smelt and three spined stickleback. Within 18 months of the breach fourteen species of fish were breeding in the marsh. Oystercatchers, shelduck, redshank and lapwing were in turn attracted by this ready food source and the speed at which the new habitat developed surprised even the most optimistic of experts.

Coastal realignment has the twin benefits of providing sea defences at virtually no cost and creating a wildlife habitat that is declining worldwide. Abbotts Hall has helped to show that this is a viable and effective method of coping with the effects of rising sea levels and helping to counter the loss of vital wildlife habitat.

I walked the mile or so down to the shore, along paths that skirt the fields. Barley, oil seed rape, wheat, oats and spring beans are all grown here, with a specific policy for diversity and to improve conditions for wildlife. Fertiliser and pesticides use are minimised and a trial 38 acres have been converted to organic. I sat for a while by Salcott Channel looking across the water to Old Hall Farm Marsh, eating some biscuits I'd bought on Romford station. It had turned out to be a hot afternoon and there was no shade to be found, but I was glad of the sit down. Heading back to the reserve entrance, I found a delightful path through some young trees, crossed a field and came out in the garden at the rear of the farm buildings. This was a fine garden with a pond, attractive shrubs and flowers. A man was cutting the lawns and several people, who I assumed to be staff from the Trust's offices, were sitting outside drinking tea. What a lovely place to work.

I called back in the office to see if they sold drinks. They didn't, but suggested I went to Abberton a few miles away, where there's a visitor centre. However, once I explained that I was on foot, the lady filled my water bottle and chatted for a while about the walk. She wanted to know why I wasn't continuing along the sea wall, as she thought these were free for anyone to walk. I explained about the fences, barbed wire, soldiers and irate farmers, but forgot to mention the explosives factory or adders. There wasn't a path marked on the sea wall from Abbotts Hall and with the various breaches it was unclear if there was a way through. I'd decided not to take the risk. I showed the lady my planned route via Salcott and departed, with her good wishes and a warning not to overdo it, which left me wondering whether I didn't look up to completing the remaining miles.

Less than a mile further on and just after the Colchester Road leaves on the right, a footpath is marked on the map. I found the sign clearly indicating 'Public Footpath', but it headed straight into brambles and tall stinging nettles. Obviously no one had used it for some time and there was no way I could get through to the field beyond. On returning I looked up the Ramblers Association website, which advised contacting the relevant county council to report problems with blocked paths. I followed the appropriate link and sent an email pointing out the problems to Essex County Council. A month later an acknowledgement arrived, but that was the last I heard.

Fortunately there was another path a few hundred yards further on, and although its entrance was also getting overgrown, it was at least passable. Once through the hedge it led to a perfect path cut along the side of a meadow, this farmer obviously taking seriously his duty to maintain the right of way.

To the right of the path was a mound, covered in the white flowers of cow parsley. Marked on the map as 'Mill Mound', this was, as you might have guessed, the site of an old windmill. The next field was of corn and again a perfect path had been cut through the middle. At the end a sign indicated that the path continued through

Impassable Footpath – Great Wigborough

a gap in the fence. Following this and ducking under the low hanging branches of a small clump of trees, I emerged into someone's back garden! It was a very big garden, but clearly that of a private house, with a sun lounger under a tall tree and cricket stumps set up on the neatly cut lawn. I returned quickly to the field. While checking that the sign did indeed point into the garden, two small black scottie dogs appeared, barking madly and most upset that I was even near their territory. Not fancying having my ankles nipped, I sought an alternative way round. Going left it was possible to skirt the cornfield for a while, before the hedge jutted further out and the only way forward was to trample the corn. As a good citizen and the farmer having made such a good job of cutting the footpath further back, I didn't want to damage his crop. Once again I surveyed the garden and considered the possibility of legging it across the wide lawns. However with two yelping little dogs intent on ankle gnawing, it was unlikely that this could be achieved without attracting attention of the householder. Preferring not to be the subject of a manhunt by the local constabulary, I tried the right hand option. This was more promising, with a field of relatively short grass and the semblance of a path along the edge. Rather than taking me to the road, this however led into another back garden, from where loud barking indicated the presence of an unmistakably larger dog. Now I'm not that confident with dogs at the best of times and facing a fierce animal defending his territory was most certainly not an option. Turning back across the field I eventually found another path. This led round the houses and at last got me to the road with all limbs intact.

Here I turned left, which turned out to be 100% incorrect, with the lane ending at Virley Hall Farm, where a notice advised that there was no access to the sea wall. Walking isn't easy in this little area of Essex. Following the lane back and turning left into The Street, I walked through the little twin villages of Salcott-cum-Virley. Like most coastal villages in this part of Essex, both are steeped in legends of smuggling, with the tower of Virley church said to have been used for flashing messages to Tiptree Heath across the Blackwater estuary. Apparently there was always a good turnout here, with the congregation boosted by local smugglers, present to keep an eye on contraband concealed in various places within the church. According to one tale, villagers once found a customs boat drifting near Sunken Island in Salcott Channel. All 22 men on board were lying dead with their throats cut from ear to ear. It is said that they were buried in the churchyard, with the upturned hull of their boat covering the graves.

Both Virley and Salcott churches were badly damaged in 1884 by probably the largest earthquake to hit the UK in the last 500 years. Measuring 6.9 on the Richter Scale and with its epicentre four miles south of Colchester, the quake caused widespread structural damage within a 20 mile radius. It was felt as far away as Yorkshire, Devon and even across the channel in Ostend. St Mary the Virgin in Salcott had to be largely rebuilt, although the 15th century tower and porch are original. St Mary's at Virley was never repaired and is now just a ruin. According to local legend, on its walls were claw marks put there by the devil himself.

Apparently a medieval lord was attempting to build himself a new manor house, but was making little progress. Every night he left his tools and materials, but every morning found they had mysteriously disappeared. The nobleman was convinced that somebody was creeping up under cover of darkness and stealing his goods. Presumably he wasn't the brightest of lords, because he was trying to build his house on a deep marsh and everything was simply sinking into it. One night he decided to keep vigil and catch the culprit red-handed, however, instead of a thief, up strode the Devil, accompanied by two dogs. The Devil took one of the nobleman's house timbers and threw it into the darkness crying, `Where this beam doth fall, there build Barn Hall'. The chosen spot was indeed sound and the nobleman was able to complete his house. In return for this favour, the Devil announced that man owed him his soul and vowed, 'Where you are buried on land or sea, there I will come to fetch you'. The terrified man decreed that when he died, his body was to be kept in a coffin embedded in the walls of Virley church, trusting that he would be protected by the sanctity of the church. The power of God and the church proved to be too much for the Devil, who could only claw at the walls trying in vain to claim his prize. Whether he eventually got his man when the earthquake struck will never be known.

The lane ends at Marsh Farm, where a short path finally took me to the sea wall. A footpath is signed to the right, but although none is shown on the left, it did look possible to walk this way. Whether one could go all the way back to Abbotts Hall I couldn't tell. For just under a mile the sea wall is pretty well straight, along the narrow Salcott Channel, before turning sharp left, as the channel widens. Rather than following this round the five mile perimeter of Old Hall Marshes, an RSPB reserve, I took the direct route on to Tollesbury. It would have been a rush to catch the last bus at 18.20. I was hot and running out of water, so decided to take the advice of the lady at Abbotts Hall and not overdo it.

The path heads inland across fields, passing Old Hall Marsh Farm and the adjoining Old Hall Farm (I bet that causes some confusion when student postman is on duty). Time was getting tight for the early bus and another decision was needed. Whether to take the safe, but slightly longer and less interesting road route, or stay on footpaths with the risk of them being non existent or impassable. A lady got out of her car to open the gate at Old Hall, but whilst she responded positively to my question as to whether the sea wall path would lead me to Tollesbury, her lack of conviction only served to increase my doubts. I opted for the paths however, following the sea wall for half a mile or so. To my left was the salt marsh around Old Hall Creek, its channels rapidly filling with the incoming tide. To the right was a large meadow. Here two hares scampered, chasing each other like a pair of kittens, then stopping abruptly and sitting back to back, where they remained dead still until I was out of sight.

At the most inland point of the creek a path departed to the right, through fields and up a gentle slope towards Tollesbury. With time running out for the 4.00 bus, I quickened my pace, overtaking two couples, walking according to normal convention – the men ahead and the ladies engaged in conversation following about 100 yards behind. At a little bridge I had the choice to go left or straight on. I took the former, which brought me out on a road that led to the main village square, where I arrived with five minutes to spare.

Tollesbury has a somewhat sporadic bus service. There is a reasonably regular service to Maldon, although for some reason this stops running at 2.30, an occasional bus to Colchester and a few to Witham. However when I arrived the square was a hive of omnibus activity. Ancient vehicles were moving in all directions, dropping school children, who headed either for the village shop, or the chip van that was doing a roaring trade. The Witham bus, which I shared with one other passenger, pulled in bang on 4.00 and took us a pleasant ride through this most rural part of Essex. At one point in the middle of nowhere, the bus lurched to a sudden halt, allowing a mother duck to cross the road with her ducklings following in a line behind. We passed the famous jam factory at Tiptree (famous in these parts anyway) and its jam museum, which is apparently marginally less boring than it sounds. My fellow passenger got off here, but I was not alone for long as several others boarded before Kelvedon, where I was to catch the train. The bus timetable had said 'Kelvedon Railway Station', but there had been no sign of it as we reached the end of the town. The driver explained that the bus merely 'passes the station', telling me it was 'way back there'. Fortunately there was just time to walk back down the long main street, find the station and catch the hourly London bound train.

## CHAPTER TWELVE

# AROUND TOLLESBURY

(11 miles)
30th May

Headingham Omnibus's service from Witham really is a most friendly affair. I was the only passenger the driver didn't know and almost everyone got a little chat as they stepped on or off. It was quite busy too, mostly with people returning from early morning shopping in Tiptree. One young girl was put on the bus by her Mum, who told the driver she was staying until the 12.30. This was the sort of journey that you could let a child do alone without worrying. The more I travel on rural buses, the more I like them.

Today was a figure of eight walk around the village of Tollesbury, mainly to go back round Old Hall Marshes that I'd missed out last time, and for the first time I was starting and finishing at the same point. It took 35 minutes to walk the two miles back to Salcott Channel. The rain had started as soon as I'd reached the sea and by Quinces Corner it was necessary to don leggings. Remembering that mine were several inches too long, this time I'd brought my wife's, which were of better length, but a rather fetching shade of purple. I should have put them on earlier, as the long grass had already soaked my jeans to the knee, but at least another layer allowed them to gradually warm. It had been difficult to predict today's weather. The nice lady on the television had confidently said that it would be wet in the morning, but dry in the afternoon. The Met Office online forecast said exactly the opposite. It turned out that neither would be correct, with rain falling on and off all day – more on than off.

Old Hall Marshes is a nature reserve of over 1,000 acres. Bounded by water for 90% of its perimeter, the reserve is almost an island, and has been embanked to keep the sea out since the end of the 16th century. Purchased by the RSPB in 1984, it has developed into a series of outstanding habitats, regularly hosting up to 20,000 wintering wildfowl. The site consists of grassland, reed bed, salt marsh and open water, and is grazed by cattle and sheep to provide the right conditions for a number of different bird species. The central core of grassland represents the largest remnant of traditionally managed reclaimed grazing marsh in Eastern England. The area of reed beds is said to be the biggest in Essex, although I was later to find that Stanford Warren makes the same claim. Old Hall Marsh is recognised as being possibly the best grazing marsh in the country and almost unique in the context of present day coastal wetlands.

The reserve supports internationally important numbers of wintering dark-bellied brent geese (around 2% of the total world population) and of migrating ringed plover. A further seven species of wildfowl and wader; curlew, dunlin, goldeneye, grey plover, shelduck, teal and wigeon, reach nationally important numbers in winter. The grazing marsh is a locally important wintering area for hen harrier. As well as the migrants, the marsh has nationally important breeding populations of marsh harrier, pochard, barn owl and bearded tits.

I saw a greater variety of birds today than anywhere else on the walk so far, although I have to admit to being unable to name most of them. There were herons, oystercatchers, shelduck, brent geese, various types of gull and some swallows, but most of the rest were beyond my still poor recognition skills. It's difficult to say exactly why, but even if you're not a spotter ticking off each species, knowing the name of a bird adds to the enjoyment of seeing it. If I return here in more clement weather, I would be sure to bring binoculars and RSBP book.

The southern side of the marsh runs along Salcott Channel, opposite Abbotts Hall Farm. With the tide at its highest it looked very different from the expanse of mud I'd seen from the far bank the previous week, and when the rain relented for a few minutes I sat on a stile, hoping to see a seal bobbing in the still water. Both grey and common seals can be seen around the Essex coast, but despite many hours by the sea, keeping an eye open in likely spots, I hadn't spied even one so far and nor was I to today.

On the grassland was a large herd of dark brown cattle, many with young calves. They stood firm as I approached, each one standing dead still and watching me intently. Then when I was about 20 yards away the whole lot turned and legged it to the other side of the field. Cows aren't the brightest of creatures are they? Firstly, there was about ten yards of deep water between them and me. Secondly, if they didn't think it necessary to run until I was almost upon them, why retreat hundreds of yards? Why not simply maintain a considered safe distance as birds tend to do? If evolution should one day lead to the cow possessing sufficient brain to realise that its bulk actually makes it capable of inflicting far greater damage to an unarmed man than we could do to them, their days of subservience could be over. No longer domestic, they could roam free, up hill and down dale, nibbling grass and squashing walkers to their hearts content. Or could it be that our bovine friends do actually possess greater intelligence than we give them credit for? That they have realised that domestication takes the stress out of life, and so long as they do nothing to upset the status quo, fine grass and hay will continue to be provided by their human 'masters'.

Towards the end of the reserve is an area of salt marsh. Beyond this, sitting low in the water is Sunken Island, where the men from Salcott had found the customs cutter and its unfortunate crew. After this a notice asked us to walk below the sea wall for a short length to protect wildlife, however I regained the wall near the tip of the Old Hall Marsh. This was the most remote point I'd yet been to and at three miles from a road, house or even a building, there can't be many more isolated spots in the South of England. There is closer civilisation, but that's across the water on Mersea Island.

Rounding the headland into the Blackwater estuary the wind immediately picked up, the sea was rougher and the smell of salt in the air. Whilst this still wasn't open sea, there were waves splashing, the first I'd seen since Jaywick. So far I'd walked something like 140 miles and only about 10 of those were alongside what you might call real sea. The rest being the quieter, but in many ways more interesting creeks, backwaters and estuaries that make up most of the county's coast.

A small red and white boat was towing a line of six small yachts along the Blackwater towards Mersea Quarters (the channel that separates the island from the peninsular of Old Hall Marsh). Here the wind or currents must have changed, as one by one the yachts started to capsize. Time and again the little boat had to turn back and the two men aboard lean over to right them. At first I was quite concerned they might be in difficulties, but they seemed to be coping OK. I kept watching however until they were in the calmer water near the island, lest it should prove necessary to call the Coastguard.

Across the Blackwater was the vast grey bulk of Bradwell nuclear power station, about five miles away by sea, but a lot of walking by land. At the entrance to Tollesbury Fleet is Great Cob Island, part of the RSPB reserve and a well established roosting area. Once alongside the more sheltered fleet, the wind dropped again.

The sea wall was easy walking, with grass nicely cropped by sheep. Even the rain ceased and at last I was able to stop and eat lunch. I'd had a bacon roll in the excellent buffet on Witham station, but by now was quite hungry. Sitting on a concrete block beneath the wall and looking across a small lake, I just managed to finish before the rain returned.

After Joyce's Head, Tollesbury Fleet opens out into an extensive area of salt marsh, creeks and mud banks. Across the channel were lines of fascines; wooden breakwaters constructed with twigs between the vertical supports. I didn't know whether these were remnants from old sea defences, or a traditional method used by more modern engineers.

Other wooden structures were the remains of jetties, once used by the many smugglers who took advantage of the sheltered inlets of the Blackwater and that the nearest customs house was some miles away in Maldon. Its staff were greatly overworked, so Tollesbury smugglers were more or less free to come and go as they pleased. Once the authorities became more vigilant,

Fascines – Tollesbury Fleet

contraband was simply thrown overboard in one of the creeks, to be collected when the coast was clear. However, there was always a risk that goods could be found by 'honest' men and turned in. In 1819, one such man, Daniel London, was dredging for shellfish and hauled up a large number of tubs of spirit. He spent most of the night loading 152 tubs into his boat, which he took to Maldon Custom House. However he left 11 in the water, presumably for collection later. When he got home a reception committee of smugglers was waiting for him, not unnaturally wanting their property. Being reasonable men, they offered to pay London half the value, but he foolishly declined. At this point the angry mob threatened to lynch him and he retreated indoors. The Maldon Controller of Customs arrived and London, in fear of his life, owned up to the other 11 tubs. He was promptly accused of smuggling and thrown into Chelmsford jail. Petitions were made for his release, but the fact that he had a previous conviction for smuggling weighed against him and his boat was eventually confiscated. Having upset both the authorities and smugglers, his time in prison was not pleasant and he received regular beatings from other inmates.

The circle was completed close to Old Hall Farm at Ship Ahoy Quay, where the attractive Old Hall house, formerly the Crooked Billet ale house, looks out across what appears to be a still functional quay. In its heyday this was a busy landing place for barges and coasters, with a coal wharf and lime kiln, but now just the old pub remains. For half a mile I retraced my earlier footsteps, but rather than taking the path up to Tollesbury, continued on the sea wall. Soon the path switched to a lower secondary wall, half a mile or so inland. The map didn't suggest why, but this was soon apparent as a large gap in the main wall came into view – another example of managed realignment of the coast. The breach having taken place in 1995, it seemed strange that it wasn't shown on the Ordnance Survey map from 2000.

This was actually one of the first places that this 'soft' engineering

Coastal Re-alignment Near Tollesbury

option had been trialled, with the aim to reduce the cost of maintaining embankments and at the same time deliver environmental benefits. As at Abbotts Hall, this has been successful, with the vegetation and invertebrates quickly colonising the newly forming salt marsh. However, twelve years after the sea was allowed to flood what was then farmland, the field boundaries were still clear, with lines of trees and hedges, long dead thanks to the salt water, making for quite a surreal landscape. I imagined a dark night, with the skeletons of trees peering out of the mist, as the incoming tide swirled around them and was glad that I was in this quiet spot on a clear, although damp afternoon.

Passing a particularly smelly sewage works, the path soon took me to Tollesbury Waterside, a busy little area with a few light industrial units, boat repairers, quay and marina. Moored in Woodrolfe Creek is the 119 foot two masted steel Trinity lightship, an icon for the village. Almost every picture seems to show this bright red vessel, which surrounded by salt marsh, appears from many angles to be in the middle of the land. Built at Dartmouth in 1954, at a cost of £80,685, she first served as the Scarweather Lightship off the Tyne Estuary, before moving to Swansea where she performed duty in the Bristol Channel until 1980. Originally named Lightvessel Number 15, in 1988 she was purchased by the Christian charity, Fellowship Afloat, and renamed Trinity. She is now used as a centre for relaxation, adventure and exploring the environment, for youth organisations, churches and special needs groups.

Dominating the waterfront is a line of restored wooden sail lofts. Built at the turn of the 20th century to serve the local fishing fleet, they were later used as stores for the wintering of J class yachts. These fast and elegant racing yachts, which were owned by wealthy Edwardians, have a long association with Tollesbury. They had their roots in the America's Cup challenge, twice being skippered by Tommy Sopwith, better known as the aviation pioneer who developed the Sopwith Camel.

By Woodrolfe Hard is the old granary, a 150 year old Grade 2 listed building, which in July 2006 was featured on the BBC's Restoration Village programme. The timber framed building is of typical Essex design, although was modified in the 1920s when the barge trade declined, a corrugated iron roof replacing the original wood. After falling into disuse in the 1950s, repeated flooding damaged the lower level, but there are now plans to restore it to form a local maritime and history centre.

Behind the sail lofts are some flats, which like the lightship, had been visible from several miles back. Fairly new, their clean white paint didn't quite fit with the slightly faded and more ramshackle buildings around them. I followed the path which runs in front of the flats, stopping for a while to watch birds feeding from a table on the grass. The usual suspects were there; sparrow, starling and chaffinch, and on the ground picking up the crumbs they dropped, was a pheasant.

Tollesbury Cruising Club, a posher looking affair than the sailing club by the Hard, sits back from the marina. Opened in 1971, it boasts a heated swimming pool, tennis courts and restaurant, and clearly caters for the upper end of the boating fraternity. As I passed a ginger cat appeared, walking purposefully towards the marina. He sauntered down the slope onto the floating pontoon and hopped aboard the first boat, an expensive looking three masted wooden yacht, then jumped down the hatch, turning to look out with just his head showing. Whether he was a resident of the yacht returning after a foray ashore, or a land based visitor, he certainly looked at home.

Following the path beyond the marina, I paused on a seat at the top of a small hillock to look at the map. The concrete seat was the most rickety affair, moving alarmingly as I sat down and I kept very still for fear the whole thing would collapse. The next section of coastline is a five mile circuit of Tollesbury Wick. Given the

Tollesbury

still inclement weather, I opted to leave this for today and once again get the early bus home.

With more than an hour to kill, I wandered a little more around the marina. A man was washing his boat in the rain and another (boat not man) hung from a crane, waiting to be returned to the water. I walked round the marine lake, a sea water filled pool constructed in 1907 and still open for swimming in the summer, read the information board on the Hard, then took the only road up into the village. A young lady offered me a lift, provided I could put up with the mess in her car. I declined of course, although explained that my refusal had nothing to do with the state of her vehicle.

The main village square is both attractive and historic. On the west side is the Kings Head, one of the remaining two of Tollesbury's original six public houses, and traditionally the pub frequented by seafarers. Opposite are several old cottages and by the church wall, the village lock-up in which the local constable would have incarcerated drunks until they sobered up. A small wooden shed like building, it was constructed around 1700 and restored in recent years. With just a grill for air and light, it couldn't have been a pleasant night for those detained, although most were probably too intoxicated to notice. I must say it seems an awfully good idea and a few of these in our towns and cities might help deal with our modern day drunk and disorderlies.

I bought a drink and some chocolate in the village shop and ate it sitting on a seat under a tree in the corner of St Mary's churchyard. A couple of teenage girls stared as they passed by, almost as if it wasn't a normal occurrence for a rather wet and somewhat scruffy middle aged man in bright purple leggings, to be seen eating snacks amongst the grave stones.

I was pleased to see a notice saying that visitors were welcome inside the church, both because I was interested to look round and as it provided a refuge from the continuing rain. Two ladies were arranging flowers for a wedding the next day, but one stopped to chat for a while. She agreed what an interesting village Tollesbury is and confirmed my observation that it didn't appear to attract tourists. This she put down to geography, as it is not a place one passes through, but saying 'sssshhh' she told me they wanted to keep it that way. I would add that tourism tends to be self perpetuating. People don't go Tollesbury, because although it has the setting, views, history and buildings that many would find enjoyable, it is not marketed as a tourist destination. Nor does it have the cafes, caravans, car parks, ice cream vans, craft shops and associated 'attractions' that visitors expect. If the village set out to sell itself to tourists and put in some of these services, then visitors would start to come. Once some came they would create custom for other attractions and soon more would visit. Tollesbury could easily become another day trip and long weekend destination, but it wouldn't be to the Tollesbury that's there now. Like the lady arranging the flowers, I hope it doesn't change.

I bought a small guide to the church and a parish magazine and had a wander round. The church was built around 1090, although various additions and alterations have taken place over the years. The lower, Norman, part of tower is made from septaria (nodules of stone) and the upper brick built part is Tudor. Parapet walls and pinnacles were added to the top in the 17th century. Restoration took place in 1872, at which time the chancel and south porch were built and the fine east window dates from 1902. Internal doors from the south porch were the Millennium gift of 'Friends of St Mary's' and are engraved with the dove of peace, plus the inscription 'Jesus 2000'.

I hope the lady in the church won't mind me saying how much I liked Tollesbury. It's a self-contained village in an isolated position, but gives the impression of being far more of an outpost. The centre is historic, attractive, but lived in. As shown by the chip van, the school buses, the hairdressers, butchers and Post Office,

Trinity Lightship - Tollesbury

Tollesbury is a community – a home to 3,500 souls. The waterside is what you might describe as unspoiled, although not in the idyllic picture postcard way. It hasn't been redeveloped like say Wivenhoe, or even tarted up, but remains genuinely a place where local people make their living or enjoyment from boats. The yacht club obviously caters for quite some well to do visitors, but nothing like say Torquay or Brighton, and the working marina enhances the whole waterfront. With typical Essex countryside to its west, nature reserves on either side, and standing at the head of the mysterious channels that lead to the Blackwater estuary, Tollesbury epitomises the unique attraction of the county's coast. As I've said about several places on my journey, if this were in somewhere like Devon it would be overrun with tourists. Don't bother with going to Tollesbury if you want to do much more than just look, walk or sail, but should you choose to visit and should anyone ask, please don't tell them I recommended it.

# CHAPTER THIRTEEN

# TOLLESBURY to MALDON

(16 miles)
19th June

Why is it so uncool to travel by bus? As I've commented before, most bus passengers seem to be either too young or too old to drive. Generally people consider the train as an acceptable way to travel, even if they don't use it much themselves, but the poor old bus is looked down on. A mode of travel the majority don't choose unless they have no alternative. In towns like Nottingham where trams have been brought back, far more travel on them than previously used the buses, and if a railway closes far fewer will use the replacement bus.

I regularly travel on business and wherever possible use public transport, although this is increasingly earning me a reputation as being slightly odd. I recently travelled by train from London to Milan for a meeting, which my hosts commented was 'unusual'. Once I visited a customer in the West Midlands. Chatting on arrival, he made the usual polite enquiry as to whether my journey was good, to which I replied in the affirmative. He asked which route I'd taken, presumably meaning M1 or M40, to which I responded that I'd taken the train to Wolverhampton. He appeared slightly surprised, but we commenced our meeting.

After a while he interjected, 'How did you get here from Wolverhampton?' My answer, 'On the bus', he really couldn't comprehend. I felt obliged to almost apologise, explaining that I'd intended to get a taxi, but instead got a bus as there was plenty of time and it ran from outside the station. We completed our meeting and as final pleasantries were exchanged, he invited me to come again, adding 'but don't come on the bus'!

After leaving Headingham's number 91 for the final time in Tollesbury square, I purchased an extra bottle of water from the village shop. Currently a Post Office, this is one of many under threat of closure. The Government say they're not needed now that pensions are mainly paid direct into bank accounts, but ignore the social benefits of what is often the centre of village life. Like public transport, rural Post Offices provide a service and their indirect benefits to the community should be considered. It is not a simple matter of profit or loss. And anyway, you might be able to bank online, but how can you send a parcel through the internet?

Rather than going back down the road to the waterside, I turned left just after the village school, then right into Woodrolfe Farm Lane. This soon became a track, then a path, coming out at the south end of the marina, by the entrance to Tollesbury Wick, another Essex Wildlife Trust nature reserve. A box by the gate contained information leaflets, so I stopped for a few minutes to read one and apply the day's first coat of sun cream.

The main area of the 600 acre reserve is grazing marsh, which was reclaimed from the sea by construction of the sea wall, probably in the late middle ages – certainly before 1777, when it was shown on the Chapman and Andre's map, the first large scale map of the county. It is a Site of Special Scientific Interest and a wetland of international importance, mainly because of over-wintering birds. Lapwing, brent geese, golden plover and wigeon are some of those who feed or roost on the wet grassland. The large areas of rough pasture suit small mammals such as pygmy shrew and field voles, who in turn attract hunting hen harriers and short eared owls.

A path runs on the top of the sea wall and makes an excellent circular walk from Tollesbury. Initially alongside the expanse of salt marsh that protects the village, it soon turned right along South Channel, opposite Great Cob Island and Old Hall Marsh. The grass was quite high, suggesting that the path was not well trod. The long dry grass and wild flowers on the sea wall support a wide variety of insects and I saw more butterflies enjoying the sunshine here than anywhere else on the walk. It was perfect walking weather. The sun shining, but not too brightly. Warm enough for shorts and T-shirt, but with a pleasant breeze of perfect strength. Strong enough to be cooling, but not to be successful in its attempts to steal my hat.

To the right of the path is a fresh water channel, 10 metres or so across, with fringes of reeds providing nesting sites for reed warbler and bunting. I'd noticed these lengths of water running inside the sea wall in many places, but hadn't known their origin. The reserve leaflet gave what now I realised was the obvious answer – they were simply the result of digging out earth to build the sea wall. It told me their name – borrowdyke, so hence forth I shall use the correct terminology.

At the tip of the reserve and marking the end of Tollesbury Fleet, is Shinglehead Point, a most attractive little area of shingle and shells. The leaflet asked visitors to keep off from late April to the end of July so as not to disturb nesting oystercatchers, ringed plovers and little terns. On the corner of the sea wall is a Second World War pillbox, which would have made a good bird hide, had the entrance not been concreted over.

Back on the main Blackwater Estuary, I could once more hear the gentle lapping of waves. The stronger wind here was welcome as the midday sun gathered strength. Heading up the estuary, the wall runs almost dead straight, with views across to Bradwell Power Station. Just off the shore is an area of shingle which originated from dredging work in Harwich Harbour. With most of the salt marsh eroded away and a risk that the sea wall would be undermined, thousands of tonnes of material were spayed here, in a process known as 'Beach Recharge'. So far this appears to have been successful, with the added bonus of creating an ideal nesting area for little terns.

The sea wall runs inland around Brockhouse Bay, another area of salt marsh. It appeared that even less people came this way, as the grass on the path came up to my waist in places. Running from the apex of the little bay is the counterwall, a secondary sea defence, built fairly recently to protect the bulk of the reserve should the main wall be breached. Looking inland is traditional grazing marsh which has never been ploughed. Small lumps and bumps are the long established ant hills of the yellow meadow ant. The most skilled nest builder of the 50 species of British ants, these little chaps can dig more than a metre underground, but other than for mating flights are rarely seen on the surface. A larger mound is of human origin and believed to have been made to provide a safe refuge for grazing sheep in case of flooding.

A second pillbox marks the end of Blockhouse Bay and another straight section of embankment. At the head of Mill Creek is the remains of Tollesbury Pier, relic of a dream to develop Tollesbury as a continental port and once the unlikely terminus of a railway. Built in 1904, The Kelvedon to Tollesbury Light Railway was better known as The Crab and Winkle Line, on account of it regularly carrying shellfish. The same name was used for the Brightlingsea branch, but Tollesbury is generally accepted to be the original. In 1907 an extension was built from Tollesbury village to Mill Creek, with a station just inside the sea wall to serve the pier. On this unusual railway, the steam locomotives had to be modified to allow them to negotiate the line's sharp curves and coaches were fitted with smaller wheels to enable passengers to board from the low platforms. Travel wasn't fast, with a maximum speed of 25mph and trains having to slow to 10mph through villages and ungated crossings. The fare from Kelvedon to Tollesbury was 9d (about 4p). Many trains were 'mixed' with both passenger coaches and freight trucks, usually carrying fish from Tollesbury and jam from Tiptree Britannia Preserves. So important was it to the jam factory to have a rail link, that the owner had threatened to move to Dagenham if the line was not built, as they could no longer rely on using horses and carts on the rutted tracks to Kelvedon.

The Great War caused the ambitious plans for the port and yachting centre to be shelved and after just 14 years the pier extension was closed in 1921. The rest of the line continued to run until 1951 when it closed to passengers, although the section from Kelvedon to Tiptree remained open for freight until 1962. The pier deck was removed in 1940 to hamper landing should the Germans have chosen this remote spot to invade, but the uprights remain. Along the way I had passed many mysterious wooden remains in the sea and it was nice to know the story behind this one. I'm glad that the port idea failed and this remains another unspoilt piece of Essex coastline, but it's a shame there are no longer little steam trains carrying their mixed loads across the countryside.

By the pier I met the only other person walking the marshes this morning. A most friendly gentleman who lives in Shropshire, but had been brought up nearby and was visiting his mother in Tollesbury. After the usual weather related pleasantries and general agreement as to the niceness of the coast, he told me how much the area had changed. It used to be very poor, but now there is a lot of money around. He recalled how as children they used to watch the huge lorries full of building materials on their way to Bradwell Power Station, but that they didn't really understand what was being constructed. I wondered why it is that almost

Tollesbury Pier

everyone one meets while walking is both friendly and interesting. Does walking attract the nicest of people, or is it that spending time in the countryside imparts additional pleasantness and knowledge? Maybe it is just that they are indulging in the same activity as me, so will tend to share interests, but I cannot recall meeting a grumpy walker.

For those wishing to complete the circuit back to Tollesbury a path leaves to the right at the end of Mill Creek, but I continued on the sea wall towards Maldon. Presumably very few come this way, as the vegetation here was even higher than around the reserve. For some miles the path followed an unusually featureless, but typical in and out route, as it headed generally westwards. As it was simply a matter of following the sea wall, I made the mistake of not bothering to look at the map. Lost can be defined as 'Unable to find one's way' or as 'Uncertain of one's location'. I plead guilty to the latter. I'd mistaken Rolls Farm for Joyce's Farm and thought I was almost at the village of Goldhanger, when it was actually still some way on. At least this made up my mind that I had to continue to Maldon, as I'd missed the 15.29 bus from Goldhanger, the only possible option to cut the walk short.

For some stretches the path barely existed, being overgrown with long grass and vegetation. Sometimes there was an easy path at the foot of the embankment, but sheltered from the wind it was much hotter here and of course with no sea views. Out of the breeze I changed my West Ham baseball cap for the wide brimmed sun hat that I'd bought some years ago in Scarborough. This provides good protection from the rays, although much embarrassment to my children. It is also a tempting target for the wind. Back on the wall its repeated efforts were finally successful, a particularly strong gust depositing it on the salt marsh below. Fortunately it was an easy climb down from the wall, so a favourite piece of headgear could be retrieved.

Somewhere near Gore Saltings there was a new bench beside the path, with the inscription 'Nick Felsted 1977 – 2006, His Thinking Place'. On the seat was a home-made Fathers Days card, in adult writing, but signed by the hand of a young child, Jessica. Another lay on the ground, the name smudged by rain. I picked it up and wedged it back into the seat. It's always sad when you see a memorial to someone who died young, but the children's cards made this so much more poignant. It was really quite moving to think of them coming out to this isolated and beautiful spot by the sea, a place so loved by their Dad and leaving their cards for him. When I got home I found a notice in the local paper's internet archive; 'Nick lost the fight and passed away peacefully on 1st August 2006. Much loved Husband of Kate and Daddy to Andrew and Jessica. Adored Son and Grandson.' I sat thoughtfully on the bench for a while, although unsure whether I was intruding into a very special and private place. I hoped however that the family would have been pleased that the seat was being used by someone walking and enjoying the coast that their lost one had obviously found so special.

Other than the gentleman from Shropshire, I had seen no one since leaving Tollesbury. However approaching Goldhanger I passed several people out for a stroll, or sitting on seats around the narrow creek that leads to the village. Fishing boats used to unload their catch at the quay, taking them up Fish Street which leads to the village square, but today a couple of rather elderly windsurfers were the only ones on the water. I would have liked a look at the village and its 11th century church of St Peter, but with still some way to walk, decided to press on.

For a while the path was made up, but as I moved further from Goldhanger it became grassy once more, although much easier walking than the overgrown sections I'd covered earlier. The tide was high and the strengthening wind bringing waves into the shore and white horses out in the estuary. A mile or so off the shore and roughly mid-channel, is Osea Island. Like most Essex islands, this can be reached without need for a boat for part of the day, although with the sea covering the mile long causeway, it was hard to believe that cars may cross two hours either side of high tide.

Osea was occupied by the Romans, who appeared to use it as a major pottery production centre. It is recorded in the Domesday Book as having a well stocked fishery and enough pasture for 60 sheep. Agriculture has always been its main activity and a third of the island is still used for sheep farming. The island is inhabited, but privately owned, so permission must be sought to visit or use the causeway.

In Victorian times Osea was the base for a remarkable institution, a 'Home for Inebriates'. This was founded by Nicholas Charrington of the famous brewing family, after he witnessed a drunken man punch his wife because she asked him for money to provide food for their children. So shocked was Charrington that he sold his brewery shares, spending much of the £1 million proceeds on encouraging people to give up alcohol. He selected Osea, as a secluded and self contained island, with no public house, for his 'House for gentlemen suffering from the baneful and insidious effects of alcohol'. Initially the idea worked well, with those who we would now refer to less colourfully as alcoholics, unable to feed their craving. However local boat owners soon saw an easy opportunity for profit. Liquor was smuggled onto the island, bottles being hidden beneath bushes under cover of darkness and boats hired out to enable the 'inmates' to row across to the inns of Maldon. Charrington did his best to try to keep his charges' minds off the demon drink, even setting up a small zoo on the island, with emus, kangaroos and cockatoos. Unfortunately and probably inevitably, the drinkers lack of desire to abstain meant that the scheme was doomed to failure.

After Decoy Point, where the Osea causeway leaves the mainland, the fields on my right gave way to chalets and caravans. This was the first significant built up area along the shoreline since Tollesbury and before that as far back as Rowhedge. There were

View to Osea Island

more people around and even a few on the beach. A lady in a pink costume was just going for a swim, walking slowly but confidently into the water, as females tend to do. Us men either charge straight in, or take it gingerly, one toe at a time.

It was hot walking on the sheltered concrete path and I stopped for a quick drink at the Mill Beach Inn. When I came out 15 minutes later, the sun had gone and it was distinctly cooler. It looked as if the rain that had been forecast may be imminent, although this never arrived, so the waterproofs I'd carried all day weren't needed. The path goes round a small bay before coming to Heybridge Basin, a picturesque lock where the Chelmer and Blackwater Canal meets the sea. The 13 mile canal to Chelmsford opened in 1796, with Heybridge Basin dug out to enable lighters to enter the lock and transfer their cargo for the journey inland by barge. The sea lock is still used for pleasure boats in summer months, although can only operate from one hour before high water until half an hour after. Flanked by two hundred year old cottages and with an assortment of boats moored up, Heybridge Basin was another pretty spot to add to my list.

The Basin was somewhat unfortunate to be targeted by a German air raid in the Second World War. William Joyce, better known as the Nazi broadcaster and British traitor, Lord Haw Haw, decided to make up some strategic military sites in order to gain brownie points with the Germans. He had holidayed at Heybridge before the war, so knowing the location and that there were marine workshops here, decided to say that it was a submarine base. One night the German bombers came and all but destroyed a row of cottages. The unusual shape of the only one to remain is a result of the bombing. Next to it is a garden made in remembrance of a couple who were in bed when the bomb hit and were blown across the road, bed and all.

For the next mile and a half the path runs along on a narrow strip of land between a lake and the sea. Unusually for the size of water, the O.S. map gives it no name, although locally it just seems to be known as Heybridge Lake. Initially the path faces Northey Island, before turning sharp right at a headland and running opposite the attractive waterfront of Maldon. After an area of salt marsh the River Chelmer heads off to the left and Heybridge Creek to the right. From here the waterfront is far from attractive, with an industrial area, part active and part derelict. There's no access by the shore, so I continued on the path into the village, but hadn't realised it was going to take so long to get into Maldon. After walking all round the road, over the Chelmer Bridge and up the market hill, (the steepest B road in Essex), I reached the High Street just as the 6.30 bus was pulling away. With an hour until the next one, I found a little café and enjoyed a pie and chips. My legs were grateful of the rest. They'd completed 16 miles, the longest I'd walked for about 30 years, when I used to walk on Dartmoor with my father.

# CHAPTER FOURTEEN

# MALDON to MAYLANDSEA

### (8 miles)
### 13th July

I could almost live in Maldon. It's just the right size for a town. Big enough to have a reasonable selection of shops, two supermarkets on the outskirts, schools and some industry, but small enough to have its own identity, character and community. However I wouldn't live there because there's no railway station. Although the Essex branch lines to Southminster, Braintree and Sudbury survived, the line from Witham to Maldon closed in 1964. This was a sad loss to the town and although there is a good bus service, I wouldn't want to live somewhere you can't just jump on a train.

Arriving early and thinking that there was plenty of time for today's walk, I stopped at Tesco for breakfast. Then I wandered around for a while, looking at the town and for a nice bakers shop to buy lunch. I found just such an establishment, the very friendly lady serving contrasting with the impersonal automatic checkouts installed in our local supermarket over the previous weekend. I refuse to use them of course.

Maldon is an attractive town with old streets, inns and towers clustered on the hill, and a picturesque quay on the Blackwater. The town has a number of old and interesting buildings. Outstanding on the High Street is Moot Hall, the centre of local government since the 1576. Designed by Sir Robert D'Arcy, it has its own prison and a courtroom which was added in the 18th century. All Saints church has a most unusual triangular tower. Built in the 12th century and a result of French influence, this is unique in England. There used to be two Anglican churches in the town centre, but in the 17th century the nave and chancel of St Peter's fell down. The tower still stands, but the building attached that appears to be a church, is in fact a library. This was commissioned by Archdeacon Thomas Plume of Rochester in 1704, to provide accommodation for his collection of 7,000 books which he bequeathed to the town of his birth.

A number of annual events add to the town's character. Each year around New Years Day is the Maldon Mud Race, where competitors race across the Blackwater estuary at low tide, mostly on their hands and knees! In December it holds a Victorian Evening, with local people dressed in costume selling traditional food and crafts. Every summer there is 'Taxi Day' when London Black Cabs bring disabled children for a day out. The event goes back to 1952 when a cab driver visited the Elizabeth Fry Special School in London and wanted to do something special for the young patients he saw there. He wrote to every one of Essex's seaside towns and apparently the only one willing to help was Maldon.

Its claims to fame include being the first town in England to have a Tesco supermarket. Not the big new one where I'd had breakfast, but the current Iceland store. It was the home of reputedly the fattest man in England, Edward Bright, the so called 'Fat Man of Maldon', who was born in 1721 and weighed in at 47 stone. It was said that his coat would encompass seven men of normal girth. Maldon is said to have the driest climate for any town in England, although I had read a similar claims for both St Osyth and Brightlingsea. Most obscurely it claims to be the place of origin for the phrase 'To go like billio'. The story goes that the first minister of the Congregational Chapel, a Reverend Joseph Billio, preached with such gusto that anyone being advised to do something well was told to 'go like Billio'.

After spending more time than anticipated in the town, it was almost eleven by the time I was walking down the High Street towards Hythe Quay. This historic area has recently been done up and is a real credit to Maldon. Eight old Thames sailing barges were moored at the quay, two of them full with passengers ready for a cruise on the Blackwater.

Opposite the quay is Promenade Park, with a lake that used to be a large sea water swimming pool, having been made by closing in one of the tidal inlets in 1905. It has now been landscaped with fountains, although it appears this wasn't universally popular, as back in the town I'd seen several signs in windows asking for the swimming pool to be reinstated. Each of the several refreshment huts had tables outside, full with either young mums and their small children, or groups of older kids who I assumed were off school supposedly revising for exams. There's an excellent new play area, with a big wooden galleon and a good sized model boating lake, where an elderly man in a motorised wheelchair sat controlling his little boat.

Beyond the promenade is a short breakwater, at the end of which stands a bronze statue of a warrior, sword held aloft. A lady with a young baby in its pram was looking up at the fighter. She told me that not all the townsfolk liked it, although we agreed that we did. We both found it strange that there was no plaque explaining that this was Bryhtnoth, the Saxon warrior who fought the Vikings in 991AD. It was not as I thought a millennium project, but had been handed over to the town by the Norwegian Ambassador, His Excellency Bjarne Linsdstrom, in October 2006.

The breakwater protects a small harbour used by Maldon Yacht

Club, which has its clubhouse in an old barge. There's no public access along this bit of shore, so I followed a grassy path. This runs through an avenue of trees, at the edge of a large field used for parking cars, and for picnics by those who don't wish to venture more than a few yards from their vehicle. Beyond the field I found myself back on the now familiar rural coast, with the pools and inlets of salt marsh to my left. To the right was a high metal fence, topped with barbed wire and protecting the town's municipal dump. I never have understood why councils make refuse dumps so secure, when all that is there are things that people have thrown away.

I watched the two Thames Barges slip by, initially under engine power with no sails raised. I was to catch sight of them on and off for much of the next couple of hours as they cruised round Osea Island, looking most impressive with sails now aloft. A mile on from the quay is the causeway to Northey Island, which is best known for its role in the Battle of Maldon. I got talking to a retired history teacher and was glad that I'd read up on the battle the night before, so didn't appear too ignorant as we chatted by the causeway. He obviously had a great interest in the battle and used to bring his pupils here for history lessons.

At the end of the tenth century England was ruled by King Aethelred 2nd, now more commonly known as Ethelred the Unready, from the Saxon 'unraed' meaning 'ill advised' or 'no counsel'. His reign coincided with a period of regular raiding parties from Scandinavia, the ravaging and pillaging Vikings. Ethelred had no military or diplomatic answer to the raids, so simply raised a tax called Danegeld to pay them off.

In August 991 a large body of raiders appeared on the English coast and having plundered Ipswich, made their way to the Blackwater estuary. Here they camped on Northey Island, with the important strategic settlement of Maldon in their sights. A defending force was quickly gathered, led by Earl Bryhtnoth, who although in his sixties, was a strong and skilful fighter, greatly respected by his fellow soldiers.

While the tide was high the Vikings shouted across the water demands for gold and silver in exchange for leaving, but Bryhtnoth refused. As the waters fell the raiders began to stream out along the causeway, but the narrow strip was easily held. With the causeway defended and the thick mud either side almost impassable to a heavily armed warrior, the English held a virtually unassailable position. No doubt realising this, the Viking leaders made the rather cheeky request to be allowed to cross unhindered, in order that a fair fight could ensue on the mainland. In one of the less inspired military decisions of our history, but in keeping with a very British sense of fair play, Bryhtnoth agreed to their request.

With surrender not an option so far from home, the Vikings were ferocious fighters and a fearsome battle took place. The invading forces were considerably the larger and despite heroic efforts by the English, the battle was lost when Bryhtnoth himself was killed and many of his men took flight. The Vikings however had suffered heavy losses and rather than continue further inland, they returned to their ships, sailing to another base on the Island of Sheppey. Eventually King Ethelred paid them 5 tons of silver to leave England, but of course having been once successful they returned many more times to seek fortune.

As for Bryhtnoth, the English took his body to Ely Cathedral for burial, but not before the Vikings had cut off his head as a trophy, a wax ball being made to take its place. His bones were examined at Ely in 1769 and his height was estimated at 6 feet 9 inches, which at a time when the average height was considerably less than it is today, would have made him an extremely tall man. His statue can be seen above the entrance door to All Saints Church in Maldon High Street, and as I saw at the end of the promenade, his bronze figure now stands sword aloft guarding the entrance to the town.

One can speculate as to what would have happened had Bryhtnoth not treated war as if it were a game of cricket and refused the Viking demands for a 'fair fight'. Given the difficulty in crossing from Northey Island, it is probable that neither side would have been defeated. The Vikings would most probably have eventually withdrawn, but not until Bryhtnoth had been able to gather forces of far greater strength. Any battle on the Essex coast would then have been far from a foregone conclusion and the invaders may have been defeated or returned home. Perhaps a more prepared, confident and braver England would have withstood another invader 75 years later – William the Conqueror – and how different our history would then have been.

Half a mile on from Northey causeway, Limbourne Creek is the first of many inlets between Maldon and Bradwell. This is why the Essex coast is so long. Not only are there five major estuaries, but these have many creeks and inlets and I rarely went in a straight line for more than a mile. The remains of an old canal can be seen at the eastern head of the creek. Built in 1832 and just 1¼ miles long, this was a private canal that linked White House Farm in Mundon with the Blackwater. Although it became disused as long ago as 1880, the course is still clearly visible heading back from the shore. Just past here was a line of square ponds in the salt marsh. They looked to be man-made and I assumed they were old oyster beds.

Stopping for a drink, I found that I hadn't properly closed my rucksack and a bottle of water had fallen out. Fortunately nothing else seemed to be lost, but I was annoyed at not having enough drink on what was becoming quite a hot day, and that I had inadvertently left litter behind. I had another small water bottle, which I'd kept in the freezer overnight to give a refreshing drink as the ice melted, but so far it was still a solid lump.

Since Northey Island causeway the path had been getting more and more overgrown and my progress was slow. It was usually

Brythnoth

easier going beneath the wall, but here there was rarely a proper path and of course no view of the sea. I tried to stay on top of the embankment where I could, but it was becoming more of a trudge than a pleasant walk. My legs were getting scratched and I wondered what nasty little creatures may be hiding in the undergrowth, waiting to bite as I passed. I'd decided to travel light today, so had no long trousers to put on and no choice but to keep pushing on through the vegetation. Every few minutes I had to stop to remove sharp seed heads of grass from my shoes and I was forever pulling pointy bits out of my socks. This was worse than walking in the rain and somewhat disgruntled, I stopped earlier than planned to eat some lunch.

The spot I chose, opposite Coopers Creek, reminded me of the place on the Stour where I'd had lunch on the first walk back in September. It was equally deserted, with just the occasional yacht sailing by and no one on the shore. Again there were good views up and down the river and across to the far bank. The weather was similar; very pleasant to sit in, but just a little too warm to be ideal for walking.

Lunch completed, I continued my trudge along the sea wall towards Mundon Stone Point at the head of Lawling Creek. There wasn't a path at all here and I alternated between pushing through the vegetation, to scampering down the bank and making use of any shorter grass beneath it. Across the water I could see the village and marina of Maylandsea, but as usual it wasn't a straight route to get there.

Near Brick House Farm the edge of the field had been cut, so walking here was quite easy. After a while the sea wall moved away from the field, but I stayed on the cut strip, assuming the two would converge at some time. I realised I was heading back in the direction of Maldon, but kept going, thinking there would soon be a way back to the sea wall. Then it dawned on me that the nicely cut strip actually ran round the perimeter of the field and nowhere else. To continue on it would take me round a long circle, so I had to find a way back to the wall. Unfortunately there were now several areas of water barring my way and no possibility of crossing the 300 yards or so back to the shore. The only option was to return to where the field had diverged from the sea wall. Not happy about either the wasted time and effort, or the prospect of more slogging through the vegetation, I stopped to drink some of my now thawing water, although with the result that with every step the remaining lump of ice bounced annoyingly against the bottle.

Back on the sea wall I could again see across the creek to Maylandsea, although this appeared to be one of those frustrating places where you think you're nearly there, but don't actually seem to get any closer. The 'path' follows the ins and outs of Mundon Creek, which is really just an extension of Lawling Creek and eventually became a little easier going. Here I passed a couple and we chatted for a while. They were walking the whole coast of Britain, although in summers only. Last year they'd done the South West Coast Path and this year had continued on from Poole. Today they were going to reach their thousandth mile for the summer. The couple had a caravan and drove this to their destination each day, then got the bus back to the starting point. Today they'd parked at Maldon and caught the 8.00 bus to Bradwell.

The man told me that the footpaths in Essex were by far the worst they'd encountered. Yesterday they'd done the long stretch from Burnham to Bradwell and the paths were awful, but they weren't much better this side of Bradwell. I had to tell them that much of the rest of their walk today wouldn't be easy and neither was the section from Goldhanger to Tollesbury. They blamed the state of the paths on lack of maintenance, but I suggested it's simply that people don't use them. All that really keeps down the vegetation on a country path is the footsteps of those treading it, and in most of Essex these seem few and far between. I'd broken several silky spiders webs across the path this morning, so assumed I was the first to pass this way and it was likely that this couple were to be the only others on this stretch today. One could understand if we were in a wilderness somewhere, but nowhere on the Essex coast

Maylandsea Creek

is that far from a town and there are large centres of population within easy reach. Is the reason that most Essex people aren't interested in walking their own coast because they don't realise how beautiful it is, or that they just aren't into walking?

Just before Maylandsea there was at last a real path, as I joined St Peter's Way, a 45 mile footpath linking Chipping Ongar with the ancient chapel of St Peter at Bradwell. On 25th August a group of Essex walkers (yes there are some) planned to walk the entire length of the path as a 'challenge event'. Starting at 4.30am, breakfast was to be served at 15 miles, lunch at 28 and afternoon tea at 37 miles, with the whole walk, including stops expected to take 14 hours. And I thought I was doing well to complete a third of the distance in a day.

Maylandsea was bigger than I'd expected and best of all there was a pub yards from the sea. The question wasn't whether I should be venturing into The Horny Toad, but how long I would stay. It appeared to be fairly new and according to reviews I found on the internet, is quite different to the other pub in the village, The General Lee on the main street. The Horny Toad is apparently, 'the more lively pub where every one walks out wobbly', 'a top place with friendly staff and punters' and 'where all the young ones hang out'. At the General Lee however, 'you might have trouble distinguishing the bar from the toilets', 'you wont get served if you don't fit in (old, boring, prepared to lick landlords boots)' and 'you'd have more fun and better company in a cemetery'. I'm not sure whether this says more about the pubs or those posting on the internet.

I stayed for just one drink, before returning to the footpath which runs between yellow lines through a working boatyard, then along the shore by the small marina. After another short section of sea wall a decision had to be made as to whether to continue round the next headland to the village of Steeple, or to stop for the day and catch the 15.33 bus from Maylandsea. It had been my intention to catch this service further down the route at Steeple, however too much dallying in Maldon, a couple of stops to chat, and most of all the hard going due to lack of path, had meant the walk took much longer than anticipated. I could have caught the next bus two hours later at Steeple, but just didn't fancy any more trudging through vegetation, so wimped out, having completed a mere eight miles for the day.

I turned inland towards the village centre. Passing the General Lee, (which looked OK to me, as a member of old and boring category), I found the bus stop opposite Maylandsea's surprisingly long parade of eight shops. Stephensons' D1 service arrived five minutes late, with the customary handful of elderly passengers, all carrying shopping from Morrisons in Maldon. This was another friendly country bus and the lady driver stopped right outside one couple's house, put the ramp down for them and helped carry their shopping. By Southminster I was the only passenger and although a few minutes late, was in plenty of time for my train.

The village of Southminster is at the end of the branch line from Wickford and rather an unlikely terminus for trains from London.

On the station are two most impressive mosaic murals. These were produced by the local community and school children and won an award for art under the Community Rail Partnership. The once boarded up station buildings have been refurbished and are now in regular use for various activities – amongst others, a Citizens Advice Bureau, toy library, cycle hire shop and café. The project has reduced the incidences of vandalism in and around the station area to the point where graffiti is almost non-existent.

Just outside the station is a crane gantry over a short section of track, surrounded by a high security fence. This is used to transfer loads of nuclear waste from Bradwell Power Station to the train used to take them to Sellafield for reprocessing. It runs once a week, but the time is kept secret for security reasons. I can however tell you that there's normally an hourly service from Southminster, but that the timetable shows that on Thursdays the 13.17 doesn't run, leaving the line clear. Why it is kept clear I cannot say.

# CHAPTER FIFTEEN

# MAYLANDSEA to ST LAWRENCE

### (8 miles)
### 19th September

A trip to hospital for a hernia operation meant it was two months since the last walk. I'd hoped to have been back on the coast sooner, but recovery had taken longer than expected. I'll spare you the details, but suffice to say that the surgeon's warning that the bruising may 'travel south' proved to be correct.

Steady rain was falling as I boarded the Southminster line train at Shenfield, but this soon gave way to a dry day with the sun popping out to show its face just often enough to validate the 'sunny intervals' forecast. Marketed as Crouch Valley Line 'passing along the banks of the River Crouch, affording fine views across the river and of gently rolling countryside', the branch line to Southminster provides a pleasant ride. Less scenic than the Harwich branch, mainly because for most of its length you can't see much water, (although every so often a sail can be glimpsed appearing to be in the middle of a field), it is nevertheless pleasingly rural and provides an excellent link into this quite remote corner of Essex.

Five minutes after alighting from the bus in Maylandsea I was back by the sea, although with the tide down, there was little water to be seen. The rotting wrecks of several small boats lay partly submerged in the mud and a curlew moseyed around looking for lunch. A concrete path ran as far as the Harlow (Blackwater) Sailing Club, with its attractive wooden clubhouse, which replaced an old ferry that originally housed the headquarters. Leaving Maylandsea the path was easy going, with nice short grass. A pleasant change from much of the last two walks. Towards the head of Lawling Creek it ran along the edge of a field, which although raised above the shore, unusually had no sea wall. Further along the bank was protected by concrete slabs, but erosion had caused many of these to fall into the sea. The dried earth banks showed more erosion here than I had seen anywhere so far, with big overhangs that looked ready to drop at any moment.

Heading inland once more, this time along Mayland Creek, the path runs inside a large area of salt marsh. The tranquillity was rudely interrupted by a loud siren sounding for at least 10 minutes. I had no idea what this was for, but hoped it didn't signify some unfortunate mishap at the nuclear power plant. By the first of three small lakes to the right of the path was a tent, out of which protruded three fishing rods, pointing over the water. Whether anyone was at home I couldn't tell. Heading towards the village of Mayland the path ran between hawthorn hedges, coming out at the old jetty at Pigeon Dock. The dock at the head of Mayland Creek is long disused, but the remains still stand in the mud. With the subtle late summer colours of ground cover plants, this was a most attractive spot, another hidden little gem of Essex.

It is interesting that the places I'd found most attractive were not the wholly natural, but all had some man made element. Yachts bobbing in the Stour at Wrabness, the tide mill at Thorrington, the old granary at Kirkby Quay, and a wrecked boat at Beaumont Quay. Generally I would have said that the greatest beauty comes from nature – the mountains of Scotland, glaciers of the Alps, bubbling streams of Dartmoor, but maybe the relatively bleak Essex coast needs something extra to bring out its splendour.

St Peters Way rejoined the coast path at Pigeon Dock, running along the sea wall for half a mile or so, before going east into the village of Steeple. The pointed tower of the village church of St Lawrence had been visible for some time. Built in 1882, it looks far older, as it was constructed largely from materials taken from an earlier 12th century church.

Approaching Steeple Bay Caravan Park at the mouth of the creek, I noticed an increasing amount of litter. Beer cans on the beach, chocolate wrappers, crisp packets and cigarette ends. This continued until a couple of hundred yards beyond the now deserted park. Why come to such a nice spot then spoil it by leaving litter? I simply cannot understand the selfishness of these people. Back in the summer we'd been at Meadfoot Beach in Torquay, another beautiful place. As I followed three lads of about 15 eating chips, one casually dropped his wrapper on the beach. I picked it up, saying 'Excuse me but you dropped this'. His response was that he no longer required the paper and spurned my kindness in returning it. Keen however to reunite paper and owner, I popped it in his bag. Needless to say, Mr Litter Lout was not happy and I departed to a barrage of naughty words and flying chips.

For the next mile I was back on the main Blackwater estuary and again the path was easy. I'd been expecting to be pushing through long grass again today and it was a pleasant surprise to find proper paths. I suspected that this was due to a combination of dry weather having slowed the growth, and that a few more people walk this less remote stretch, although I believe that some stretches of the wall are cut once the nesting season is over.

At Shoat Farm Sluice I got slightly lost. The path was blocked by a gate and barbed wire, but I found another which crossed a little bridge and ran between two hedges before coming out in a field. Here there was no indication of which way it went, but I walked diagonally across the field and found a gate to Stangate Road. A close inspection of the map revealed that instead of crossing the bridge I should have taken another path through a gate, which came out on the road just after Steeplewick Farm. I had added an unnecessary half mile to the walk.

The private road was paved, surprisingly for what the map showed to be a farm track. It was lined with blackberry bushes, all heavily laden with ripe fruit. I ate as I walked, gradually perfecting the art of picking without breaking my stride, like a relay runner taking the baton. The map showed the road ending at Stansgate Abbey Farm, but just beyond this was Marconi Sailing Club, which the Ordnance Survey seem to have completely missed.

Located at a strategic point on the Blackwater Estuary, Stansgate was an important position in both World Wars. Relics of this are the Launching Hard, now used by the yacht club, and the gun emplacement on which the club's race box now stands. Back in the 19th century Watch Vessel No. 21 was permanently moored here and used by the Coastguard to supervise all craft using the river.

An easy path along the sea wall took me the mile and a half to Ramsey Island. Most Essex islands are joined to the shore at low tide, but Ramsey is all the time. A series of land reclamations which started in the 10th century and included blocking up Ramsey Creek, mean that it is now a permanent part of the mainland. Only at times of severe floods, such as those in 1953, does it regain its former island status.

A line of expensive looking houses fronting onto the shoreline mark the start of the village of St Lawrence. A popular location for water sports, its summer population is boosted by caravaners and many second homes. The point where the only road to the village meets the shore is known as The Stone, where there is a small car park and pub of the same name. The exclusive Tinnocks Private Estate, with some very nice houses surrounding a green, stands just back from the sea. Housing is another of the coast's contrasts. Either it's top end of the market, expensive houses and apartments, or its caravans and chalets. There's very little in between.

Approaching St Lawrence I'd starting to feel the first twinges from the operation, so my decision to stop here had been correct. With good paths and ideal weather the walk had been short in both time and distance, but I was at least moving forward again and on schedule to complete the long Bradwell section before winter.

# PART FOUR

## St Lawrence
## to Hockley

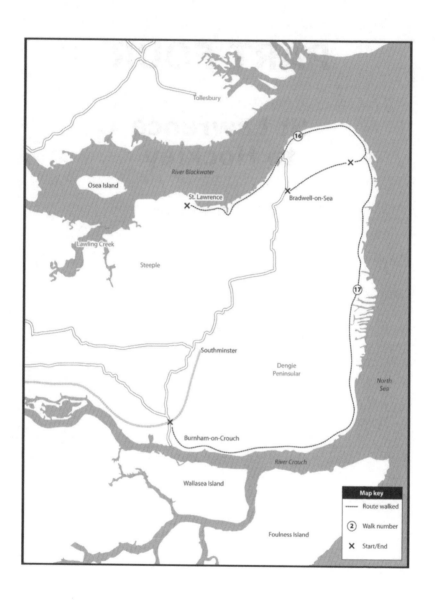

# CHAPTER SIXTEEN

# ST LAWRENCE to
# BRADWELL ON SEA

### (10 miles)
### 10th October

It made my blood boil. As the Southminster train pulled out of Shenfield station the platform attendant nonchalantly kicked a polystyrene cup onto the track. There was a bin a few yards away but this man, an employee of the railway, chose to litter the track. I gave him a hard 'Paddington Bear' stare and vowed to write to One Railway (but never got round to it).

No other passengers joined me on little green and white bus at Southminster, so the very helpful driver had plenty of time to explain that I should change at The Star in Steeple. He told me where the bus stops in Bradwell and that a Day Rover ticket for £4.00 was best for my needs. The buses on Dengie are operated by Stephensons, with subsidy (no doubt considerable) from Essex County Council. Their friendly and punctual service is an example of how rural buses should be run.

The 20 minute wait at Steeple gave me time to look at the old village pump now in the bus shelter, and take a wander down to the most attractive church, which I'd seen from Mayland Creek last time out. A man pulled over in his car and asked if I knew the way to St Lawrence. He'd been sent in the wrong direction, but with the help of my map I was able to direct him.

St Lawrence isn't the easiest place to get to by public transport. With three trains and two buses, it took me 2¾ hours from home, but again I'd shown that it can be done. The D1 arrived opposite The Star bang on time and its single passenger disembarked, giving me another solo journey. I walked down to the sea at The Stone, but despite what the map showed, found no path heading east beyond the green. A wooden fence running down to the shore stopped anyone walking in front of the water-ski club or the next few houses. Returning to the village I tried to find my way round the roads, but seemed to be heading in circles. An elderly lady appeared from behind bushes in the driveway of her house, then stepped back, saying I'd made her jump. Apologising profusely, I took the opportunity to ask her how to get to the sea wall path. She explained the way back to the shore in great detail and said that I could walk along the beach for a couple of hundred yards, then climb back up to the wall. Her grey cat joined us as we talked, and we parted with me patting the cat and her telling me not to get stuck in the mud.

However, back at the shore I found her advice impractical. The tide was up and there was no beach at all. Scrambling on the sloping outside of the sea wall looked too dangerous, so I got out my map and surveyed options. A gentleman walking his dog said I looked lost and was most helpful, telling me to take the second road on the left, which led to the sea. Another helpful lady standing at the corner of this unmade-up road confirmed I was heading the right way, so after wasting 30 minutes I was once more on the sea wall.

The path was good and I was by the sea, so all seemed well, however this lasted for just a few hundred yards. Then a large sign asked people to avoid the sea wall during winter months, which it

Village Pump - Steeple

defined rather broadly as 1st October – 31st March, so as not to disturb nesting birds. It asked walkers to use an alternative path, which went back to the road, but then showed no indication of where to go. I walked back to the main road, but realised this was going to take me in the opposite direction to Bradwell. Returning to the sea, I could see no other way, so decided I had to proceed along the path. I promised the birds I'd be very quiet and look away should they wish to engage in any intimate activities. For a short distance I could walk on grass below the sea wall in front of the caravan site, but then had to climb up to the wall. There were no signs asking people from the caravan site to avoid the sea wall, or indeed anywhere else, so what was the point of stopping people joining at just one end?

I was walking to a deadline today, aiming to catch the 15.02 bus from Bradwell on Sea. The timing for this had seemed about right, but with the delay at St Lawrence it was now going to be very tight. I set off at a pace to catch up time. A good path with short grass ran along next to the sea, then went inland around St Lawrence Creek. Here the grass was both longer and wetter, so after a few minutes, realising that my jeans were soaked to the knees, I put on waterproof leggings. Unfortunately this was a few minutes too late and with the damp sealed in by the rubbery purple leggings (I was still borrowing my wife's pair) they stayed wet for most of the day.

After less than a mile I decided to give up on the 15.02 target and dropped to a more comfortable pace. It would mean a long wait in Bradwell, but there were things I wanted time to see on this walk, and to treat it as a race would spoil it.

At the end of the salt marsh around St Lawrence Creek a sign advised that due to sea wall damage the path was diverted. It gave a phone number in Ipswich to call for information, but quite what anyone could add is unclear. The sea wall was breached here in 1995 and for more than a mile the path ran inland. There was more vegetation here, but it wasn't hard going, however I could see why the couple I'd met back at Maylandsea had had such trouble getting through in the height of the summer. At the far end of the diversion, the high tide covered much of the area inside the sea wall, making a most attractive water meadow. This was another nice little spot to add to my collection.

It was a misty morning and the grey hulks of Bradwell Power Station loomed out of the gloom ahead. Tollesbury Wick could only just be made out across the Blackwater and Mersea was beyond view. It is hard to believe that in Roman times, at low tide it was apparently possible to cross the estuary on a horse. Approaching Bradwell, the coast is sheltered by Pewet Island, a low lying marshy strip. A dozen or so small yachts were moored in the calm water between the island and shore.

After a short section along the sea wall I reached Bradwell Marina. Privately owned since 1984, this caters for good sized yachts, which can be berthed at most states of the tide. Having given up on the early bus and with soaking wet trousers, the possibility of lunch in a pub at Bradwell had been tempting me for a while. I knew there was just one pub, but did it serve food? From the marina paths were signposted both towards the sea and straight into the village. Taking the former, I found it stopped at the shore and a no entry sign prevented people passing in front of the Bradwell Outdoor Centre. This was one of the annoyances of the whole walk – people with waterside properties who don't allow others to pass in front.

The Green Man is an unspoilt 16<sup>th</sup> century pub, with the usual smuggling connections. Some would say it has character, but others that it is boring. Either way it was warm and had a surprisingly extensive menu. Fortified by an excellent bacon baguette and with trousers nicely drying out, I set off on what was to prove one of the nicest stretches of the walk so far. The path on the sea wall was perfect with easy walking short grass and this morning's mist had given way to a sunny autumn afternoon.

As I approached Bradwell Power Station it at last started to appear as more than the two huge faceless blocks that I'd been seeing across the water for many miles. From closer quarters it actually seemed of less character, the detail somehow detracting from its personality, which seemed to suit being a dull grey faceless megalith. Construction of the power station started in 1957, but it wasn't until 1962 that it started to produce electricity. The site was apparently chosen because the land had minimal agricultural value, was geologically sound, offered easy access and had an unlimited supply of cooling water from the North Sea. What isn't officially mentioned is its remoteness from centres of population, lest any little mishaps should allow radiation to escape.

Indeed there were a number of 'incidents' that could have caused alarm. Twenty uranium fuel rods were stolen in 1966 and in 1999 a security guard hacked into the computer, deleting records. The incident was kept secret for some time, but it was eventually leaked to the Guardian, after which it came to light that the employee had never been vetted and had two undisclosed criminal convictions.

One of eleven Magnox stations commissioned in the UK, and generating 60 TWh of electricity, enough to supply at least ten towns the size of Chelmsford, the plant had an operating life of just 40 years. The two reactors were shut down in March 2002 and decommissioning commenced. By the end of 2006 all fuel had been removed and 41,000 radioactive particles been transported to Sellafield in Cumbria. Only 1% of the site's radioactivity was said to remain.

The next couple of miles to the head of the Blackwater estuary at Sales Point, were amongst the most enjoyable of the whole coast. The afternoon sun shone brightly on the almost white beach, where waves gently lapped. The weathered remains of a series of World War Two gun emplacements added interest without spoiling the beauty. I jumped down onto the beach for a few minutes to look at the shells. This was the sort of beach one expects to find on a holiday island, not next to a nuclear power station in Essex. After a while the path moved slightly inland around an area of salt marsh. Seven egrets stood in the shallow water. As I approached they flew off, landing in a ploughed field where they stood together, their bright whiteness standing out against the brown earth.

Beneath the sea wall just before Sales Point were two mechanical diggers, paired with their arms face to face and surrounded by temporary wire fencing. They looked like a couple of monsters in a cage at the zoo. A sign on the fence advised that this was a 'Hard Hat Area'. Why the current obsession for protective headgear?

Shell Beach Near Bradwell

How often on TV do you see reporters or politicians wearing these big plastic hats in a place where they are patently not necessary? The other day I saw someone interviewed at an archaeological dig, where everything was taking place at ground level, the biggest tool a small trowel and barring a stray meteorite, absolutely no risk of anything landing on the persons head, but of course he had the hard hat. Safety is important, but protective clothing for the sake of it is plain daft.

Sales Point marked the end of my long trail round the Blackwater Estuary and a rare section of open sea. Now it was due south along the North Sea shore of the remote Dengie Peninsular to the next estuary, the Crouch.

At very low tides a number of wooden stakes are uncovered in the mud off Sales Point. These are the remains of a fish weir built by the Saxons in the 7th century. Investigation by archaeologists and extensive aerial photography has shown that there are up to 20,000 stakes on the site. Branches were weaved in and out of the stakes to form walls on three sides, with a funnel shape at the entrance, directing fish into the trap. There were several traps facing different directions on the mud flats, designed to catch fish on both the ebb and flow tides.

In an isolated spot, half a mile from the end of the nearest road, is the Othona Community. Hidden amongst a rare patch of trees, the community was founded in 1946 as a place to explore peace and reconciliation after the war. It is run by a small group of permanent residents, but in the busy summer months as many as 80 people from many different countries stay here. Although an ecumenical Christian community, people of all faiths, or of none, are welcome to enjoy the peace, fellowship and nature of this beautiful location

After walking through the trees I emerged in a grassy clearing. In the middle of this is St Peter on the Wall, the oldest church in England. In AD 653 an Anglo Saxon by the name of Cedd sailed down the coast from Lindisfarne in Northumberland, where he had been educated as a priest in St Aiden's monastery. Invited to Essex to spread the Christian faith by King Sigbert of the East Saxons, he landed at Bradwell and built a small wooden church. A year later Cedd used stone from a nearby Roman fort to build the chapel, which he modelled on the style of churches in Egypt and Syria, and which still stands today. Cedd was successful in his mission, establishing other Christian centres at Tilbury, Prittlewell and Mersea and was soon made Bishop of the East Saxons.

Despite coming to Essex at the invitation of King Sigbert, Cedd was not afraid to chastise him. One of the king's relatives had unlawfully married a member of his own family and Cedd banned him from his church. He told Sigbert not to enter his house, but the king disobeyed. Cedd lowered his staff to the ground as a sign of God's disapproval and told Sigbert that he would die in that very house. Such was his authority that the king fell to his knees seeking forgiveness. Whether this prophecy came true is unknown, but what is recorded is that the king was eventually murdered by this same relative.

St Peter's Chapel continued to be used until the end of the 14th century, however with the population having moved inland around the newly built parish church, it fell into disuse, eventually to become a barn. In 1920 it was handed back to the Diocese by the farmer, restored and rededicated. It became a place of pilgrimage and services are held here each Sunday and Wednesday during the summer. A notice inside said that communion would be held at 8am on Wednesday, unless very cold. Churches visit for special services and 'Quiet Days', and an annual pilgrimage is held on the first Saturday in July, which is attended by large numbers of

St Peter on the Wall

Christians. I know there were 20 coaches a few years ago because my wife drove one of them!

The interior is simple, but larger than I'd expected. The crucifix, which hangs behind the altar was designed by Francis Stephens and dedicated by the Bishop of Chelmsford in 1949. The stone altar is supported by pillars, into each of which is set a stone representing the three other communities involved in Cedd's ministry. The left hand stone was a gift from Holy Island Lindisfarne, where he was trained. The centre stone is from the Island of Iona, where the Celtic mission in Britain began and from where the St Aiden was sent to Lindisfarne. The right hand stone is from Lastingham in Yorkshire, where Cedd built a monastery after leaving Bradwell and where he died of the plague in AD 664. Hearing of his illness, thirty of his monks from Bradwell travelled to be with him, but they too caught it. Just one young boy survived to return to Essex.

Having missed the 15.02 bus and with 2½ hours to the next one, I spent a while leisurely exploring. Two ladies were sitting chatting in the church, which rather detracted from the serenity and peacefulness that many had commented on in the visitors book. I bought a couple of postcards, but after a quick look left to return later when the gossipers had gone. Bradwell Cockle Spit nature reserve lies between the church and sea. This is jointly run by Essex Wildlife Trust and the Essex Birdwatching Society and supports a host of bird species, with up to 20,000 waders roosting at high tide. Oyster catchers, little terns and ringed plovers breed on the shell banks and salt marsh supports redshank, linnet, reed bunting, yellow wagtail and meadow pipit. In winter hen harrier, merlin, peregrine and short eared owl can be seen, and sparrow hawk, hobby and marsh harrier are among the raptors who feed here.

There is an old wooden hide, but the access ladder had been removed, presumably as it is no longer safe, however hidden beneath the trees I came across the Bradwell Bird Observatory. A gentlemen was sitting outside with a long lens trained on the marsh. We said our hellos, but unsure of the bird watching etiquette, I didn't like to start a conversation. Is silence de rigueur, or is it polite to ask what one has seen in the way you start chatting to a fisherman by enquiring as to what he has caught? With time to kill I walked back to the beach, sitting on the shells and looking at the strange mud formations. A few hundred yards out to sea was a line of 11 sunken barges, positioned here to help protect the salt marsh and sea wall from the ravages of the North Sea.

After another look in the now quiet chapel, I headed along the Roman Road into Bradwell on Sea. By now the sun was quite hot and I was glad to have brought a cap. It's a couple of miles into the village along what is a very straight road. To the right were views of the old Bradwell Bay airfield, which was built in 1930 to service aircraft using the offshore sandbanks for target practice. In 1941 it was enlarged to a full scale airfield and used as a fighter base, initially by 418 Squadron Royal Canadian Air Force. Bradwell's location right by the North Sea meant that it was often used as a landing place for planes unable to reach their home base. The runways and control tower are still in place and a mosquito plane stands as a monument to those who lost their lives flying from here.

Bradwell on Sea is just a small village, but still has its own school, where a few youngsters were playing football. Opposite is the impressive St Thomas's Church, which has a 14th century nave, to which was added a tower in 1706. Built into the outside wall of the Church is a block of five stone steps at the top of which is an iron post. These were for the benefit of the wealthy churchgoers who arrived for services on horseback or by carriage.

I would have liked to spend the remainder of my wait in the Kings Head, however this didn't open until five. The bus timetable was unclear as to exactly where the 17.15 stopped. Most services were shown calling at the Kings Head, but not this one. I asked a lady who told me it would pass here on its way back from a loop round the village, but to be safe I jumped on when the bus went by in the outward direction and was glad to have done so, as it didn't return through the village. Needless to say I was the only passenger to Southminster, but was pleased to see several boarding for the return journey when the London train pulled in. I hope that Stevensons' little blue buses continue to provide such a useful services for the Dengie residents.

# CHAPTER SEVENTEEN

# BRADWELL ON SEA
# to BURNHAM-ON-CROUCH

(14 miles)
17th October

Today I cheated. Having vowed that I'd only use public transport, my good wife gave me a lift to Bradwell. I could have got here by bus and train, but only with a very early start and relying on tight connections – 5 minutes at Shenfield and 2 minutes at Southminster. Missing either would have meant a lunchtime arrival Bradwell, with insufficient time to do the walk. This was one section that had to be completed in full, with no villages en route, or possibilities for curtailment. I was heading to the remotest part of Essex.

Anyway, my wife was pleased to visit Bradwell and from her bus driving days, knows that it's at the end of the road. One morning a young lad got on asking for 'After Bradwell'. She rightly replied that there was nowhere 'after Bradwell', it being the end of the route. No, 'After Bradwell' he repeated, to which the response was of course, that's where the bus stops. 'After Bradwell' he asked once more, to be told again that there's nowhere after Bradwell – 'Bradwell's the end'. Eventually the penny dropped – 'After Bradwell' was actually 'Half to Bradwell'!

We parked near East Hall Farm, saving the walk along the Roman Road from Bradwell, my wife accompanying me as far as St Peter's Chapel. I'd misjudged the weather, forgetting that an autumn morning by the sea would be cooler than a mild inland town, so was glad to borrow her jacket. We parted, she heading back to the car and me along the sea wall towards the wilds of Dengie Marshes.

The next 14 miles were to take me through not only the remotest part of Essex, but one of the most isolated areas in southern England. Only on Dartmoor are there areas so far from roads or villages. This is the longest stretch of coastline without any kind of settlement in the whole of England and I didn't expect to meet anyone on it. Hence I took the precaution of carrying a torch and survival blanket, just in case.

The St Peter's Way runs south along the sea wall from the chapel. It was an easy path with short grass, inland of an area of salt marsh by Gunner's Creek. Further out in the sea was another line of sunken barges. On the marsh stood 24 mysterious metal constructions, a sort of X shape with horizontal top piece, all in a line parallel to the shore. I had no idea what they were, but once the path turned towards the sea, found part of the answer. Behind a high razor wire fence were a number of big grey metal boxes, quietly humming to themselves. A sign warned of RF Radiation and indicated that they belonged to the world's third biggest defence company, BAE Systems. Their website failed to shed any light on the purpose of this installation. It did however tell me that the company was giving free breakfasts to all staff who cycled to work in National Bike to Work Week, so it can't be all bad. An email address was given to request information on the company, so I wrote asking about this installation. I shall take it from the lack of reply that this is a top secret national defence site and that no one is to know anything about it.

Leaving the mysterious humming boxes behind, the path turned

Defence Installation - Dengie Peninsular

right, parallel with the sea again. This was one of a number of places on this section where there are two sea walls. It appeared that the original one ran pretty much in a straight line, but that later extra marsh had been enclosed by building a new wall to reclaim more land. The new defences were higher, with borrowdykes running alongside them adding to the beauty of the area. In most places it is possible to walk on the old walls, but the going didn't look so easy and although more direct, they didn't meet the criteria of 'nearest path to the sea'.

Below the sea wall I saw an old football, presumably washed up by a high tide. Also a bunch of about 20 balloons. Blown here from some misguided celebration, these now littered the coast and would remain for years as a hazard for wildlife.

At Glebe Outfall I stopped to take photos of the sun shining across the mud, a view just as beautiful as if the tide had been in. At Sandbeach Outfall St Peter's Way continues on the old wall for a short distance, before heading inland to Tillingham. I took the outer wall, which once more headed towards the sea, then turned right to Marshhouse Pumping Station. Surrounded by flat marshes and two miles from the nearest road, this is the only building between St Peter's Chapel and the Crouch. Its red bricks could be seen for some miles and with the various bits of antiquated machinery lying around it, added a bit of human interest.

For a short way, in a rare section without the extra protection of salt marsh, the sea wall was concrete, but soon reverted to earth with grassy top. There was no path as such, but with grass only a few inches high, walking was easy, although I would imagine that with more vegetation in the summer it could be a struggle. Once St Peter's Way had departed inland the path had pretty much disappeared, suggesting that most walkers follow the long distance footpath. As expected I hadn't seen anyone out on the wall today.

Near Howe Outfall is an octagonal World War Two pillbox. Constructed from concrete, the five apertures facing south have been bricked up, but the one in the northern side remains open. It seems strange that the pillbox was built in this location, as the side with the most firing positions faces inland across seemingly impenetrable marshes. The northern side aperture was of limited use, its field of fire being much restricted by the sea wall. Close by are the remains of a wooden tower, which it is thought was used for observation in the war.

Between Grange and Bridgewick Outfalls I found a sheltered spot for lunch. Sitting on the sea wall, before me was an expanse of salt marsh, stretching for a mile towards the sea, and as far as one could see to the left and right. A blend of delicate autumn browns and yellows, with patches of purple, this looked more like moorland than sea shore. Out of site, were the mud banks of Dengie Flat and Ray Sands, and beyond that the North Sea. Behind me were occasional farms dotted around the marshes, but there was probably no other person within two miles of this isolated spot. This could be National Park country. Not the picture postcard beauty of the Lakes or Dales, but the wilderness and desolation of Dartmoor or Rannoch. Maybe it's best as it is, without the car parks, the visitor centres and trails that attract people. A white area on the road map, that few give a second glance. Another gem of Essex that hardly anyone knows.

Unusually I lingered over lunch, reluctant to move on, but eventually conscious that it would be dark before six, continued south. It was a perfect day for walking. The sun shone, but it wasn't hot, the wind was moderate, but following and the air clear, allowing undistorted views for miles. St Peter on the Wall was still visible as a distant speck behind me, although at one point this almost caused me to come a cropper over the sea wall, as I walked backwards looking at the view. This probably wouldn't have been the best place to break a leg.

At Bridgewick Outfall I realised to my disappointment that today's walk was almost halfway through. This was a rare combination of perfect weather, beautiful coast and solitude and I didn't want it to end. I'd planned the date for each section of walk a week or so in advance and to go ahead regardless of the weather. Hence I was extremely grateful that for this, the longest and most remote section, it was clear and most of all dry. Essex doesn't sound the sort of place where one has to worry about dying from exposure, but in bad weather, on these isolated walls that could be a real risk for the unprepared rambler.

Although it was obvious that the way forward was always to follow the sea wall, I'd kept a close eye on the map. As I'd learned, it's always good to know where you are. The main reference points were the outfalls, where the marshes drained into the sea, the last of which was Coate Outfall. Soon after here the salt marsh ended and I was back by the sea. The tide was up, and real waves were splashing on the white shell beach below. Without natural protection, the sea wall was once again concrete. A gate stood across the path, attached to which were an array of strange items; boots, trainers, seaweed, driftwood. I wondered if these had all been picked up on the beach, although there seemed an inordinate amount of footwear for it to have all been found here. I have no idea whether this was the work of one person, or a tradition for some of the few who visit this remote bit of coast.

At Holliwell Point the path turns inland and once again I was heading down an estuary. It was to be many miles before I was by the open sea again. Unlike the Stour, Colne or Blackwater before, the Crouch has no town at its mouth, and the five miles to Burnham are the most remote river walking in Essex. Opposite was Foulness Point and far beyond, a wind farm which sits on Foulness Sands.

In the more sheltered estuary the path became grassy once more. With warm afternoon sun I was glad of the cooling breeze that now blew across me from the north. This however led to another hat incident, when a gust grabbed my hat and I had to literally dive, goalkeeper style, to save it from permanent loss in the river. The Crouch must have been considered a more likely landing point for the Germans than the Dengie Marshes, as I passed several pill boxes facing across the river. One larger defence structure, set back just behind the sea wall, stood out as a landmark for some miles.

Near Holliwell Farm I met the first people since leaving my wife at Bradwell. Two men were fishing and I stopped to chat to the older one, who wore a woolly Arsenal hat. He advised that neither of them had caught anything, blaming too much weed in the water. With miles of sea to choose from, I wondered why they didn't move to another position.

I stopped for a snack by a sheltered little beach and retrieved another balloon, this one black with BHS printed on it. I could

Essex Mud - Dengie Peninsular

feel a letter coming on. In the distance could be seen some modern tall buildings, which I eventually worked out must be Basildon. How many of the town's 100,000 population have visited this coastline I wondered?

Opposite was Foulness, another Essex island which remains connected to the mainland. With an area of 10 square miles, Foulness Island is the county's largest island and the fourth largest in England. Finds of pots and several 'Red Hills' (mounds of reddened earth oxidised by heat from salt production) show that the island was occupied by Romans. It was the first site of land reclamation in Essex, with the practice known locally as 'inning' starting in the 15th century. The reclaimed land was of excellent quality for agriculture, for which much of the island is still used today.

Foulness is best known for its military use and it is still owned by the M.O.D., with access to the island requiring a pass. A number of the mysterious looking installations can be seen from across the Crouch. The army started using the island in the 19th century, making use of the extensive Maplin sandbanks, which allowed shells to be fired out to sea then collected when the tide was out. The first access road and bridge was built in the 1920s. For a short while the island enjoyed a tourist trade, but the tea rooms which opened to serve visitors soon closed down as military activity increased. Trials for the Normandy Landings were carried out here, an anti-tank range set up and weaponry tested to combat the German V1 flying bombs. An Atomic Weapons Research Establishment was opened in the 1950s, although this is now closed, and an Environmental Test V1 Centre (whatever that may be?) established in 1963. The M.O.D. now uses Foulness mainly as a gunnery and explosives centre.

The church of St Mary the Virgin was built in 1853, partly financed by a donation from Trinity House, given on the condition that the steeple was high enough to act as a landmark for shipping. A lock-up cage was also built for the detention of miscreants. This was later used as a mortuary, but was a little too small, and the practice stopped as the feet of the deceased could often be seen protruding into the road!

The previous church was timber framed, but in 1553, soon after it was built, its patron Sir William Stafford sold all but one of the bells. His purpose was to raise money for repairing the sea wall, reasoning that 'the parish needs but one bell to call the islanders to prayer'. This upset the local witch, who is said to have cast a spell covering his lands with mice. Undeterred, Stafford then sold four of the five bells from nearby Rochford church, for the same purpose.

Foulness and the whole area around it was nearly ruined in the early 1970s, when Maplin Sands was proposed as the site for London's third airport. A new motorway and sea terminal would

Gate - Dengie Peninsular

have been built, with one scheme having a runway across Foulness and neighbouring islands. Contrary to the findings of the Roskill Commission, which had been set up to investigative four possible sites, the Government announced that the airport would be built on Maplin Sands. An organisation 'The Defenders of Essex' was formed as an alliance of conservation groups, parish councils and others opposing the development. The wild bird population on Foulness and their surrounding mud flats is of international importance, with the second largest UK colony of avocets and huge numbers over wintering waders and brent geese. Although an initial Bill successfully passed through Parliament in 1973, the airport plans were eventually rejected on environmental grounds.

It would be nice to say that such a scheme would not be considered in today's more environmentally enlightened times. However Maplin Airport was mooted again in 2002, and construction of an airport proposed in another hugely important wildlife site at

Cliffe on the Kent side of the Thames Estuary. Fortunately this too was rejected after a concerted local and national campaign, for which the environmental argument was paramount. Hopefully one day Governments will realise that ever increasing air travel is simply not sustainable for the planet. Low cost airlines have opened up new markets in travel, but is this necessarily a good thing? Can there be any justification in flying from say London to Manchester, Paris or Brussels, when the train is as fast and ten times less damaging to the environment. Rather than more airport capacity, do we need to use appropriate taxation and investment to move passengers to the railways?

The path on the Crouch's northern bank continued in pretty much a straight line towards Burnham. It was a long walk and my legs no longer felt that they wanted it to carry on for ever. On the opposite bank the river splits, Brankfleet running between Foulness and Wallasea Island. Wallasea is connected to the

Beach – Holliwell Point

mainland by a causeway, although as this is passable at all but the highest tides, its true island status could be questioned. The only settlement, containing a few houses, timber yard, marina, hotel and pub, is in the north west corner. The rest of the island is just shown as white on the map, with a single track running across it. Colin and Rosemary Fretwell, a couple of senior citizens walking the British coast, made particular mention of Wallasea as containing the most boring map square in the whole Ordnance Survey system! A ferry runs to Burnham on summer weekends, useful for those coastal walkers who prefer to avoid a 30 mile detour inland. The couple I'd met at Maylandsea had told me they arrived here midweek, and on finding no ferry, persuaded a local boatman to take them across the Crouch.

Wallasea's outline resembles that of an easterly swimming whale, although whether that is the derivation for its name is unknown. Much of the island is farmland, although part of it is returning to salt marsh after 300 metres of sea wall were bulldozed in July 2006, easing the flood risk on the Crouch and providing winter grounds for wading birds. As with Abbotts Hall, this managed retreat appears to be working well, with sediment being deposited at a rate of two inches per year. The RSPB has put forward plans to allow the sea to take back three quarters of the island, using spoil from the Crossrail project to create hillocks and dips into which sea water will ebb and flow. A haven for wildlife would be created, but some local farmers believe that the agricultural land should be defended. However the Environment Agency have already decided not to maintain the sea wall and the RSPB argue that it is only a matter of time before it is breached, so best for everyone that this is done in a managed manner. A debate that we will surely be seeing more and more as sea levels rise.

The approach to Burnham is marked not by the usual Essex caravan sites, but by a sewage works. The path becomes paved, running past boat yards with their cranes and slipways, then the impressive 1930s clubhouse of the Royal Corinthian Yacht Club.

Mine Watching Tower – Crouch Estuary

With tired legs and a train due soon, I left exploring the town until next time. Twice I had to ask the way, as the many sign posts around the town pointed to yacht clubs and parks, but not the railway station. The only sign showing this was of little use, being only about a hundred yards away. At least it said railway station and not the increasingly used 'Train Station'. I know language evolves, but not necessarily for the better. Hurrying up the hill, I arrived a minute before the train, having completed 14 miles of the most remote but enjoyable walking in Essex.

CHAPTER EIGHTEEN

# BURNHAM-ON-CROUCH
# to NORTH FAMBRIDGE

(9 miles)
3rd November

An easy walk, with easy transport. The half mile from Burnham station to the riverside seemed much shorter than it had in the opposite direction, up hill and at the end of 14 miles walking. The town was busier on a Saturday too, with people pottering about the shops, eating in the many cafes and pubs, or just sitting in the sunshine watching the boats go by. Four bikers sat having lunch at a table outside the Cabin Dairy Tea Rooms, their big shiny bikes standing opposite.

The town's best known landmark is the red brick octagonal clock tower, which stands on the High Street. Built in 1877 as an addition to Burnham Endowed School, it was dedicated to the memory of Laban Sweeting, a well known oyster merchant who was renowned for his philanthropy to local residents. A historic and most interesting town, Burnham has no less than 117 listed buildings, however it is to the river that most visitors head.

Burnham-on-Crouch is a yachting centre of international repute.

Unlike many of the other places I'd passed, it's not really a holiday haunt for Essex man and his caravan. The town attracts plenty of day drippers, but mostly they are how shall I say it, more genteel, than the hoards who visit Clacton or Southend. It has been suggested that there are probably more boats on the water than cars in the car parks. The water front has fairly recently been done up. The red brick walkways enhance the riverside with its mostly white old buildings – so much better than the concrete which would have been used 30 years ago. A walkway runs along the whole of the front, with little bays for people to sit and view the river. Five yacht clubs have their headquarters here, and the Burnham Week of racing and regattas at the end of August is claimed to be second only to Cowes.

The grandest is probably the Royal Corinthian Yacht Club, which was founded on the Thames in 1832 and has its splendid club house at the sea end of the town. As 'Corinthians' the members are strictly amateur and no professional seaman or paid hands are allowed. The Club was asked to help prepare the British Olympic Team for the 1936 Games and at that time rules defined Corinthianism rather grandly as 'That attribute which represents participation in sport as distinct from gain and which also involves the acquirement of nautical experience through the love of the sport rather than through necessity or the hope of gain'.

The Royal Burnham Yacht Club was founded 1895, receiving Royal Patronage in December 1927. For most of the Second World War it was taken over by the Royal Navy, who used Burnham as a training centre for landing craft, although the club was determined to continue on a social basis and some sailing took place.

The Crouch Yacht Club dates from 1907 and the white weatherboard club house seemed to be the liveliest spot on the waterfront. As I walked past its bistro restaurant was packed with people eating lunch, and their happy chatter drifted out through the large windows overlooking the river. Burnham Sailing Club, the last building on the front, was in contrast to the rest of the busy little town, silent and deserted. This is a more recent addition, being formed in 1930. It is renowned for its Wednesday evening racing programme, which attracts boats from all clubs on the river.

Five large house boats are permanently moored opposite Burnham Riverside Park, with its sports pitches and play area. I recalled visiting Burnham probably 40 years ago and a dog licking my grandfather's bald head as he lay on a grassy slope in the park. We used to come here every so often, as an easy day out by train (ours was the only family I knew not to have a car). On another trip I remember my Great Uncle Hal feeding Polos to a donkey, but being too scared to do so myself.

The path heads inland around Burnham Yacht Harbour Marina, a large and modern facility, which was constructed in 1989 and has pontoon berths with services for 350 vessels. You have to walk through the boat yard where some pretty impressive yachts stood. One was for sale at £160,000, which isn't much less than our house is worth.

Leaving the marina and people behind, I continued along what was an easy going grassy path. This was my first walk at the weekend and I thought I'd have seen a few people on what was a most pleasant autumn afternoon. Outside of the town however I saw no one else walking all afternoon.

Half a mile on from the marina walkers have to divert inland by Creaksea Yacht Club. A sign showed the footpath heading into a small field, with a notice warning of livestock and asking for dogs to be kept leashed. The livestock consisted of a single large and rather ugly pig, who grunted noisily as I passed. The path seemed to be heading too far inland, so I turned left onto a roughly made up road. A sign at the end of this informed that it was private, but too late, I'd done it now. By The Lodge, a small house at the head of an avenue leading to The Tideways, a footpath was signed heading along the side of a field. This runs by the grounds of Creeksea Place, a large Tudor mansion and reputedly the home of Anne Boleyn. The path came out by the sea wall, so despite some doubt, I had been going the right way. The diversion past the pig and private road could probably have been avoided by continuing right up to the yacht club, but I had been misled by the footbath sign. Creeksea is reputed to be the place where King Canute attempted to hold back the tide, although this is also claimed by Bosham in Sussex. Had he have been around to more successfully perform the feat today, it could have saved me a long walk up to Battlesbridge.

Back by the river I found a sheltered spot for lunch. As I munched my way through a cheese roll, ten yachts sailed past, racing upstream. With the wind facing progress was slow as they tacked to and fro, the three man crews working hard to gain maximum advantage. From the big D on their sails and with a bit of research, I identified these as Dragon Class, presumably from the Royal Corinthian Fleet. This thoroughbred racing boat was designed in 1929 and adopted as an Olympic Class in 1948. As the yachts disappeared up the river, the only sound was once again the gentle lapping of tiny waves.

A mile from Creaksea the path heads up a small hill, in a rare departure from the horizontal. Marked on the map as 'The Cliff', this is one of the few cliffs in Essex. There was one at Wrabness and some on the section from Walton to Clacton, but since then the coast had been almost totally flat. Sharks teeth and bird skeletons can be seen in the face of the cliff, evidence of life 50 million years ago. The tide was high so I couldn't walk on the little beach and had to take the gentle slope up to a grassy meadow over the top. Although only 20 metres high, the view from the peak was quite different. It reminded me of the difference between watching football in a park from the touchline, to viewing it from raised stands in a stadium. For almost all the walk I'd been at

Clock Tower - Burnham on Crouch

'pitch level' and it was nice to get a bit higher and take in a different perspective.

At Stokes Hall Sluice, the remains of an old wooden jetty stand in the river. This was used by sailing barges which bought materials from Kent and London for construction of the railway in the 1880s. Here the racing boats came back into view, now heading downstream. With the wind behind them, each had a brightly coloured spinnaker unfurled at the front, with the blue sail of number 722 leading. In contrast to the activity on board as they tacked up the river, the crews were all just sitting, or leaning on the masts, with little they could do to enhance the speed of their vessels.

Soon after here the river divides, with Althorne Creek to the north of Bridgemarsh Island and the wider main stream running south of the island. It seemed hard to believe that this low lying island, now interspersed with little creeks, was once occupied. There used to be a brickworks using its deposits of clay and a tramway to take product to a quay, where it was loaded onto Thames barges. The last clay extraction was after the Great Flood of 1953, when it was used to fill sea wall breaches on the banks of the Crouch. This was once good farm land, with pasture for sheep and cattle, and crops growing on fertile soil. However the sea walls were neglected and when an exceptional tide inundated the island, drowning the livestock and ruining the soil, the farmer, Stan Clarke, moved to the mainland. Information varies as to whether the flood was in 1928 or the late 1940s, although most local sources suggest the former. Since 1953 the island has been largely left to nature, and the newly formed salt marsh became home to wildlife. It is now owned by Bridgemarsh Island Trust.

Opposite the end of Bridgemarsh Island a footpath heads the mile or so into Althorne, a small village with 14th century church and three pubs. Of most note is the impressive war memorial, with an ornate metal plaque built into a shelter of massive oak beams. The villagers did not simply pay for this memorial to their heroes, but built it with their own hands. A tribute to those who went away but did not return.

I continued along the sea wall alongside Althorne Creek towards the small Bridgemarsh Marina and boatyard. Signs indicated private either side of the path, although a track leads the short distance inland to Althorne station, a mile or south of the village. Beyond the marina was a very posh house, with a lake and swimming pool in its grounds. Then some distinctly less salubrious pre-fabs and caravans. From here were several miles of quite remote riverside, with no settlement until North Fambridge.

For some time I'd been hearing the sound of gunshots and as I rounded the creek just after Althorne the source became apparent. A group of men with guns stood abreast in the corner of a field, while two lines of men waving flags walked slowly towards each other across the field. A couple of dogs nosed around in the longer grass and a man at the end of the line seemed to be directing operations with various arm signals. The whole thing seemed very organised and disciplined. Every so often there'd be a flurry of activity, then the flag waving would stop, a few shots let off, then it would all start up again. Rabbits and birds were being disturbed and would cross the line of guns, but nothing actually seemed to be being shot.

A well spoken man, who was standing on the sea wall and seemed to be in charge, told me they were shooting pheasants and partridge. He said there were 9 guns, but rather perversely, that they were bad shots so I didn't have to worry about being hit! They were paying £250 each and got to keep the birds that were killed, which were of excellent taste. The 25 or so beaters with the flags got a token £20 for the day, but had to walk for miles across ploughed fields. Someone was making a lot of money out of all this. He said they release young partridge, but shoot only 70%, and although buzzards take some, this more than maintains the population. There are two types of partridge, the English (grey) and the French (red-legged). He told me that the former had greatly declined in numbers and releases for shooting were helping to increase it once more. I could have suggested that not shooting them might have been an even better idea, but this wasn't really the place for a debate. Maybe shooting the birds for food isn't necessarily bad, provided they die humanely, however there must be some that just get injured and endure a slow and sad death. What I question is why anyone should gain pleasure from killing wildlife?

We moved on to the customary talk about how nice the weather and countryside were and that so few people bother to come to see it. The salt marsh he said would be gone in 50 years, as global warming raised the sea level. They would have to strengthen the sea wall as the railway line was apparently a metre below the water level. Walking on, I soon disturbed a partridge, which popped out the hedge and I was pleased to see it fly off in the opposite direction to the guns. I hoped he had the sense to keep flying away from the bangs.

As I walked along the straight section of river known as Longpole Reach, the low afternoon sun lit up Canewdon church on the hill opposite. With early winter nights, darkness as well as transport, was once again becoming a determining factor in the length of walk. A stile led me into Blue House Farm nature reserve. A 600 acre working farm, this was purchased by Essex Wildlife Trust in 1998, and is a Site of Special Scientific Interest for its wetland bird species and rare water beetles. Originally salt marsh, the land was converted to grazing pasture after the sea walls were constructed and is still used for this today, with the Trust working to maintain a balance between good livestock farming and conservation. The flat fields are used by brent geese and widgeon for winter feeding, with upwards of 2,000 birds commonly seen. A variety of diving birds can be seen on the fleets, including teal, the smallest UK duck and shelduck, the largest. Otters lived here until the mid 1960s and it is hoped that in time they may return.

The creeks and ditches are important habitats for the water beetles and other water insects such as the hairy dragonfly and the scarce emerald damselfly. As its name suggests, this is a rare insect and was in fact thought to be extinct in 1980, before being rediscovered in Essex three years later. Both this and the more common emerald damselfly are metallic green in colour and the two species are difficult to tell apart. Anyone wishing to make positive identification should know that the inferior anal appendages are straight in the emerald, but curved inwards in the scarce emerald.

The sun was setting as I reached North Fambridge, where there is a quay and small marina, around which were moored a dozen or so yachts. There used to be a ferry across the river to South Fambridge, which is known to have operated as far back as the 14th century, but ceased running some years ago. Despite their names, there is no evidence of there ever having been a bridge linking the two villages. Fambridge Yacht Club has its headquarters in a white wooden building on a pier over the river. Behind this is a boatyard, through which I walked into the village, letting myself out through a metal gate in the high security fence, then realising that I should have continued on for a few more yards on the river bank and followed the road.

Behind the boatyard is the Ferry Boat Inn, a 500 year old free house, serving a range of real ales. These included Shepherd Neame, Bishops Finger, and Spitfire, which I though could just as easily been the names of plants in the nature reserve. The inn also offers accommodation housed in a single storey building which was built around a courtyard in 2001. It was originally a row of three small cottages and the low beamed ceilings, with an open fire, give it a cosy country atmosphere. The inn was once on the river bank, but sea defences and the changing river bed have altered the coastline, so it now stands a couple of hundred yards from the water.

North Fambridge station is a mile from the river and it suddenly dawned on me that I hadn't left much time to catch the 16.34 train, so as with the last walk I ended the day rushing. The train arrived just as I did, so the hurrying was worthwhile. An hour's wait on a dark and deserted country station wouldn't have been the best of fun.

The station had until recently been simply Fambridge, but on 12th July 2007, a ceremony attended by One Railway and North Fambridge Parish Councillors had been held to celebrate its change of name. One Railway took the decision to alter it to North Fambridge, because as Mr David Winder, the Business Director for the Metro and Southend route said 'it more accurately reflects the geographic area in which the station is situated and community it serves'. Given that it's a fifteen mile walk to South Fambridge, I think he was right!

# CHAPTER NINETEEN

# NORTH FAMBRIDGE to SOUTH WOODHAM FERRERS

(10 miles)
19th November

This should have been the first starting point within an hour of Upminster, but for the first time for many trips, the train was delayed, arriving half an hour late. There's a path towards Woodham from just north of the station, but in order to stay closest to the river, I headed down into the village. Rather than take the road back down to the quay, I continued into a short lane with signs to Fambridge Hall and Church.

Hidden away at the end of the lane, I found the beautiful little brick built church of Holy Trinity. It has no spire or steeple, but just a tiny wooden tower. The inside was simple, with chairs rather than pews, and the most striking feature a stained glass window behind the altar. Inscribed 'To the Glory of God in loving memory of Henry John Barrett of North Fambridge Hall 1870 – 1958', this was a relatively recent addition. The window showed the hands of God, the Holy Dove, Pascal Lamb and a pelican. The significance of the last of these being that according to legend, in time of famine a mother pelican would draw blood

Village Sign – North Fambridge

from her own chest to give to her chicks, so the bird symbolises the sacrifice of Christ on the cross. The church dates back at least to the 1200s, but is thought to have been rebuilt in the 16th or 17th century. Its walls are over two feet thick, with flint boulders under the brick. Services are held every Sunday, but visitors seem few, as I was the first person to sign the visitors' book for 5 weeks.

A sign showed the footpath heading up the lane, however there was no indication where it left the road, and on reaching the entrance to West Wick Marina I realised I'd missed it. Turning back I soon found the path running along the edge of a field. With almost continuous sea wall walking since Tollesbury, it was some time since I'd been in the fields and it made a pleasant change. After crossing the railway, the path meets up with the one from Fambridge Station. It continued straight on, but the 'nearest to the coast' route was to turn left, where the path led to The Old

Rectory. Built in 1830, this was later extended using money from land sold for building the railway. There is a well outside the front door and three old fire engines were parked in the garden.

The railway runs along the next section of low sea wall, alongside the salt marsh at the end of Stow Creek, but with no path a detour has to be taken inland. A little lane, with patches of grass in the middle, runs north, past Rookery Farm. I ambled along, being in more of a wandering than speedy mood this morning.

Turning left onto the busy B1012 Burnham road, I commenced probably the least enjoyable and most dangerous section of the whole walk. There is no pavement and not much in the way of verges. I had to walk at the side of the road, squeezing into the hedge and facing the traffic as it roared towards me. Most cars moved over politely, but some were going so fast that it was very much a last minute manoeuvre. At one point, on quite a tight bend, bushes ran right to the edge of the road. There was no way drivers could see there was a pedestrian until they were almost upon me, when they had to swerve hastily. This road was certainly not designed for walkers. At Great Hayes Farm, where it makes a sharp right turn, piles of old tyres had been placed on the corner. Presumably I haven't been the only person concerned at speeding motorists.

A footpath is shown diagonally across the field from Great Hayes, but it wasn't very clear and as I couldn't see a way out the other side, chose to stay on the road for another couple of hundred yards, before taking the lane on the left. After passing some huge piles of manure, this led towards the river and to Little Hayes Farm. The forecast had been for heavy rain and cold, so I'd come suitably attired, but despite having shed several layers of clothing, I was now quite hot. With the low sun in my eyes I wished I'd brought a cap. This was the first walk where summer baseball cap had given way to winter woolly hat, although I was soon glad to have had the latter.

After crossing the railway once more, the path reached the sea wall of Stow Creek. Here it was immediately cooler and on went the clothes once more. On the right are two tumbling down old barns, presumably once used by Little Hayes. In the mud to the left is the wreck of a Victorian sailing barge, the Cerf, which was built at Frindsbury near Rochester, but must have lain here for many years. Standing on the mud beyond were 15 splendid shelduck. After passing the yachts of West Wick Marina, I was soon out of the creek and back on the bank of the Crouch.

Finding a spot for lunch wasn't easy as the sun and wind came from the same direction, so anywhere sheltered was also in the shade. Heavy rain in the night meant that the ground was wet, so sitting places few. In the end I found some dry concrete on the sloping sea wall opposite Clemuntsgreen Creek, although as the sun went in the moment I sat down, it wasn't particularly warm. It was hard to believe that half an hour ago I'd have been happy in shorts and T shirt.

On the opposite bank a man with a long lensed camera was photographing birds. I hoped he'd still be there when I passed, as it would be interesting to talk to someone who could identify them. My recognition skills remained rather limited. There was no water at all in Clementsgreen Creek, which runs almost back to the railway. I was walking faster after lunch, not consciously, but because that seemed the most relaxed pace. Its strange how one's preferred pace changes, but that to try to go any faster or slower doesn't seem so comfortable. It took the best part of an hour to get round the creek, by which time the photographer had gone.

For the next couple of miles it was back to the sea wall on the gradually narrowing Crouch. On the opposite bank a large area of salt marsh was followed by the rather run down looking chalets and caravans of Brandy Hole. North of the river is Marsh Farm Country Park, a 350 acre grazing marsh owned by Essex County Council. Rare coastal plants including grass vetchling and sea

Holy Trinity Church – North Fambridge

barley can be found, their growth encouraged by the sheep who keep the grass cropped in summer months. The Country Park is visited by hundreds of wildfowl and waders, and is recognised as an internationally important site for over-wintering brent geese. Over 150 species of birds have been recorded here. It has a visitor centre, shop and café (closed midweek in winter, otherwise I would have been in for a snack) and the working farm is open as a children's attraction.

A slipway runs down to the water by the headquarters of South Woodham Ferrers Yacht Club. Formed in 1975 this is a far more modest affair than the grand clubs of Burnham. The map showed the dotted green line of a footpath crossing the river here and a signpost duly pointed across the water. It gave no indication however of how one was supposed to get to Hullbridge on other side. It was low tide, but the river was still something like 30 yards wide and of unknown depth. Furthermore, a flock of about 25 swans were swimming back and forward from one bank to the other and beneath each of their serene exteriors was no doubt a vicious bird ready to break a man's arm. I stood surveying the situation, considering whether I could come more suitably attired next time and save ten miles by wading across. A man in full length waders came along the mud. He had been repairing his boat and the told me that the tide was at its lowest now, so the river would be about 2 feet deep. What he didn't know was whether you'd sink another 2 feet in mud, but we agreed it would be too cold to wade anyway. Although with suitable clothing and at the lowest tide, one could probably shorten the walk this way, I preferred the longer, but dryer option of staying on the bank.

Soon after here the river splits again. The main Crouch continues up to Battlesbridge, but I followed the bank of Fenn Creek heading to South Woodham Ferrers. Houses are set back a little way from the creek, and although overlooking it, they can't really be said to be riverside properties. In fact despite being surrounded by water on three sides South Woodham Ferrers has no real riverfront. The town grew up around the railway station, which was built in 1889 to serve the village of Woodham Ferrers, a mile to the north. It was greatly expanded as a 'New Town' in the 1970s, with more recent development added near to Fenn Creek. It is only in fairly recent years that many towns have realised the value of their waterfronts and that so many have 'done them up', so maybe the 1970s planners didn't think of using the river to give character to the town. It is a shame that it seems to largely ignore its main natural asset.

The town has little of architectural or historical interest and its recent claims to fame are somewhat negative. In the 2003 Idler publication 'Crap Towns', South Woodham Ferrers was ranked

33rd worst place to live in the UK. Two years later things hadn't improved, with Idler's website saying of the town, 'Its nauseating red and yellow brick housing estates were completed mainly in the 80s – hardly a time known for tastefulness. The centre piece of South Woodham is in fact the Asda Clock Tower, where heathen residents go to worship the God of groceries. I doubt there are any more miserable places on this earth to grow up than South Woodham. It's not poor, or underprivileged, or even rough, it's just utterly, utterly soulless.'

The town briefly made the national news in April 2005 in a 'Man hurt by flying sausage' story. The incident which brought South Woodham to the nation's attention, featuring on the TV quiz, 'Have I Got News for You', involved a group of local teenagers. Bored with their bar-b-que, they began hurling spare frozen sausages over the garden wall, one of which passed straight through the open window of a passing car, breaking the nose of the unfortunate driver.

As I passed Eyotts Yacht Club the rain which had been promised all day finally started, although not heavy enough to spoil the last mile of the walk. I followed a path around a loop in the river which almost encloses a piece of land shown on the map as Eyotts Faron. This looked a classic meander that could one day form the geography teacher's favourite feature, the ox bow lake. A fence barred access to the creek in front of the next couple of houses, so I had to complete the whole circuit and leave the 'Faron' by the same path by which I'd arrived. Just as it seemed it would be roads back to the station, I found the path that was marked on the map continuing along Fenn Creek.

The river split again, with Woodham Creek leaving to the left. Soon after a here a small bridge crosses what remained of Fenn Creek, which was now little more than a stream, much of which seemed to be coming from the outfall of a large sewage works on the right. Checking my watch as the path crossed a field towards another railway crossing, I realised I could catch the train an hour earlier than planned. Once again I quickened pace, hurrying along the path that runs parallel with the railway and this time arriving a whole 3 minutes before the train.

CHAPTER TWENTY

# SOUTH WOODHAM FERRERS to HOCKLEY

### (11 miles)
### 30th November

Today's walk round the end of the tidal Crouch was to be more fields and roads than river. Much of it could have been avoided had I chosen to wade from South Woodham Ferrers to Hullbridge, although with rain pouring as I left the station, the longer route didn't look to be a much drier option. It turned out to be one of those days when the weather changes every five minutes. One moment cold, wet and rainy, but the next warm and sunny.

Taking the path alongside the railway, I was soon back at the grassy area at Woodham Fenn. This is an Essex Wildlife Trust reserve, which they manage on behalf of the local council. It is an SSSI and 'Ramsar' site of international importance. The reserve's significance is as one of the few remaining places where salt marsh blends naturally into dry grassland, and for its eleven species of dragonfly and eight rare species of spider.

A wooden bridge crosses the end of Fenn Creek, with the path then running by the railway line along the edge of a field. A sign warned that dogs should be kept on leads as the crop had been treated with toxic slug pellets. At the end of the field the path ends at the A132, the main road into Woodham. Although this is the closest to the river, I chose to avoid more than a mile of busy road with no pavement and continued opposite into Tabrum's Lane. This is marked on the map in white, meaning 'Other road, drive or track', but also with green dots indicating 'Other route with public access'. To confuse matters, after a few yards the road narrowed, looking more like a driveway. A sign said no motor vehicles and a barrier was down across the road, but there appeared to be no restriction for pedestrians. In any case I had little intention of turning back.

The little lane goes through Grange Nurseries, with greenhouses on either side and a sign warning of fork lift trucks crossing. At Woodham Road, the old route prior to the A132, I turned left, passing several more nurseries and garden centres. Meadow Croft Garden Centre promised the additional delights of a Garden Tool Museum. A path running between two hedges goes off to the left just after Croft Cottage, the last in a line of houses after Smithfield Nursery and Catkin Cattery (not the most original of names – in one minute on Google I found 25 others in England). The path crosses the A132 again, where I had to wait ages for the road to be clear, then takes a bridge over the railway, before heading into another field towards the river. The entrance to this, like many of the fields, was blocked, the metal barriers or concrete blocks deemed necessary in these parts to keep 'Travellers' out.

At the bottom of the field a sign advised 'Private – No Trespassing on the Marsh – SEWCC'. I was unable to find out what this stood for. The way to the left was blocked with a fence and another Private sign, confirming that I couldn't have walked round the coast from Woodham. To the right the path indicated on the map as heading towards Battlesbridge, didn't appear to exist. However I made my way down to the river where a very narrow path ran along the bank. This soon changed to a gravel path, passing several old barges, which appeared to be permanently moored as houseboats. There was quite a modern wooden jetty at the head of the little creek which leads to Woods Farm and I believe that occasional boat trips run to here from Burnham. A fence and yet another Private Property sign barred entry to the sea wall on the opposite bank, although there seemed no reason why the public should be denied access to this little stretch of coast. Instead I had to take the lane into Battlesbridge, passing a selection of typical Essex cottages. The early nineteenth century weatherboard Malting Cottages, with steep tiled roof, small paned timber windows, and white painted picket fence, are typical of the county's rural dwellings. I came out by the village green, a pleasant spot, with a pond and several old cottages.

In medieval times Battlesbridge was a small port. Its activities expanded over the years and by the 19th century the village was a thriving community of mills, farms, coal yards, lime kilns and maltings. Coal came from the north, and flour and hay were taken to London by barges, the latter to feed the capital's huge horse population. Small fishing boats plied the river, catching smelt, whiting, flatfish and even the occasional salmon. The complex included a drying kiln and granary, which still survive, a tide mill, which was mostly demolished in 1902 and a steam mill built in 1896. By the First World War the traditional riverside industries and goods transport were in decline and in 1932 a major fire destroyed one of the remaining mills. Since the 1960s Battlesbridge has been reinvented as a popular centre for antiques, with many properties on the north side of the river used for the sale of antiques and collectables.

My wife loves the antique centres here, so we arranged to meet for lunch. This we had at the top of the Old Granary, in a strange rectangular room with windows both sides and views for miles across the flat Essex countryside. It reminded me of the passenger capsule in an airship. We looked round the five floors of the Old

Battlesbridge Antique Centre (Old Granary)

Granary, purchasing a small fish fossil for our youngest son who is fascinated by rocks of all sorts.

With no path on the southern bank of the Crouch, it was back to road walking once more, leaving Battlesbridge on the impressive Grade II listed Victorian bridge. Built by William Webster in 1872, at the cost of £3,500, it has a cast iron central arch, with brick side arches, parapets and pillars. After about a mile the lane turns sharp right and a footpath leaves on the left, running down to the river. It was a pleasant walk from here to Hullbridge, although the constant traffic noise from the busy A130 behind Battlesbridge was an unwelcome intrusion. Opposite a caravan park a sign warned of 132,000 volts in cables 62 feet above. These used to take current from Bradwell Power Station, but even with this decommissioned one assumes they'd still give you a nasty shock. The path was quite muddy, but seemed to be reasonably well used. Nearer to Hullbridge and judging by the many dollops of poo, it appeared that it is frequented by dog walkers. Unfortunately some are too inconsiderate to clear up their mess, despite signs warnings of a £1000 fine.

Hullbridge starts with The Esplanade, a row of newish houses, each with a little terrace by the river, where their owners could enjoy the view across the Crouch. The path runs between the houses and their terraces, then enters Kendal Park, a small wooded nature reserve managed by the parish council. By the wood's entrance a squirrel sat on a post and allowed me to approach within a few feet, before scampering up a tree. Here he sat nibbling a nut, while another bustled about in the undergrowth nearby. Walking through the woods I counted 14 more squirrels, all in pairs.

Just beyond the wood is the 'crossing point' to South Woodham Ferrers. The tide was higher today and wading certainly not possible, but the swans still patrolled. A signpost pointed across the river from this side too. Although the map's green line with bars across it denoted 'Byway open to all traffic', with the tide higher today there was no way this could include the pedestrian. There was a bridge here in Roman times, from which the town gained its name and another which was built in the 13th century, but apparently disappeared in the 17th. How can you lose a bridge? In later years a ferry carried people over the river and children from Woodham Ferrers used to be rowed across to the Old School House, which still stands in Hullbridge. Here's a snippet of useless information for you – the last of the ferry men, a gentleman known as 'Jock' was a stand in for Johny Weissmuller in the Tarzan films.

Beneath the river there is a tunnel, which at seven feet in diameter is large enough to walk through, but carries water, not people. A circular brickwork structure at the end of Ferry Road is the head of a vertical shaft 54 feet deep. This leads to the brick and steel lined tunnel, which was built in 1926 to take fresh water from the River Chelmer to the expanding Southend.

Hullbridge has two waterside pubs. The Smugglers Den is at the eastern end and stands where a barn was used to store the coal unloaded from barges at a wharf by the slipway. The Anchor is next to the slipway, with a large garden running down to the river. I don't think I've ever seen so many wooden tables outside a pub; 92 at a quick count, and on this winter's day none were occupied.

The path continues along the river bank to Brandy Hole, where new and rather ugly metal flood defences have been erected to protect a holiday park and some very posh houses. These were seriously expensive residencies, many with large yachts moored on private jetties. As seems normal for such properties 'Private' notices abounded, but as with The Esplanade, they had to put up with a public footpath at the bottom of their gardens. A sign advising that the public right of way existed for only 36 inches either side made sure any outsiders knew their place. On the fence of one of the larger houses were the remains of a fireworks display, which looked to have contained enough explosives to demolish a couple of tower blocks and must have cost the owners a fortune. It is my firm belief that big fireworks and large cars have something in common. The man who buys a mega whopper starburst moonraker bazooka rocket and the man who chooses a 16 valve, fuel injection, super thrust, GTI, is almost certainly compensating for one thing and one thing only – that he has a particularly small willy.

Brandy Hole gained its name from a smuggling reputation. It is thought that tea, rather than liquor was the main contraband that passed through here, enabling many of the locals to become rich. After Brandy Hole Yacht Club the path becomes part of the 'Hockley Centenary Walk', a route commemorating the centenary of the transfer of the civil administration of Hockley from the Church to Parish in 1894. The path however seemed to be little used and I was soon to find out why. After pushing my way through an overgrown section through low trees and bushes, I came out on a rather desolate section of low sea wall. Unusually there was salt marsh both sides of the path, which perhaps should have given me a clue as to where it was heading.

A metal sign indicated that the marsh on the inland side was private, belonging to the B.W.A., the Blackwater Wildfowlers Association, who purchased 60 acres in 1993. This organisation does much to conserve ducks and geese on the eight sites it owns on the Crouch and Blackwater estuaries – managing ponds and marshes, rearing and releasing mallard to supplement the wild population, providing additional feeding in harsh weather, disposing of litter and maintaining access routes. Then at dawn and dusk, between the months of September and February, its members creep out and shoot them.

The path came to an abrupt end opposite Brandyhole Reach. I say came to an end, but according to the map it continued straight across a creek. With the tide just turned this was an expanse of fast flowing water that even the strongest swimmer would have been ill advised to attempt. At low tide there is less water, but a hundred yards of mud, far too soft to support the weight of a man. How anyone is supposed to walk across this I've no idea. It was my plan however to take another path which runs inland along the side of the creek to Lower Hockley. What I hadn't noticed was that this too crosses a channel of water. That this was a tenth the width of the other was irrelevant. With the mud so soft, any channel too wide to be crossed in a single leap was an impassable barrier. Perhaps at low tide and if suitability attired one could wade through, although I would suggest that for the lone walker, this could be highly risky. With no dwelling within a mile and slim chance of anyone passing, who would pull a stuck walker from the mud before the tide engulfed them?

So once more it was retrace my steps time and a long diversion. By the posh houses I passed an elderly couple walking with their dog. Usually I greet people with 'Good Morning' or 'Good Afternoon', but as more often than not the response is a less formal 'Hello', this time I just said 'Hi'. The gentleman replied with 'Good Afternoon'. It was a mile back before there is a route inland, through the Shangri-La chalet park and out onto a little lane. From here another byway made a very pleasant walk up a gentle slope between two hedges. I imagine that this is an ancient track, maybe used by the smugglers with their tea and brandy. Near the top of the hill I took advantage of a little wooden seat for a short rest and drink, before reaching Cracknell's Farm, where the path changed to a paved road. Here I passed an old man on a bicycle who looked a 'Good Afternoon' type, so this was the greeting with which I bade him. His response, a very cockney 'Alright- How you doin!'

A footpath across a field cuts off a corner and leads to Lower Road. This is the closest route to the river and the most direct route to South Fambridge. Unfortunately the southern side of the Crouch lacks the convenience of the Southminster railway. There are buses to Hullbridge, but none to South Fambridge and the next village of Canewdon was too far for today. I therefore headed some way inland to Hockley. I could have stayed on this road for a mile before heading south, but with the light already beginning to fade, preferred the safer and far more pleasant option of the path. This continued after a few yards on the opposite side of the road, running for about a mile before crossing the Southend railway line, then passing Blounts Farm. Signs at the entrance to this advised both 'Public Footpath' and 'Private Keep Out', plus more worryingly 'Guard Dogs Loose After Dark' – on a public footpath?

About a mile and a half of road walking took me to Hockley Station, where it was a welcome change that a 20 minute service meant that there was no need for my customary rush for a train. I was doubly glad that the wait was short after finding that One Railway chooses to play piped music on the platform. Lest it should fill several pages I shall spare you my thoughts on such matters.

# PART FIVE

## Hockley to Benfleet

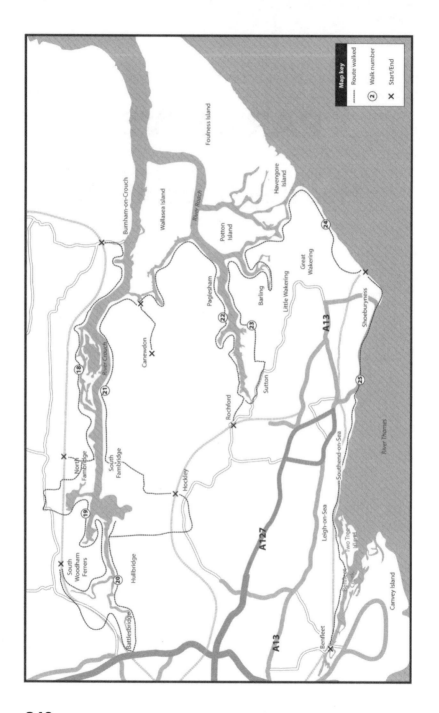

# CHAPTER TWENTY-ONE

# HOCKLEY to CANEWDON

(11 miles)
7th December

It took 40 minutes to walk from Hockley station, over the hill and back to the Canewdon Road. The footpath (not signposted) starts by a parade of shops, crosses the railway, then runs alongside Maryland Nature Reserve. With a number of paths across farmland, not all of which were marked on the map, the route wasn't always clear. I realised I'd gone wrong at the summit of Plumberow Mount, where a notice advised that the woods ahead were private. It was however worth the detour to inspect the mysterious ancient mound at the top of the hill. Assumed to be a burial chamber, it was excavated in the early 20th century in the hope of uncovering treasures, but all that was found were a few broken pots and a Roman coin. The true purpose of this ancient mound is still unknown, although it may have been a pagan altar, or a Saxon beacon to warn of invading Danes.

Walking round the wood and following the edge of the fields, I regained the main path just before it reaches the road. A short distance on, just after The Dome Village of chalets, was the path that I would have come out on last time had I chosen to wade through the mud at Brandy Hole Reach (assuming I hadn't drowned in the process). Not surprisingly this path looked little used. I walked another mile along the road, passing Riverside Nursery and a house whose owners had chosen to ignore the convention to name after romantic places, and had called it 'Rochdale'.

Opposite a sharp right turn, a path heads off on the left, passing some farm buildings, running between two hedges and coming out in a field next to a huge pile of manure. Two brown cows stood next to it, staring at me as I passed and looking most proud to have produced such a monster heap. For the most part there was no clear path, but easy walking over the ideal surface of short, springy grass. The route was remarkably well signed and maintained by Essex County Council, who had even gone to the trouble of placing a marker post in the middle of the field, so one could see the direction to head when a slight rise hid the exit. New wooden gates had been erected at each field boundary, even though most of them were superfluous, being adjacent to a wide unfenced opening.

The path comes out by a little green in the small village of South Fambridge. A white cottage, The Willows, stands in one corner and an impressive wooden village sign in the other. This was erected to celebrate the millennium and has carvings of a duck, a boat and a plane. The last of these commemorates the little known role of this corner of Essex in aeronautical history, for in the early 1900s South Fambridge was at the forefront of the development of the sea plane. Several pioneers worked on their aircraft at hangars in the village, using the wide, straight and calm waters of the Crouch to test take offs and landings. The Howard-Wright biplane was produced in 1908 and Jose Weiss developed his No. 1 monoplane the same year, returning in 1909 with powered gliders. Robert McFee flew his monoplane in 1909, and in 1914, the aircraft depicted on the village sign, the Talbot Quick Water Plane No. 8, was built here.

The village is a mixture of old cottages, some with the traditional

Essex weatherboard, with quite a few newer homes. The centre used to be almost a mile inland, where the small early 19th century All Saints church now stands alone. The original houses and farms have all gone. The ferry which linked North and South Fambridge ran from the late 1800s to around 1950 and the Old Ferry House still stands at the foot of the village. This red brick building looked most attractive with bright orange berries growing on shrubs along its front. Less attractive was the new Mews Bar. This was previously the Anchor Hotel, but seems to have lost character in conversion and looked a little out of place in a small village. It was closed at lunchtime, otherwise I may have been tempted by a cooked meal in the warm. A sign in the window implored the reader to 'Say No to the Cockle Shed Bar and Restaurant', but gave no clue as to where this may be.

A short path leads to the river and after a gap of two miles I was once more back on the sea wall. The tide was high and three men

Village Sign – South Fambridge

were fishing at what is a popular spot, with a small car park nearby. A fourth was fishing from the top of a Second World War pill box, on which I would have liked to have sat to eat my lunch. I was hungry, but dry places were few and far between, however a bit further on I found some metal steps leading down to the water. The Crouch was flowing quickly and it was strange to be sitting almost at river level. Whilst dry for my bottom, it was freezing and there was to be no lingering over lunch today. My hands, for once released from warm pockets, objected to the unaccustomed cold air and far from being sheltered, the wind seemed more biting so close to the water. Although there was a pleasant view across to North Fambridge with its selection of white sailing boats, I was soon glad to get moving.

The next two miles is a pretty much straight walk along the embankment, with little of interest to note. Every so often on the far side of the river the Southminster train could be seen sliding along silently like an oversized caterpillar. In a field to my right a flock of maybe 200 brent geese squawked to each other as I approached, presumably passing round the message that there was a man on the sea wall, but it was not until I had almost passed that the decision was made to scarper and off they flew.

At Landsend Point the river curves slightly. Opposite, on Bridgemarsh Island the short chimney of the brickworks on the low lying marshland could still be seen as evidence of the island's former industrial past. At Upper Raypitts Farm the sea wall runs inland of an attractive salt marsh area and from here a path leads up the hill to Canewdon. This would have been my 'early bus' option, but with transport opportunities limited I preferred to complete the next section, so that the following walk would not be too long. A sign on a stile indicated that I was now joining the 23 mile Roach Valley Way, a circular walk set up by Rochford District Council's Conservation Group in 1986.

After a mile the river turns right at Black Point, opposite the end of Bridgemarsh Island. Near The Cliff, a black dingy with three men dressed all in black sped past me. Who they were I had no idea, but assumed it was probably not the S.A.S. patrol they resembled. By now the sun had gone. It was windy and very cold, and unusually I was wearing every item of clothing that I'd brought. Generally I pack too much, working on the basis that one can always carry an extra item if hot, but can't put more on if you don't have it. Today I was glad of every layer and one more wouldn't have gone amiss.

I climbed down to read a sign beneath the sea wall and found that I was at Lower Raypitts, another Essex Wildlife Trust reserve. Purchased by the Trust following an appeal in 1991, the 137 acre reserve contains salt marsh, intertidal and grazing habitats. Nationally scarce plants can be found on the dykes and sea walls, including curved hard-grass, sea barley, grass vetchling and beaked tasselweed. Having come across many plants of strange name I thought it was time to expand my knowledge, so undertook a little research on the last of the list. Latin name, ruppia maritime, it is found in brackish waters particularly in estuary areas and has slender bright green stems up to 40cm long. A system of slender rhizomes (horizontal stems) and fine roots hold the plant in mud and the small flowers which grow on coiled stalks develop into dark brown pear shaped seeds. The Trust's work in managing this reserve has included action to raise the water table on the marsh pastures to attract wildfowl and waders, plus sheep grazing to keep the grass short for visiting birds.

I left the Crouch at Lion Creek, as from here to the North Sea its southern banks are islands; Wallasea and Foulness. The end of the creek has been cut off by a new sea wall, forming a salt water lagoon around which the Roach Valley Way runs. This is another Essex Wildlife Trust reserve, also notable for its salt marsh plants such as sea spurrey, golden samphire and sea lavender, which in late summer make an attractive border around the lagoon. However as the lagoon is no longer strictly part of the coast I took the short route to Lion Wharf. Sailing barges used to unload their cargoes here, but little evidence now remains.

I made use of the steps of a little white wooden boat house as a dry and vaguely sheltered spot to stop for a drink and considered my forward options. The choice was between walking the couple of miles up a lane to Canewdon, or continuing on the sea wall to Paglesham. The latter was my preferred choice, but transport dictated otherwise. Two buses per day leave Paglesham, but only one arrives (presumably there is a bus factory there?). The outgoing services leave at 8.00 and 16.44, and incoming arrives at 16.41, allowing the visitor a stay of just 3 minutes. Whilst the 16.44 would have been OK, as I would have had to start the next walk at Canewdon anyway, it seemed sensible to end there today.

As I stood up after a brief rest, a gust of freezing wind snatched my two sheets of bus timetables, carrying them away across the marsh. I gave chase, but the spot they settled was in the middle of deep mud, so feeling rather guilty I had to leave them there. After the lost water bottle near Maylandsea this was the second bit of litter I'd left on the coast. I felt guilty about both, but at least no one else knows. There's a footpath part of the way up to Canewdon, but it didn't look very clear. Not wanting to risk going the wrong way and possibly missing the bus, I stayed on the lane. This passes an 'Off Road Centre', where men take their Landrovers to play, then post videos on the internet of them getting stuck in the mud.

I could have stopped at Loftmans Corner and caught the bus there. However with time to spare I chose to walk the extra mile into Canewdon and visit the church which had been a landmark for much of the last three walks. Continuing up the gentle slope a view opened up to Southend, the Thames and beyond this, across to Kent.

Canewdon is a pleasant little village, which I was surprised to find still had its own school, where a group of mothers stood waiting for their children. Opposite is a tiny house, Rose Cottage, which with its high chimney is much taller than it is wide. From here the intriguingly named Gays Lane, part of the Roche Valley Way, runs down the hill to the Crouch.

At the crossroads in the centre of the village is The Anchor, for which a website guide to pubs gives Althorne at 2.3 miles away as the nearest railway station. True if you are a crow flying in straight lines, but not so for human customers, unless they are willing to wade through the marshes of Bridgemarsh Island then swim the Crouch.

Canewdon is steeped in folklore and The Anchor is said to have witnessed some seriously strange phenomena. Knives have been reported travelling across the kitchen, TV remotes flying through the air, a baby's crying heard and unexplained perfumes smelt. The ghost responsible is said to be that of a young woman named Sarah, who had a relationship with a wealthy landowner in the 1500s. When she inevitably became pregnant the man's wife found out and told him to lock her away. This he did in the building that was later to become The Anchor, but after giving birth poor Sarah was cruelly murdered. The BBC Inside Out programme followed a team of ghost hunters as they investigated The Anchor, but their results were inconclusive. Initial excitement at the Electro Magnetic Field detector going off the scale was tempered when it was realised that this could simply be an effect of the electrical wiring within the building's walls.

Passing the village's other pub, The Chequers, I walked up the quiet High Street to the church, outside which stands the old village lock up and stocks. These were restored in 1983, the stocks dating back to around 1775. Built in the 14th century upon earlier Norman foundations, St Nicholas Church is most notable for its massive tower. At 75 feet high, this commands outstanding views of the Crouch and Thames estuaries, and a light used to be

The Anchor - Canewdon

maintained here as a guide to shipping. The tower, along with the south porch, was added in the 15<sup>th</sup> century and is said to have been built by Henry V in thanksgiving for his victory at Agincourt. Both the English and French coats of arms can be seen on the west doorway, giving some credence to this theory. Legend has it that so long as the tower stands there shall be six witches in Canewdon, but if a stone falls from it one will die.

Also according to legend, if you run three times anticlockwise round the church you will go back in time. If only I'd known this I could have caught the early bus. On Halloween however, running in this direction round the church is said to summon the devil himself. Canewden used to have a sinister reputation, with all its residents considered as possible witches and outsiders unwilling to visit. It was believed to be an unlucky place for wheeled transport and wagoners avoided it for fear of having their wagons bewitched. There is though just one documented accusation of witchcraft in the village, when a Rose Pye was accused of bewitching to death a baby girl, but she was acquitted on trial in 1580.

I walked back down to the bus stop by the school in plenty of time for the 15.40 to Rochford. Whilst waiting I was 'entertained' by an outdoor Christmas decoration which, whilst not as tacky as the inflatable Homer Simpson that has sprung up outside a house near to ours, wasn't quite Jesus in the manger – a snowman and Santa standing in a large plastic dome, with artificial snow falling on them. Lovely.

There was no mention of the number 515 on either of the bus timetables; the 2005 version on the bus stop or the 2003 issue on the shelter, but at 15.40 a big green double decker appeared. I held out my arm and the driver looked at me, but drove on. I assumed it would return on the other side of the road, which a few minutes later it duly did. This time the driver shook his head in response to my stop signal, although as I persisted he halted. Opening the door he said that this was a school bus so he couldn't take me and that I would have to wait for the number 60. At the time I wasn't certain that this was the 515, or whether the lack of mention on the timetables meant this no longer ran. As the timetable with which I could have argued my case was lying in the mud at Lion Creek, I didn't make a fuss when he drove the empty bus away, leaving me in the cold.

According to the timetable on the bus stop the next service was at 16.30 to Southend, although if I preferred to believe the one on the shelter it was 16.37 to Rochford. Either way it was a best part of an hour to wait, so I retired to The Anchor for warmth and drink. Returning in plenty of time and having witnessed absolutely no paranormal activity, the next decision was on which side of the road I should wait, as I had no idea from which direction the bus would come. The westbound stop is outside the

Canewdon Church

Spar shop by the school, but for the other direction the stop is not opposite, but around the corner about 100 yards away. This being the last bus of the day I couldn't afford to miss it, so positioned myself on the corner outside The Anchor, peering one way then the other for signs of the bus. It was dark and I had no idea whether it would be another double decker or a small vehicle like those on Dengie, so on seeing what I thought was a bus, I ran down to the stop and put out my arm. It was only as the vehicle passed that I realised I was trying to hail a builder's van. However within a few minutes an unmistakable double decker came up the hill, which I boarded, being the sole passenger to Rochford. Here the very helpful driver gave me directions to the railway station, where with impeccable timing a train pulled in as I stepped onto the platform.

The next day I emailed the bus company to ask if the 515 service still ran, explaining that I'd found the timetable on the internet, but it wasn't shown on the stop, and that the driver had declined to carry me. The Managing Director replied, saying that yes this service does run and that he had spoken to the driver who recalled me. He claimed however that I had asked to travel to Southend, so he couldn't take me as he was only going as far as Rochford. This I reiterated to the Managing Director was most certainly not what had happened. Now being a bus driver, my wife is well aware of some of the tricks certain drivers (not her I hasten to add) use to enable them to get home early. Cutting out the last run is apparently not uncommon with certain companies, although the operator of this service has a very good reputation. A few drivers seem to care little that they are providing an important service to the public, and it appeared I had encountered one who was prepared both to refuse to pick up passengers and lie to his employer. It was a disappointing end to my 100% reliability record on the country buses. Perhaps I should put it down to the influence of Canewdon's witches.

# CHAPTER TWENTY-TWO

# CANEWDON to ROCHFORD

(11 miles)
14th January

Rochford is a pleasant town to pass half an hour waiting for a bus and I spent the time wandering around the town square. Doing the same were a class of school children, with clipboards and questionnaires to fill in as they discovered the various sites of interest. One little girl was most interested seeing the butcher in his shop and asked her teacher if he made the meat there! The square has a good selection of independent shops, with several selling crafts or gifts and a welcome lack of chain stores.

For many centuries Rochford was the most important town in the area, its first market charter being granted by Henry III in the 13th century, when Southend was a mere hamlet on the edge of Prittlewell village. Surrounded by fertile land, with a rich farming community, some of the best oysters in England and comparatively fast river transport to London, Rochford was a thriving and relatively prosperous town. Many of the ancient buildings, narrow streets and alleys survive, and it has far more character than the newer Essex towns nearby. The market town cross pattern comprising North, South, East and West Streets is one of the few of its type remaining in England.

The Manor of Rochford was once owned by Sir William Boleyn, grandfather of Anne, who is said to have first met Henry VIII at Rochford Hall. Little did they know what impact this encounter would have on the history of England – Henry's divorce, their marriage, break with the Catholic Church, start of the Reformation and the birth of Queen Elizabeth I. However, after just 3 years of marriage Anne was accused of adultery, plotting to murder the king and incest. With neat symmetry the last of these was said to have taken place within Rochford Hall. It was not long until she was beheaded and Henry moved on to wife number three. The hall, some of which dates from 1216, still survives, part of it being the clubhouse of Rochford Hundred Golf Club. Henry VIII wasn't the only ruler of England to find his partner in Rochford, Oliver Cromwell meeting his future wife Elizabeth Bourchier whilst walking beside the River Roach not many years later.

After a minor panic when I saw a bus turn the other way at the crossroads and thought I was at the wrong stop, the number 60 to Canewdon arrived right on time. The route continues on a further mile from Canewdon village, terminating at Loftmans Corner. I suspect that this is more for ease of turning, rather than to serve the five terraced cottages and a very occasional walker. However it saved me retracing the last mile of the previous walk, and from here it was just twenty minutes along Creaksea Ferry Road and back to Lion Wharf.

The forecast was for heavy showers and I'd been watching a dark cloud creeping up for a while. This arrived as I approached Lion Creek, depositing its cold and wet contents upon me. Sheltering as best I could behind a hedge, I tried to remember the technique for putting on waterproof in a storm, which we'd once been shown by a mountain guide in Norway. Unfortunately I didn't really grasp it then, and it took several minutes struggling with flapping plastic before I was safely ensconced in cagoule and purple leggings (still wearing my wife's rather gaudy pair I shame to say).

At Lion House I rejoined the Roach Valley Way, which headed slightly uphill across the middle of a turnip field. I was walking directly into driving rain, each drop of which stung as it battered against my face. This was the worst weather since Walton-on-the-Naze, but at least then the wind had been behind me. It was only half a mile through the mud and turnips, but this was not pleasant walking, although a pair of swans standing in the field seemed rather more content with the conditions. With 10 miles to go, I thought back to my warm office and it did cross my mind that running a glue factory might have been a more enjoyable way to spend the day. At the end of the field the path leads onto the sea wall at the head of Paglesham Creek. The Roach Valley Way continues south into Paglesham Churchend, but I stayed on the embankment, where a good path follows the creek. As I turned virtually 180 degrees to go up the creek, the rain stopped and out came the sun. With the strong wind now behind me walking was enjoyable once more.

To my right was the tiny village of Paglesham Churchend and the attractive St Peter's church. Of Norman origin, this was restored in 1883 by Zachary Pettit, who had a beautiful stained glass window built in memory of the five of his nine children who died in childhood. To my left the timber yard and cranes of Wallasea could be seen over the creek, and beyond this the waterfront of Burnham and the Royal Corinthian Yacht Club were just visible. After a mile Paglesham Creek becomes Paglesham Pool, and the view across the low lying and apparently featureless Wallasea Island explained the plain white squares on the map. Like much of the Essex coast it may look dull from afar, but as one of Britain's largest artificial wetlands Wallasea is actually a haven of fauna and flora, much of which can only be fully appreciated by those few who take the trouble to get close to it.

At Clements Marsh I stopped to look at the map, but struggling to refold it in the wind, soon wished I hadn't. It was virtually impossible to fold. Throughout several minutes of wind assisted origami I constantly said to myself, don't let go and it can't blow away. Why I loosened my grip I've no idea, but the wind didn't wait to ask and in seconds Ordnance Survey Sheet 176 was flying towards Paglesam Pool. For most of the last mile the sea wall had been right next to the water, or rather with the tide down, the mud. Had the map landed on this there was no way I could have retrieved it without risking sinking to my waist or beyond. Fortunately on this stretch a narrow band of salt marsh lay between sea wall and creek. Whilst still muddy, there were sufficient patches of vegetation for me to hop across towards the map, which in the lee of the sea wall, was flapping only gently, although ready to resume its flight at a moments notice. Good fortune prevailed and as with previous escapes of maps and hats, I was able to retrieve it.

Map safely in bag I continued for about 10 minutes to the end of Paglesham Pool, where turning right by a well preserved pill box, I started out along the fifth and penultimate river of the walk – The Roach. Originally called the Walfleet (meaning creek of foreigners), the name was changed on the incorrect assumption that Rochford means ford over the Roach (it doesn't – the name is derived from Rocheford, Old English for the Ford of the Hunting Dogs). Once more the strong wind was blowing directly in my face, an invisible force slowing me as I pushed on towards pub and lunch. The wreck of a large barge lies in the Roach, one of a number of vessels ending their days in the Essex mud around Paglesham. What looked like the hulk of a small steam ship sat just off the bank by the boatyard and another vessel lay decaying just downstream. Passing a line of old oyster beds I reached the waterside of Paglesham, which is basically a small boat yard. A sign indicated that the Plough and Sail was 400 yards inland and I headed up the lane looking for lunch.

An inn for at least 300 years, much of the white weather board pub is original and a typical example of a rural Essex hostelry. I wasn't sure that it would be serving cooked food, but it is in fact

Plough & Sail - Paglesham

more restaurant than pub. The menu is extensive and I enjoyed a really excellent homemade steak pie. I was sorely tempted by the deserts, but with still a fair way to walk, declined, knowing I would soon regret being too full. The pub was surprisingly busy, however from the number of cars parked I assumed the clientele were mostly outsiders. The Plough & Sail has been the centre of village activities for centuries. The 1841 census records that its accommodation consisted of a parlour, keeping room, pantry, taproom bar, four bedrooms and a cellar, plus several out buildings, including two piggeries, a ten-pin bowling shed and bakehouse with oven. This could be used by villagers upon payment of one penny, to cook their bread, pies or Sunday roast.

Paglesham has a long history of oyster fishing, with over 30 smacks working in 1890 and the Plough & Sail was the meeting place for their hard working crews. Fishing acted as excellent cover for the village's other main activity; smuggling. The whole area of the Roach was said to be rife with illegal trade, but Paglesham was the district's smuggling capital. It was so much part of village life that contraband would be hidden in the church vestry and the most notorious miscreant was William Blyth, the church warden. He was also the village grocer and evidently found it difficult to separate the two roles, sometimes wrapping groceries in pages torn from the parish record books.

Blyth used to enjoy a game of cricket with fellow smugglers, although they always took the precaution of laying out their weapons ready for immediate use, should there be an unwelcome visit from the excisemen. According to local legend, on one occasion the match was interrupted by a charging bull, which Blyth grabbed by the tail and set about with his cudgel. The terrified animal fled with Blyth hanging on, vaulted a hedge, then promptly collapsed dead. Another story tells how Blyth's boat was captured during a run and the cargo transferred to a revenue cutter, on board which he and the crew started drinking. Able to hold his drink far better than most mortals, Blyth waited until the officers were worse for wear, then returned the cargo to his vessel and sailed off.

Resuming somewhat full, despite passing on the treacle pudding, I was soon back by the Roach. This was a nice section of coast, looking across to the north west coast of Potton Island, which is part of the Ministry of Defence Danger Area and hence has restricted access. The island has been populated since Neolithic times and was home to several arable farms before catastrophic flooding in 1884. Not only did the sea destroy the crops, it drowned most of the island's wild animals and ruined the soil, leaving it fit merely for pasture for many years afterwards. It wasn't until the 1940s that agriculture was successfully re-established, with crops planted once more and good numbers of cattle, pigs and sheep introduced. The cattle were often bought by train from Wales and were walked to the island from Shoeburyness station. However the Great Flood of 1953 inundated Potton once more, trapping 11 people who had to be taken off the island by boat, and 450 sheep which were swum to safety at Wakering.

Before the land could recover, in 1955 Potton was purchased by the M.O.D., after which it reverted to pasture and military activity. A 'Blast and Fragmentation Range' was established, where research included controlled explosion on cars, knowledge from which was later to prove useful in the Northern Ireland troubles. Information that came to light in 2005 under the Freedom of Information Act, showed that in the 1980s Potton Island was one of 12 sites considered by the UK government as a potential location for long term storage of high level nuclear waste. It was only at the fall of the Major government in 1997 that plans to bury the waste were scrapped, although the incoming Labour Government still failed to provide a real solution as to how it should be stored for its radioactive life of several thousand years. Apparently when the plans for Potton were revealed Southend Borough Council expressed their surprise and concern that they had not been party to any consultation on the matter, but I don't suppose that the Government of the day had had any intention of entering into debate. What council is going to say, oh yes we'd love to have your nuclear waste, just put in it this hole and we won't tell anyone?

The west coast of Potton is separated from the mainland by The Violet, a stretch of water which changes its name several times as it runs south, linking the Crouch and Thames and thus conferring island status on Potton and Foulness. I made good progress along the north bank of what is an easy walking and pleasant, but relatively featureless stretch of Essex river. Rising in Marylands Woods near Hockley, the nine mile long River Roach is the only significant tributary of an Essex river, and is navigable as far as

Stamford Mills, just downstream from Rochford. Whilst most of its traffic is pleasure boats, a small amount of commercial cargo can still be seen.

Probably the most famous vessel to sail these waters was HMS Beagle, the ship that carried Charles Darwin on his scientific expedition to the Pacific, which spent its final working years as a coastguard ship on the Roach. Launched at Woolwich in 1820, the Beagle was initially surplus to requirements and didn't make its first major voyage until 1826. Then, under the command of Captain Pringle Stokes, it set out to explore Patagonia and Tierra del Feugo. The trip didn't go without incident, most notably the Captain shooting himself in a fit of despair and a group of Feugians stealing one of the ship's boats. In reprisal for this the new master took hostage two men, a boy and a girl, bringing them back to England. Here they were trained as missionaries, to be returned to their homeland the following year. For this voyage, in view of the demise of Pringle Stokes and concern for the loneliness of the position, it was decided that a gentleman passenger should be appointed to act as companion to the Captain and also to have opportunities as a naturalist. The man chosen was Charles Darwin, whose observations on the five year voyage were to form the basis of his theory of evolution.

After a further voyage exploring Australia, the Beagle was refitted as a static coastguard watch vessel, renamed as 'Southend WN No.7' and permanently moored mid-river near Paglesham (or according to another source, beached in Havengore Creek). Accessible at low tide by a causeway, the ship accommodated seven coastguard officers and their families, who would have been drawn from outside the area to minimise collusion with locals. The officers used small boats to intercept the many smugglers who used the maze of waterways and creeks between the Thames and Crouch to bring ashore their illegal cargoes. Oyster companies and traders petitioned for the ship to be removed, claiming that it was an obstruction in the river, although with so many gaining from smuggling, their motives may have been less honest. However, it remained in post for some years, until finally being sold for scrap in 1870. It fetched what was then the not inconsiderable sum of £525, most of which would have been for the value of her copper plating.

At Barton Hall, walkers have to go inland for a short distance along a path covered with white sea shells. Next to the house was a huge heap of shells, presumably intended for more lengths of pathway. Here I joined up again with the Roach Valley Way, which I'd left in the driving rain near Paglesham Churchend. Since then there had been one short shower, but otherwise it had become an unexpectedly fine and sunny day. With the low sun sparkling on the still water and bringing out the colours in the marshes, Bartonhall Creek was another pretty little area of Essex coast.

The next half hour was an easy walk close to the bank of the now full river, with views towards Southend, its tall buildings standing out in the late afternoon light. Downstream of Rochford there are remarkably few buildings by the Roach. Practically nothing on the south bank and on the north just the boatyard at Paglesham, Barton Hall set back behind its creek and Great Stambridge Hall. A surprising lack of development given its proximity to the county's largest built up area. Great Stambridge Hall stands on an artificial mound a little way back from the river, adjacent to the Saxon church. It was excavated some years ago by the Southend Historical Society, who unearthed retaining walls, two gatehouses and the moat. Also a garderobe; a medieval toilet consisting of holes in the outer wall, dropping into a cess pit or moat. The village of Great Stambridge is a mile up the road and was home to John Harriot, who founded the Thames Police Force in the 18th century, some considerable time before Sir Robert Peel instituted the present day constabulary.

The Canewdon bus runs through Stambridge and had the rain continued I might have cut short the walk here. However with it set fair once more, I carried on to Rochford. At Broomhills the river divides, the Roach heading up to Rochford and the Prittle Brook down to Southend. Here the path moves away from the river, as there's no access in front of Stambridge Mills, a large but derelict flour mill. The building has dominated the waterfront for many years and inside the complex is an old tidal mill, which was built at least 500 years ago on the site of an even older construction. It is soon to be replaced by luxury flats. Hopefully these will be designed so that the public too can enjoy the waterside.

The path runs diagonally across a field, passing a cricket pavilion, then on a wooden bridge over a pond. At the road I turned left, then just before the mill entrance took the path which runs behind the mill buildings. This crosses the Roach on two metal bridges, coming out by an industrial area. It follows the bank of the last tidal section of river and then the small stream that runs into Rochford. Like several Essex rivers, the Roach doesn't have a conventional middle stage, changing almost instantly from stream to tidal. Although sheltered from the wind, it wasn't the most scenic of paths, running past a huge breakers yard, with wrecked cars stacked on racks like goods in a supermarket, then the local refuse dump, with the usual unpleasant odour. It improved slightly after the industrial area and with the approach of dusk a succession of rabbits scampered across my path.

The path ends by the Horse and Groom on the main road into Rochford. Here I left the Roach Valley Way, which goes through the town centre, instead taking the left fork to the station. From there my journey back via Southend went perfectly – right up to the point that the train pulled out of Basildon and announced next stop West Ham. In what must be several thousand previous journeys, I'd never before made the mistake of joining a train that didn't stop at Upminster, but today was to speed through my home station at 70 miles per hour. At least I realised in advance and didn't do the embarrassing get up and stand by door routine, pretending just to be stretching legs, as other passengers pretend not to be sniggering. It wasn't even scheduled to stop at the next station, Barking, although to add to my frustration it did actually halt in the platform, but only at a signal and the doors remained shut. Obviously I wasn't going to accept that it was my fault and after due consideration decided to blame the driver. True it wasn't his responsibly to check the timetable or station indicator on my behalf, but whilst most drivers announce when there's an irregular calling pattern, this one didn't bother. While annoyed at the unnecessary doubling back and waste of time, it was at least slightly mitigating to share the blame with an anonymous train driver.

# CHAPTER TWENTY-THREE

# ROCHFORD to LITTLE WAKERING

(8 miles)
5th February

The six minute ride from Southend Victoria to Rochford was to be my last trip on One Railway. After today I was to be walking the Thames estuary and using the equally oddly named C2C line. One was however soon to change its name to National Express East Anglia. National Express took over the franchises of Great Eastern Railway and Anglia, both eminently sensible names and in the case of the former, historically relevant. In what I understand it later privately admitted was in ill thought out decision, the company had decided to call itself 'one', to show that this part of the network now had just the single train operator. However, as a little forethought could have predicted, there was immediate confusion – the 1.01 One train at platform one will be leaving in one minute etc. Almost as annoyingly, the company chose to follow the trendy, but grammatically incorrect practice of no capital letter for a proper noun, which you may have noticed I have refused to use. C2C is supposed to signify Coast to City, or County to Capital, and has become a well accepted brand, however the owners apparently now want to change this too, no doubt with much repainting of trains, ultimately at the travelling public's expense.

It was a mile back to the coast, once more down the Roach Valley Way, with the high fence, stacked cars and noise of the huge breakers yard to my right. Contrasting, and infinitely more pleasant, on the left were the reeds and grasses of the river's flood plain, from where a single heron emerged, flying off lazily as I approached. Ahead stood the silent hulk of Stamford Mills, awaiting its inevitable fate once the planners work is finally done. A path on the right enters the Purdeys Industrial Estate, which blocks access to the head of the tidal Roach. I spent 15 minutes following dead ends around the estate, confirming that this is another example of the public being kept away from the waters edge for no apparent reason.

Coming out of the estate onto Sutton Road, I turned left, crossing the Prittle Brook on Sutton Ford Bridge. A tributary of the Roach, albeit hardly smaller than the main river, this rises on Thundersley Common and flows parallel with the Thames for some miles, although not entering it as some sources incorrectly state. The road was very busy and despite having a narrow pavement on one side, it was not enjoyable to have huge lorries thundering by within a few feet, knowing that the slightest lack of attention by any driver could see my untimely demise. Unfortunately with no access to the river by the bridge and no path shown on the bank for the next two miles, another diversion from the coast was necessary.

A sign welcomes you to Sutton with Shopland and a little further on an impressive village sign stands in the corner of a field. It incorporates a war memorial and was erected in 2000. It took considerable research to find out what the four pictures signified and I am indebted to Barry Summerfield, Clerk to Sutton Parish Council, for his assistance.

The 'Wheat' represents present farming practices and the 'Cow' past farming, as Shopland had a prize winning herd for many years. The 'Quill and Book' represents the historian Philip Benton (1815 – 1889), who published works on the history of the Rochford Hundreds. The 'Stars and Telescope' represents Chester Moor Hall (1703-1771), a former resident of Sutton Hall, who invented the achromatic lens for telescopes. This used two lenses made from different glass to remove colour flares and clarify the image. Hall was the first person to make a refracting telescope free from colour distortion, however he made little effort to communicate his discovery to the world. A John Dolland later tried to patent the lens and at trial in Westminster Hall Lord Mansfield granted him the rights, ruling that although Chester Hall was the inventor, it was the Dolland, who had brought it forth for the benefit of humankind and so should benefit. Maybe Chester Hall was just too busy to develop the idea, as in addition to his mathematical skills, he was a lawyer, landowner and county magistrate.

Sutton is just a small village. There is an attractive old church, a few cottages and Crowstone Preparatory School, which presumably caters for more than just local kids. Down a little road towards the river is Fleet Hall and near All Saints church stands Sutton Hall. Shopland is even smaller and is not as it suggests a 'retail experience', but appears to consist solely of Shopland Hall (now an equestrian centre), a mile or so to the south east. Although once a parish of its own, the 1881 census shows it had just 14 dwellings, plus St Mary's church, which received severe damage in World War Two and was demolished in 1957. The church's artefacts are now kept in All Saints at Sutton, but that too is under threat of closure.

The village or villages, if you want to stretch it that far, have in recent years however become quite well known for their annual festival. Held in July at Sutton Hall, the Sutton and Shopland Festival is a mixture of music, dance and 'media expressionists', whatever they may be. Initially a one day event, it now runs over a weekend, with camping facilities for those wishing to stay over.

Some of the more interestingly named acts include Biff Bang Pow, Mr Frisbee, The Legendary Undertakers, Tracksuit Awareness Campaign, Beep Beep Ritchie, Lupen Crook and the Murderdolls, Bid Dog G and Dirty Fairies.

The pavement ends after the school, but as most traffic had taken the Southend road to the right, walking became far more pleasant. After half a mile I followed the bridleway which continues straight on as the road turns sharp right. On the corner was a small green corrugated hut, with a sign saying 'Shopland Mission'. To the left and looking most attractive through the trees, was the impressive white farmhouse of Butler's Farm. The bridleway passes the farm, which has a number of interesting looking buildings. Quite unusual for Essex is a low white stone cottage which looked much like a Scottish croft.

The wide path continues across fields with views to Great Stambridge on the other side of the Roach. Here it was quiet at last, bar the occasional roar of a plane taking off from Southend Airport a couple of miles to the west. Whilst the only current scheduled flight runs just in summer, twice weekly to Jersey, the airport is increasingly busy with cargo, training, business and private aircraft. One regular service is to Cologne for Ford employees, providing a connection to their German headquarters. In 2006 by percentage of passenger numbers, Southend was the fastest growing UK airport and with services due to start to Bruges, Le Touquet and Calais, expansion is expected to continue.

At Mucking Hall, where remains of the old moat are visible, the bridleway goes right through the large, but deserted farmyard (not even the obligatory barking dog), passing under a conduit that feeds three large grain dryers from a barn. It ends at Mucking Hall Lane, at which point the rain arrived. It had been preceded by a marked drop in temperature, increase in wind and darkening of the sky, so I knew it was coming, but hadn't expected a change from dry to downpour in a matter of seconds. A speedy donning of waterproofs was required.

At Bolts Farm where lane turns sharp right towards Barling, the map indicates a footpath going straight on towards the river, however there was no sign. An impressive notice marked the entrance to Roach Farm and Stables (at first and rather hopefully I thought it was a pub) and another advised that the road was private. However, armed with my map, I walked into the farm and by the stables found a very small yellow arrow on the gate. In pouring rain I followed the grassy path until reaching the sea wall and after a three mile detour, was once more back on the Essex coast.

Despite no path on the map, the sea wall to the west looked perfectly walkable. It's not clear however whether the river can be accessed near Fleet Hall at the Rochford end, or if you could get past the marshy area directly north of Mucking Hall. (I came back here to investigate one hot July day and found that with the grass longer there wasn't really a path either east or west. However walking was still easier than some sections on the Blackwater that have a marked path and I got round the marshy bit with no trouble, but had to stop at a temporary fence and sign warning of bulls and heifers on the sea wall. I cut back through fields to Mucking Hall, so had at least walked another short piece of coastline. Unfortunately though, I'm still unable to say whether you can walk the rest of the sea wall to Fleet Hall on days when the local bull isn't entertaining his lady friends by the river).

It was good to be back by the water, especially with the tide high and the sun out once more, the rain having ceased as abruptly as it had started. My stomach had been suggesting for a while that it was lunchtime, but there was the usual winter problem of finding a dry and not too cold spot to sit. A pub would have been nice, but there was none for another four miles. Noticing three concrete blocks by the borrowdyke, I chose to forego the river view, in favour of this sheltered spot and more importantly, maintaining a dry bottom.

The next mile and a half was easy going along the short grass of a wide and relatively straight sea wall. Views across the river were of the attractive Barton Hall, then of Paglesham and in the distance Canewdon church, a landmark from all directions. For much of the walk I had been heading towards one of five milestones, all visible for miles ahead, although often requiring many twists and turns before they were reached. The first was Harwich Docks, then Walton Tower, Brightlingsea Church, Bradwell Power Station and finally Canewdon Church. All man made, with not a cliff, headland or hill amongst them, such is the flatness of the Essex coast.

The river bank was strewn with rubbish, a greater concentration of assorted debris than I'd seen anywhere else along my journey. Whether it originated from land, or had been brought in on high tides from vessels at sea, it was difficult to tell. Buckets and barrels were probably boat related, but how did a large toy fire engine and a bean bag get here? The section from Fleet Hall to Mucking Hall has been adopted by the Southend Round Table, who organise regular working parties to collect the rubbish that accumulates on the river's banks. In one short session they reported filling one and a half Landrovers, two trailers and six bin bags. Unfortunately with the map showing no path on that bit of the Roach, few people get to see the results of their efforts.

The area south of the Roach is marked on the OS map as Barling Marsh, but it is in fact Barling Tip, the refuse dump for Southend's rubbish, a brown and smelly scar on the coastline. I say brown, but much of it was speckled white by the huge numbers of gulls scavenging for any edible scraps from our dustbins. On weekdays and Saturday mornings, when fresh rubbish is being brought, the tip attracts the largest number of gulls in the Southend area, plus bird watchers who come here to observe the various species.

At Barling Ness I left the Roach and headed south along The Violet. Some of Potton Island's mysterious military installations were now visible across the marshes. The wind was no longer following and walking was less easy. A large fox sauntered along the other side of the borrowdyke, looking plumper than its urban cousins that raid our bins, presumably thriving on a whole tip full of scraps. He was the first fox I'd seen on the walk, the countryside not being overrun despite the dire protestations of those who enjoyed hunting them before the Government at last brought in the ban most of the population wanted. Funnily enough we haven't seen packs of hounds slaughtered, horses sent to the knackers, or people turned out of work. In fact the hunting ban seems to have achieved just what was intended. The tradition and social fabric of those who like to dress up to ride across the countryside continuing, but without the killing of animals for fun.

The tide was now falling, exposing the usual expanse of Essex mud on which seven oyster catchers stood with their orange beaks facing into the wind. As I approached they gradually backed away towards the water, until finally one lost his bottle, taking flight, with the others immediately following. I felt a bit guilty that I'd disturbed so many birds on the walk, but if only they'd understood I had no evil intentions their inconvenience could have been avoided.

The river splits again, with Potton Creek following the island and Barlinghall Creek running inland. It is a real maze of creeks and channels between here and the Thames and difficult to work out what is attached to the mainland and what's island. Two men wearing wellies and fluorescent jackets and carrying coils of rope passed by, with a brief greeting, but no hint as to what task they were en route to accomplish. At Barling there was the rare sight of two working fishing boats, Lady and Janeen, and behind them the even rarer sight of two fishermen mending their nets.

The small village of Barling was previously known as Barling Magna, which is still the name of the parish that includes Little Wakering, plus the smaller inland settlement of Stonebridge. The name is said to derive from the Saxon words 'ban' for a boar and 'ing' meaning meadow. Just inland is All Saints Church, which is thought to have been built in the 12th century (records were lost in the Fire of London), although Christianity is known to have been established in the village in 998 during the rein of Ethelred the Unready. In this year Barling was left in the will of Leofwine, a Saxon Thegn (official or attendant) to Lord Wulfstan, Bishop of London. Subsequently the manor became property of St Paul's, until being transferred to the Diocese of Rochester in 1846, St Albans in 1877 and finally to Chelmsford, under whose jurisdiction it still resides.

After Barling the sea wall is smaller and the path much rougher, however it was a sudden change in the weather that made walking distinctly unpleasant. The sun disappeared and within seconds heavy rain was falling once more. As I turned up Little Wakering Creek the strong wind blew the freezing rain straight into my face, making progress both slow and uncomfortable. Looking around for shelter I realised how few trees there are on the Essex coast. Maybe that's why there aren't many dogs either.

The creek runs up to Little Wakering, where the map showed a pub and I decided to shelter here. Although I had already eaten lunch, I hoped to find a nice choice of hot deserts. Fortified by the prospect of dry and warmth, I spent the next few minutes considering whether my preference would be for apple pie, a crumble, or maybe some treacle pudding. A short path from the creek led to the main road and a bus stop, where a quick glance at the timetable indicated that the number 14 would be leaving for Southend in 15 minutes. I carried on up the road to the Castle Inn, but remembering Bryson's 'knowing when to stop' advice, made an instant decision to forego the pudding and quit for the day. As I waited opposite the attractive 11th century Church of St Mary the Virgin, the rain stopped as suddenly as it had started, but my mind was made up. Although the sun soon emerged, with more dark clouds already approaching I didn't fancy another soaking. The torrential downpour that hammered on the roof while I waited on Southend station confirmed it was a good decision and I was very glad to be in the warmth of a train and not on the exposed sea wall.

CHAPTER TWENTY-FOUR

# LITTLE WAKERING to SHOEBURYNESS

(10 miles)
29th February

Today was to be the last bus journey on the walk; Stephensons'
number 14, which conveniently stops in Southchurch, just up the
road from Southend East station. It was busier than most, with a
good number of the usual clientele of over 60s returning from
early morning shopping in Southend. This bus was particularly
friendly and all the passengers seemed to know each other, with
farewells all round every time someone got off. One had even
brought a flask of coffee for the driver. Of the 29 buses I'd used to
and from various outposts of rural Essex, none had been more
than a few minutes late and the only problem the driver in
Canewdon who decided he didn't wish to carry passengers. Not
a bad record and far better than the common perception of
country bus services.

Alighting at Little Wakering, in five minutes I was back on the sea
wall, with walking somewhat more pleasant than when I'd left the
opposite bank three weeks earlier. Barlinghall Creek divides, with
Little Wakering Creek running west and Fleethead Creek south

east. Between them is an area of salt marsh, marked on the map as Brimstone Hill. This was named after a family named Brinson, who originated from Briencun in Normandy, although rising no more than a few feet above sea level, calling it a hill is somewhat optimistic. There is evidence of late 13th or early 14th century occupation, possibly with some form of hunting lodge.

I stopped at a stile to put on an extra jacket and woolly hat, glad that I'd thrown them in the bag at the last minute, as the exposed sea wall around the loop of Barlinghall Creek was quite cold and blowy. A hare, startled by my approach, sprinted round the curve for several hundred yards, almost as if it was practicing for its job at Romford Dog Track. At Barling Quay only one fishing boat lay tied up in the mud, the other one presumably away at work. Although more than two miles walk from the nearest house, this wasn't the quietest bit of coast, with the reversing bleepers of lorries on Barling Tip, the squawks of gulls feeding on its rubbish and distant bangs from the army ranges, all disturbing the peace.

Turning right opposite The Violet, I left Barlinghall Creek and set off along Potton Creek and towards the Thames. The wind was even stronger here, but I found a reasonably sheltered position to eat lunch by the causeway which crosses to Potton Island. Until the Ministry of Defence constructed a bridge this 'hardway' was the only access to the island and before it was built all materials had to be carried on a raft pulled with ropes. The causeway is still used occasionally for very large loads which are too heavy for the bridge. It's only uncovered at low tide, but even then, with thick mud at either end, is probably only passable for specialist vehicles.

The swing bridge, half a mile south, has a control tower at one end, but this appeared to be deserted, with no one to shoot me had I chosen to ignore the Keep Out signs. It can be opened on request to allow boats through, however there's only sufficient water for most vessels an hour either side of high tide, so those craft seeking to use the creeks as a short cut from the Crouch to

Causeway to Potton Island

Thames have to plan their trips with care. The map shows the large M.O.D. Danger Area extending onto the mainland for a short section after the bridge, but there were no signs so I continued walking. Just along the creek at Sutton's Boatyard several quite large wooden boats lay gradually decaying in the water. Next to them was an old barge with a modern prefabricated building erected on its deck. A long wooden pontoon with small yachts moored either side stretched down the creek as far as the inlet of Mill Head, where two old metal barges sat in the mud. 'Rotherhithe Docklands Museum' was written on the larger of these, although this no longer exists and I was unable to find out how the barge came to lie in this remote Essex backwater.

On the opposite bank was Rushley Island, which is only accessible at low tide by a ford across the creek near Oxenham Farm. Its only building, a barn, stands out on the flat, low lying land. The island is protected by a 3 mile sea wall, which was initially constructed by John Harriott of Great Stambridge, already mentioned as the founder of the Thames River Police. He purchased Rushley for £40 in 1781, with the aim to develop it for agriculture. It took several years before the land was fit to successfully grow crops, but an exceptional tide in 1791 flooded the island. Harriott had no funds left to effect repairs, so was forced to abandon his project, eventually emigrating to America.

Both today and for the latter part of my last walk, I'd been catching occasional distant glimpses of a modern looking bridge, which I guessed led onto Foulness. Now I was almost upon it I realised that it is actually Havengore Island, although this is joined to Foulness, so not a true island. The current bridge replaced a second hand one from Germany, which was transported to Essex in 1921. This was becoming increasingly unsafe, with loads having to be broken down into small packets to cross and frequent closures trapping the islanders. In February 1986 Dr Michael Clarke, MP for Rochford, presented a petition to Parliament demanding a new bridge which was signed by 98% of the residents of Foulness – 172 persons. Havengore like Rushley has just one farm. It is owned by the M.O.D. and was used before World War Two for the development of AA 'Z' rockets, for trials in tackling oil storage fires and studying the effect of bomb explosions on Anderson shelters.

Havengore Bridge marks the start of the M.O.D. Danger Area for Shoeburyness Ranges. The previous night I'd phoned the number shown on the O.S. map for access information. Expecting a recorded message like you get for the Dartmoor ranges, I was surprised to get answered by a real soldier in the control room. He told me that there is live firing every day bar Sundays, so I wouldn't be able to walk this section of coast. However, the gate in the high metal fence was open, although a sign stated 'DANGER FIRING RANGE – NO ENTRY'. Another instructed people to keep to the footpath marked with red and white poles. A third sign warned 'DO NOT APPROACH OR TOUCH ANY DEBRIS AS IT MAY EXPLODE AND KILL YOU' and a fourth was even more explicit:

**DANGER**
**M.O.D. FIRING RANGE**
**This is an M.O.D. prohibited place under the Official Secrets Act 1911 – 1939**
**Photography and firearms are prohibited under the Military Land Byelaws 1935**
**Shoeburyness Artillery Range Byelaws 1936 apply**
**DO NOT LEAVE PUBLIC RIGHT OF WAY**

I'm afraid I was unable to resist taking a photo of the sign. So should I carry on? In favour was the fact that the gate was unlocked, the sign saying stay on the footpath and that the loud military bangs I'd heard in the morning had now stopped. Against were the no entry signs, the advice from the control room yesterday and the grave warnings of exploding debris. Captain Blackadder's advice as to what one should do if they were to accidentally step on a mine came to mind – 'Normal procedure is to jump 200 feet in the air and scatter yourself over a wide area'. However on balance I decide to proceed with caution as they say on the railways, but wrote in my note book 'Gate Open' so my family could sue the army if was to be returned in small pieces.

Half a mile along the sea wall I arrived at Haven Point, arguably the start of the Thames Estuary and another milestone on the walk. The point at which the River Thames becomes sea is difficult to define, but the position used to define its 215 mile length is a line between Havengore Creek and Warren Point in Kent, which until 1964 was the seaward limit of the Port of London Authority. Daring to stray a few yards from the path I sat for a few minutes on a concrete bunker, taking in the view of the huge expanse of mud that is Maplin Sands. Had the tide been up

I could have enjoyed looking at sea, rather than creek or river, for the first time since north of the Crouch. However this afternoon I had to make do with mud and a couple of container ships several miles distant showing that there was indeed deep water between here and Kent. Not entirely at ease sitting on the bunker, partly due to a lingering doubt as the whether I should have been on the range and partly because 50 yards behind me were two large artillery guns pointing in my general direction, I set off up the Thames. Frequent notices reminded of the nasty things that might happen should I choose to stray from the sea wall. Various buildings and ruins could be seen through the bushes, but other than the guns at Haven Point, there was little to suggest what goes on in this secret area.

Shoeburyness range was established in the 1850s, as the Royal Artillery ranges near Woolwich were becoming increasingly difficult to use due to their proximity to the busy shipping route. The marshes here offered isolation, ample land and foreshore for firing, plus easy access by river for the transport of heavy artillery. Initial temporary use was made permanent during the Crimean War, with practice firing and weapon testing carried out by both the army and navy. One of the first projects was to test the recently developed Armstrong rifled guns, which rotate shells as they are fired to increase accuracy and distance. Development was taking place both to find more powerful guns and to improve the effectiveness of armour on iron clad ships, with the performance of both being tested on the range.

At 35,000 acres, Shoeburyness is the largest live firing range in the UK and is now run by a private company, Qinetiq. The main operations are still weapons testing and disposal of munitions. It is home to the Defence Explosive Ordnance Disposal School (bomb disposal to you and I), hence its reputation for loud bangs. Explosions from the range can be heard for many miles, the noise often travelling across the estuary and upsetting the residents of North Kent. The army does understand the concern of residents, so tries to minimise noise of explosions and time them to cause least inconvenience. However from comments on an internet forum it appears that some individual soldiers are more dismissive of the 'blue rinse' complainers and proud of the size of their bangs. The range was even blamed by some for the death of a bottle-nosed whale in the Thames in January 2006, with it suggested that explosions from the site may have disorientated the creature. Predictably a spokeswoman for Qinetic dismissed the claims as 'opportunistic'.

Half a mile from Haven Point and opposite an observation tower, is one of the sites of Essex that I had most wanted to see on the whole walk. It is here at Wakering Stairs that The Broomway, one of the country's most unusual and most dangerous footpaths starts. Running for six miles across Maplin Sands to Fishermen's Head on Foulness, this is not a route for the faint hearted. The path is under water for 3 hours either side of high tide, and to both left and right of the hard surface is soft sand and mud. The fast moving tides cover the mudflats as fast as a man can walk and the unwary walker can find water approaching from both sides, the conflicting flows forming whirlpools and blocking any escape to land. Disorientating sea mists often fall rapidly, leaving anyone on the path in a virtual whiteout and travellers have been known to have met their death struggling out to sea in rising water. In parish registers there are many mentions of locals and strangers found drowned having misjudged the tides or lost the path, and all in all The Broomway is not a route to the taken lightly.

Whilst it may well date back to Roman times or even earlier, The Broomway's true age is unknown, although the first written record is from 1419. To guide travellers local people drove hundreds of wooden stakes into the mud at 30 yard intervals and tied bundles of twigs to them, giving the appearance of witches brooms and the path its name. Until the first bridge was built in 1926 The Broomway was the only 'land' access to Foulness. The postman came this way to deliver the mail by horse and cart, with delivery times dependant on tides. For safety he would only undertake the journey as the tide was going out and if foggy would take a helper to look out for the markers as he drove. Sometimes he'd take passengers back to Wakering, from where they could walk across the fields to catch a train or tram to Southend. After the bridge was built The Broomway largely fell into disuse, although in recent years there have been a number of organised walks, guided by knowledgeable locals.

No one knows the path's origins, or even if it was man-made or natural, but a possible explanation is a natural outcrop of chalk just below the surface, although it seems extraordinary that this should run in such a dead straight line. The only comparable route in the UK is across Morecambe Bay. The difference is that there the route varies as the sands shift, whereas the hard Broomway is unchanging. Both have however claimed their toll of lives.

Today just a few marker poles still stand near the start, although without their twigs, but beyond this one has to follow the path and hope the mist doesn't come down. The short length of concrete by the shore is soon replaced by cobble stones, then as it turns towards Foulness these fade away, the path blending into the huge expanse of sands which stretch to the horizon. One day I shall walk The Broomway, but only in perfect weather, with suitable company and ideal tides. Despite the bold green 'byway' line shown on the map, it would be foolish to head out onto the sands without adequate preparation. However a short length wouldn't do any harm, so I set off along the cobbles. Even a few hundred yards from the shore there was a great sense of isolation, with no other person on this immense area of mud. Then it struck me that written in big red letters on the map was DANGER AREA and that Maplin Sands are very much part of the artillery ranges. Indeed one of the reasons this area was chosen was that shells could be fired across the mud and collected later. There are no red and white posts on The Broomway, so I wasn't staying on the safe route as instructed by the many warnings. Although there had been no such sign at Wakering Steps, common sense said I should return to the shore.

From The Broomway the path continues on the sea wall for another half a mile before coming up against a tall metal fence, topped with six strands of barbed wire. A selection of notices make it very clear that casual visitors are not welcome in this next area of military property. The path runs inland through rough scrub, crossing a railway track, which looked not to have seen a train for many a year. A short way down the straight track a set of gates with more barbed wire blocked the line, the scene looking more like a location for a war movie than a spot just yards from the Essex coast. This is the now disused Shoeburyness Military Railway, which was used to move artillery around the ranges. I had seen the end of the line behind the guns at Haven Point and had thought it odd that the tracks stopped with no buffers. Presumably this was to allow artillery to be simply rolled off the end. The red and white poles continued, guiding me along the path round the edge of fields, over another railway track and coming out on the road at Cupid's Corner.

The road enters the M.O.D. base, with signs saying no public access and tall fences either side. Although no one was there to stop me, it seemed most unlikely that there would be a way through to the shore. Instead I took a path between houses and the fence, which led round to Wakering Road. Turning left opposite Crouchmans Court, I continued on the road towards Shoeburyness. After half a mile it was left into Peel Avenue, opposite Pussys Palace, where one hopes the owners are better at caring for cats than they are at punctuation.

This took me past the eastern end of the Qinetiq site and another little known Essex oddity. Standing alongside military buildings were lines of old trains; diminutive Northern Line tube coaches and old Network South East slam door electrics. Known only to locals and railway enthusiasts, an extension of one of the C2C

The Broomway

sidings at Shoeburyness depot runs over a level crossing and into the M.O.D depot. Here the network of tracks is used for storage of unwanted carriages, prior to scrapping or occasional reprieve and restoration. Romantics amongst the spotting fraternity cling to the hope that these are part of a strategic reserve to be brought out in time of nuclear war or oil crisis and hauled by the steam engines they say are stored in a siding off Box Tunnel in Wiltshire.

Approaching the main entrance to the Qiniteq site I noticed a security guard come out of his building and watch closely as I walked towards him. Had I shown too much interest in the trains, had word reached him of my illicit venture onto the Broomway, or had surveillance spotted me photographing the sign back by Havengore Creek? No, he'd just popped out for a fag.

Turning left, in a few yards I was on Shoeburyness East Beach. With the tide up this is a real beach, proud of its Blue Flag, but this afternoon with just a short strip of dry sand, a length of shingle, then about a mile of mud, it wasn't the most inviting bit of seaside. At the east end of the beach are the remains of a defence boom, which was built to control shipping movements in the early years of the Cold War. The two parallel lines of concrete posts now extend about a mile to the low water mark, but used to run as far as the deep water channel and continue the other side to Sheerness. In an emergency the channel would have been blocked by moored ships. It replaced a World War Two boom, which was constructed in 1939 and stretched 1¾ miles into the Thames. Again a similar structure extended out from the Isle of Sheppey, 5 miles away on the opposite bank, with an anti-submarine net placed across the deep water channel between them. Barges were stationed along the net and the boom armed with anti-aircraft guns and searchlights. Its purpose was not only to prevent German submarines and surface ships from attacking shipping anchored in the river, but also to counter low flying mine laying aircraft.

At the other end of the beach is Shoebury Garrison, the old Royal Artillery barracks, which is now being turned into housing. With its strategic position at the mouth of the Thames, military history here goes back to the middle Iron Age (300 – 100BC), when ramparts were built to protect a village. A Roman fortified settlement known as Essobira was attacked by the British in AD50, but is thought to have survived until into the 4th century. Two centuries later Saxon invaders established a settlement here called Scoebyrig, which is believed later became a base for Danish Vikings who sought to overrun the Saxon kingdom. It was to Shoeburyness that Danish forces retreated in AD894 after defeat at the Battle of Benfleet.

The present day garrison buildings were mostly built between 1854 and 1871, to support the new ranges on the Shoeburyness marshes. Many are listed and are of architectural merit, as well as historic interest. One of the most impressive is the Garrison Hospital, which when built in 1854 was probably the most advanced barrack hospital of the time, having separate isolation, fever, casualty and general wards. It is thought that Florence Nightingale may have inspected the hospital shortly after it opened.

The dangerous nature of the work here was highlighted in 1885 when a 6 inch shell accidentally exploded during experiments on a newly invented sensitive fuse. Seven soldiers were killed, with The Times of 27th February reporting that a Gunner Allen, who was stood over the shell when it exploded, was 'literally blown to pieces' and that 'the catastrophe was the subject of lament and discussion in the town'. Such was the public concern that donations in memory of those killed were sufficient to pay for a new hospital for married soldiers.

After intense activity during the two World Wars, the garrison was gradually reduced in size until it was disbanded in 1976. The site was eventually sold in 2000 and a development plan followed. This has seen renovation of the historic buildings and erection of new housing, sympathetically reflecting, but not copying the old designs. Whilst not yet complete, the area seems to be coming back to life, an example of what can be achieved with careful development rather than the bulldozer.

The way forward was blocked by yet another high fence displaying more M.O.D. warning signs, and with heavy rain starting to fall, I decided to quit for the day. Walking back from the beach I passed the old Shoeburyness Hotel. Now closed and partially derelict, it used to be a training base for boxers attached to the garrison. Plans to refurbish the hotel as a bar and restaurant, with five flats on the upper floor and ten houses in the grounds, were refused by Southend Council in October 2006, but it will a shame if it is allowed to fall into ruin. From here it was just a short walk down the main street to the railway station and with four trains an hour running to London, an easy journey home.

# CHAPTER TWENTY-FIVE

# SHOEBURYNESS
# to BENFLEET

(11 miles)
7th March

On a beautiful sunny day I turned right from Shoeburyness Station and walked through the impressive gateway to the Garrison Estate. Although not sure as to whether it would be possible to walk by the sea, I'd decided to give it a try. The first road on the left took me to the shore, just beyond the fence that had blocked the way at the end of my previous walk. A short length of tarmac path ran in front of the new seafront buildings, but once this ended so did the easy going. In fact I suspected that I shouldn't have been going at all, but with an unusual absence of warning signs and a section of fence fallen to the ground, it seemed opportune to continue. Clearly I wasn't the only person to make the same decision, as for a while there was a path through the grass, although obviously unofficial. Various obstructions necessitated scrambling up the bank or down to the beach and another piece of fence had conveniently fallen down, but after a while even this narrow path disappeared. The only way through was along the beach, climbing over groynes, which with varying levels, meant some quite big drops down onto the shingle. Just before an old fort the beach ended and sea came up to the bank. Fortunately a rusty old metal ladder (minus a few of its rungs) allowed me to climb onto the concrete and walk round the ledge on the outside of the fort.

From here it was easy and I was soon at Shoebury Ness, the headland which many say is the end of the Thames. I tend to agree that this rather than Haven Point marks a more natural end to the river. The area is still 'out of bounds' and with no one else around the various ruined buildings were quite spooky. Walking into an old fort I disturbed a small flock of pigeons who flew out inches above my head. It could have been a setting for an episode of Scoobydoo. The remains of an old wharf, Gog's Berth, are just beyond the fort and next to this Barge Pier, which was built in the early 20$^{th}$ century, replacing Garrison Pier. All were used for unloading artillery. Two sets of railway tracks can be seen on Barge Pier, which were the start of the Shoeburyness Military Railway, the other end of which I'd seen at Haven Point.

Walking along the grassy top of the sea wall I gradually came to the realisation that there was no gate or gap in the high metal fence ahead. The section on the land was topped with sharp spikes, but the part running down the beach was less fearsome. It would still have been unclimbable had someone not left a plank of wood jammed between the posts, allowing a leg up. Avoiding glancing in the direction of the adjacent look out tower lest any occupant may tell me to stop, over the fence I went. Another fence 50 yards further on was no problem, as it ended a couple of yards before the sea, although with the tide rising this would soon have been covered. On the other side of fence was the familiar big red sign – DANGER KEEP OUT M.O.D PROPERTY.

A few yards further along the beach was a flock of at least 50 sanderling standing tightly packed by the shore, their soft grey feathers ruffling in the breeze, and all bobbing up and down slowly, as they stood on the shingle. I'd often seen sanderling exhibiting their characteristic running behaviour on sandy beaches, but never this many together. I assume they were resting, waiting for the tide to fall and expose their lunch.

Shoebury Common Beach (also known as West Beach) is a long stretch of sand and pebbles, which like much of the estuary is proper seaside with the tide up, but less inviting when the water is beyond the mud banks. The narrow grassy area of the common provides a barrier between the beach and the road which runs along the shore all the way from here to Westcliff. I walked along the tarmac path between the beach and grass, where three workmen were planting a palm tree, or more correctly one was wielding a shovel while his two mates watched. Beach huts line the foreshore, those at the east end by the path and those further towards Southend raised on wooden stilts over the sand. Several were for sale, with prices ranging from £8,000 to £15,000, depending on size, condition, location (proximity to steps) and extras like cooker or fridge.

Lying on West Knock sandbank, a mile from the shore, is a section of Mulberry Harbour, built to be used in Normandy to re-supply troops following the D Day landings. This piece of floating harbour was being towed from Immingham on the Humber to Southsea, when it sprang a leak, so was brought into the Thames estuary and allowed to sink. Here it has stayed for over 60 years, viewed by some as an eyesore and hazard to shipping, but by others as a piece of history and part of Southend's heritage. Either way there seemed little doubt that it would be here forever, or at least until eventually consumed by the mud into which it appears to be slowly sinking. However in 2002 the M.O.D. announced plans to blow up the relic, so they no longer had to be responsible for it. Fortunately a campaign led by a local Lib Dem councillor and with the support of Southend Council's Conservation Working Party, helped ensure the survival of what is not just a concrete hulk in the mud, but a part of our history.

This stretch of estuary is built up for about 6 miles and it's hard to know where one 'town' ends and the next starts. Shoebury Common Beach actually fronts on to Thorpe Bay, although this has its own beach further east. Known as the posh part of Southend, Thorpe Bay was mainly developed in the 1920s, with good sized houses in a grid pattern. Thorpe Hill Golf Club is close to the shore and one of the main clubs in the Southend area. The area was originally called Thorpe, but renamed after its railway station, which had been given the name Thorpe Bay to show it was a seaside settlement. Thorpe Bay Yacht Club is one of a line of large and expensive looking properties facing the estuary across a wide greensward. A sign warned road users of boats crossing, as the boat park occupies a concrete area on the green between club house and sea.

Approaching the centre of Southend the road was becoming busier and the noise starting to get annoying. It was nice to be by the sea, but I preferred the solitude and quietness of the more remote Essex. More people were walking here, although few without canine accompaniment, and several bike riders overtook me using the cycle track which is the start of Route 16 of the National Cycle Network. It runs to Basildon.

At the eastern end of Southend are two buildings, shall we say, lacking of aesthetic qualities. Esplanade Towers is a 1960s (I presume) monstrosity of an office block. Totally out of place on the sea front and currently sporting large 'To Let' signs. Hopefully no takers will be found and they'll let loose some of those soldiers from Shoeburyness to have a play with their dynamite.

Jutting out into the sea are the derelict remains of the Corporation Loading Jetty. Built in 1914 for the sum of £10,878, this was used for unloading Thames barges and lighters until trade declined in the early 1960s. It was then let out to private business and last used in the early 1980s for berthing two tugs. With a firing point added during World War Two visible on the top, the jetty is of some historic value, but is now unsafe and so close to the main attractions of Southend, an eyesore. At some stage a decision will have to be made as to whether to demolish or renovate.

A far more pleasing piece of architecture, its distinctive domed entrance a Southend icon, is the Kursaal, once the largest fairground in the South of England. Completed in 1901, initially as a ballroom, it expanded into a huge entertainment complex and much loved fun palace for visitors and locals alike. At its height, as well as the many amusements and rides, the 26 acre site had its own ice cream and rock factories, extensive gardens and greenhouses. It was *the* place to go in Southend and throughout the summer would be packed with thousands of holiday makers and day trippers, who would divide their time between beach, pier and amusements.

For our family however the Kursaal, like swimming pools, hot countries and theme parks, was the sort of place that *other children* went to. Our outings tended to involve trains, buses and long walks, usually in the rain, to see something like a prehistoric burial chamber or some other pile of rocks. Whilst these may not have been my preferred choice as a child, if like my friends we'd spent our holidays in Majorca, I doubt I'd have the appreciation of our countryside and preference for public transport that I do now. Parental influence often lasts longer than we realise. I went to the Kursaal once. Aged about 15, three friends and I cycled to Southend for the day and I was persuaded to put a penny into a 'What the Butler Saw' machine. My recollection is one of disappointment that he didn't actually see very much.

From the mid 1960s, like many seaside towns, Southend saw reducing visitor numbers as people started to take up cheap foreign package holidays. The Kursaal fell into decline, with much of the site sold off for housing, until it eventually closed in the 1986. For some years the listed entrance hall lay empty and decaying, but then in 1998 the newly formed unitary local authority of Southend Borough Council purchased the Kursaal as part of its plans to regenerate the sea front. After refurbishment it was reopened housing a 20 lane bowling alley and casino, and is now a thriving attraction once more.

A more recent attraction is Sealife Adventure, which opened in June 1993 and displays a wide variety of sea creatures, whilst trying to raise awareness for marine conservation. Opposite this is Southend's best section of sand, Jubilee Beach, which was created from the construction of improved sea defences and opened in July 2002.

Also relatively new to the sea front is Adventure Island, an amusement park which spans both sides of the pier. The eastern section replaced an old boating lake, which had been an eyesore for many years and the western end was formerly Peter Pan's

The Kursaal

Playground. Whilst not in the Alton Towers league, Adventure Island has 32 rides with a good selection of roller coasters and other contraptions designed to spin, invert or otherwise contort the human body.

This length of seafront is known as the Golden Mile and the 'noisy end', with the town side of the road having a selection of pubs, cafes and amusement arcades, plus the night club Electric Avenue. In our day it was Talk of the South (TOTS) and although I never ventured inside, my wife with her coach has picked up various parties of scantily clad and rather inebriated young ladies in the early hours of Sunday mornings.

And so to the pier, where I met my wife who'd come down to join me for lunch. I'd intended to walk to the end, but there wasn't time for this and to eat, as she had to get back to collect our youngest from school. In any case, it's a walk we'd done many times before. At 1.34 miles it is the longest pleasure pier in the world, a Grade 2 listed building and the town's biggest claim to fame. Sir John Betjeman once said that 'the pier is Southend, Southend is the pier'.

Originally the south end of the village of Prittlewell, Southend started to grow as a resort in the early 19th century when Londoners started coming to the seaside, which was considered to be good for one's health. However with its shallow sea and mudflats extending for over a mile at low tide, large boats were unable to stop here. Many potential visitors passed by, travelling on to Margate or other resorts where docking facilities were easier. A campaign led by Sir William Heygate, a former Lord Mayor of London, and a resident of Southend, resulted in Parliament passing an Act giving authorisation for construction of a pier in 1829. The initial 600 foot wooden pier based on oak piles was opened in June 1830, but was still too short to be usable at low tide. After several extensions, by 1848 it was 7,000 feet and the longest pier in Europe. When the railway reached Southend in the

1856 the huge growth in the number of visitors took their toll on the wooden structure and it was decided to build a new iron pier. Designed by James Brunlees, who had built the first iron pier at Southport, it was completed in 1889. The pier was extended in 1897, an upper deck added to the end in 1907 and a further extension opened by Prince George, Duke of Kent in 1929.

The original wooden pier employed a horse drawn tramway to carry visitors and goods to and from the pier head, but this was replaced with an electric railway when the new iron pier was constructed. By 1930 the system had been expanded, with four trains, each made up of seven carriages, running on double track. New rolling stock was purchased in 1949 and painted in what became a familiar green and cream.

The Royal Navy took over the pier during World War 2, renaming it HMS Leigh. Its main use was a mustering point for convoys, with 3,367 convoys comprising 84,297 vessels departing during the course of the war. Anti-aircraft guns were placed on the pier head, with the trains used to supply them with ammunition and to ferry casualties ashore from ships. After reopening in 1945 visitor numbers exceeded their pre-war levels, peaking at 7 million in 1949. Additional attractions opened, including the Hall of Mirrors, Sun Deck Theatre and Solarium Café. However, declining visitor numbers and a series of disasters almost led to the pier's demise.

In 1959 a fire destroyed the Pavilion located at the shore end, trapping 500 people who had to be rescued by boat. It was replaced by a bowling alley, but this was damaged by fire in 1977 and completely burnt down in 1995. A major fire broke out on the pier head in 1976 and despite fire fighters working on the pier and from boats, and even using crop spraying aircraft, most of the buildings were destroyed. In 1978 the railway was deemed unsafe and had to be shut down and two years later the council announced that the pier was to close. Amid much protest they agreed that it could remain open until a solution could be found and in 1983 the Historic Buildings Committee gave a grant to allow the pier to be saved. Work was completed three years later, the cost of repairs, new buildings and two new red diesel trains totalling £1.3 million.

Within months of reopening however, a ship, the MV Kingsabbey, crashed into the pier, destroying the lifeboat house, causing major structural damage and leaving the pier head cut off by a 70 foot gap. Once again the pier refused to die and in 2001 a new and impressive RNLI station opened, housing a gift shop and small museum. Thanks to grants from Europe and the UK Government, the shore end was then redeveloped, incorporating a modern tourist information centre, new lifts to pier hill and raising the bridge over the road to enable taller vehicles to pass under (prior to this double decker buses often got stuck).

On October 9th 2005 yet another fire hit the pier, severely damaging much of the old pier head including the railway station, pub, amusement arcade and café, with several of the buildings collapsing into the water. A temporary station was constructed and access restored to the RNLI station, but there is now little left to entertain visitors. There have been various plans to revamp the pier, one including a major theme park with a gigantic rollercoaster called The Swine, but every time the council has refused to sell. In public ownership it now seems unlikely that the pier would be allowed to close, but once sold and run for profit who knows what might happen. Personally I'm happy as long as one can still walk to the end of the pier, buy an ice cream and take the train back.

The mile to Westcliff was right next to the sea with the tide now high and little waves slopping up the embankment. Much of the cliff gardens on the opposite side of the road has been closed since 2003 when landslips made them unsafe. The Victorian bandstand, which had already been closed after a slip in December

New Lift to Southend Pier

2000, has now completely gone and areas of cliff have reverted to nature.

A 40 metre funicular cliff railway climbs 17 metres up the 1 in 2.3 gradient for those preferring to avoid the steep walk, although it operates less often now the new free of charge conventional lifts have been opened by the pier. It was built in 1912, replacing one of the country's first 'moving walkways', a forerunner to the modern escalator. Whereas most funiculars have two tracks, with a car on each, this has a single car, counterbalance being provided by a weight running beneath the 1.4m gauge track. The council took over its operation in 2001 and with the help of a £1.5 million grant by the Heritage Lottery Fund, undertook a major renovation of the lift and the adjacent Cliff Steps, which had been closed on safety grounds in the 1970s. Technical problems caused the lift to cease operating in June 2003, and its reopening was then much delayed by changes in European legislation. The lift had always been defined as a rack railway, but according the EU Cableway Directive 2004, it was now a cable car. A different set of regulations applied and considerable structural and mechanical work was required to meet them. It's probably best that I refrain from comment.

We often have our lunch in one of the line of little cafes under the arches of Shorefield Road at Westcliff. All offer good straightforward food at reasonable prices – all day breakfasts, fish and chips, roasts etc – the sort of food you expect to find by the sea. Today we went to Sea Breeze Cafe and had excellent omelettes sitting in bright sunshine under the awning, watching container ships on their way up river. My only complaint about these little cafes is that cars are allowed to park outside, partly obscuring the sea view. In fact cars are probably the thing I like least about Southend. It would be so much nicer without the busy road running next to the beach.

The relative quietness was noticeable, when after another 15 minutes walking the road moves away from the shore, leaving a wide concrete walkway alongside the beach. A couple of hundred yards out to sea, but more often standing in the mud, is the Crow Stone, which marks the limit of the river bed owned by Port of London Authority. This has stood here since 1837, when it replaced a smaller stone dating from 1755 that can still be seen in Priory Park, Southend.

Cliff Railway - Southend

At Chalkwell the path occupies the narrow space between the station and the sea. There can be few railway stations that are as close to the beach as this, Dawlish on the Devon coast where one platform overhangs the beach, being the only one I can think of. From here to Leigh the path runs on a narrow strip of land between the railway and sea, a walk we used to do sometimes as children, well away from the bright lights of the Kursaal.

An old Royal Navy minesweeper, HMS Wilton, is moored here. Now the club house of Essex Yacht Club, it was deployed in the UK, Europe and the Middle East, and took part in mine clearance from the Suez Canal in 1974. Wilton was the first warship in the world to be constructed from glass-reinforced plastic, giving her a low magnetic signature against the threat of magnetic mines, but nicknames of HMS Tupperware and The Plastic Duck.

I spent a while wandering around the wharves and cobbled High Street of the picturesque old village of Leigh. On fine summer days the place is packed, but on a Friday afternoon in March it was quiet and all the better for it.

Whereas Southend grew from almost nothing in the 19th century, Leigh has a long history. It was a fishing village and small port many centuries before the seaside was thought of as a place for recreation. Legra as it was then known, was recorded in the Domesday Book as a small fishing hamlet, but with a sheltered position on the shipping route to London, it grew into a fairly large and prosperous port. There was a significant ship building industry, with vessels up to 340 tons recorded as being built here. Depending on which source you choose to believe, The Mayflower was either built or owned at Leigh, or docked here to take on provisions and passengers before its epic voyage with the Pilgrim Fathers. By the 18th century ships had become larger and a change in sea level caused the silting up of Leigh's deep water channel, so it reverted once more into a fishing village. With no real rivals in the Thames estuary, mudflats offering ideal fishing grounds and oysters cultivated inshore, plus its proximity to the London markets, Leigh became a very successful fishing port.

Arrival of the railway in 1856 enabled much faster transit of catches to Billingsgate, however forced by the high cliffs to run close to the sea, the line split the village in two and resulted in demolition of many timber framed buildings. Whilst fishing has continued, the rail link to London turned much of Leigh into a dormitory town. The old village by the sea became only a small part of a much larger town, now with a population of around 21,000. A survey in 2007 by the Evening Standard newspaper named Leigh-on-Sea as the second best place to live in South East England (Christchurch was best although I'd question whether that's South East).

Bell Wharf at the eastern end of the village was constructed mainly with rubble from buildings demolished during building of the railway. Victoria Wharf was used for off loading clay for the local Victoria Potteries, as well as general cargoes such as timber and coal. A lime kiln once stood in the south east corner. Behind the wharves is Leigh Sailing Club, its clubhouse formerly part of the town's first railway station, the current one being built further west in 1936. A number of buildings on this side of the street were demolished for construction of the railway, including a pub The Smack, but its replacement, Ye Olde Smack, still stands opposite on an old wharf.

Just along from here is The Smithy, now Leigh Heritage Centre. Originally two timber framed cottages, these were brick faced around 1860 when the building was converted to a ships' smithy. Along with a number of other buildings in the High Street, it was purchased many years ago by Southend Council, with a view to a development which fortunately never took place. In 1979 the council agreed to lease it to the Leigh Society, who were given just 8 weeks to make the condemned building safe and get the demolition order withdrawn. After restoration the society used it as their headquarters, with volunteers staffing the Heritage Centre and museum. Inside is a large selection of old photos with lots of information about Leigh's history. I spent an interesting 20 minutes looking at these and the two small rooms showing how the cottages were when a family with their many children lived here. I bought a copy of *Titbits and Tales of Essex Inns* by Mavis Sipple, for which I am indebted for some of the information mentioned about the various pubs along the coast.

On the other side of the road is the old Custom House, which was built in 1815, but taken over by the railway company, who provided a new building by Bell Wharf to be shared by customs and the coastguard. Adjacent to The Strand, a medieval wharf and probably the first public landing place in Leigh, is the Peter Boat Inn. This pub was built on the site of a late 17th century building that was destroyed by fire in 1892, which also consumed a row of timber framed cottages, now replaced by the terrace of Reginald and Theobald's Cottages. The Crooked Billet, probably Leigh's most famous pub, stands at the western end of the High Street. Its rendered brick frontage covers a timber framed building from the early 16th century. Originally quite large, a section of the rear of the building was lost when the railway was built. Like the Peter Boat, there's plenty of room for drinkers to sit on benches outside when the summer hoards invade. The old wooden building next door was once St Thomas Church, which was built as a fisherman's church in 1936 and is now the headquarters of a Venture Scout group.

There is much more of interest in the higher level of the town up Leigh Hill, but I stayed by the sea, passing the famous line of cockle sheds by the railway and on to the station. Stopping here just to buy a snack from the buffet, I continued on the sea wall towards Benfleet. After miles of concrete it was good to have grass under foot once more.

For a mile there's just a narrow channel between the mainland and Two Tree Island, a marshy island with more trees than its name suggests, which was reclaimed from the sea in the 18th century. Originally rough grazing, it was purchased by Southend Borough Council in 1936, who used it as a rubbish tip until the 1970s. The island is reached by a bridge that carries its only road and which splits it into two distinct halves. The eastern part is now an Essex Wildlife Trust reserve with varied habitats. A number of interesting 'alien' plants have grown up on the old rubbish tip and a wide variety of birds can be seen on the grassland and scrub. The salt marsh on the seaward side is one of the best surviving on the Thames and the mudflats beyond, with their dense beds of eel

Leigh on Sea

grass, provide valuable feeding ground for wildfowl and waders. The thousands of dark-bellied brent geese who arrive here on their autumn migration make this a site of international importance.

The western end of the island is part of Hadleigh Castle Country Park, with a lagoon at the very tip that is home to one of my favourite birds, the avocet. This is one of only a dozen or so breeding sites in Essex, although birds here have been victims of that most shameful act of egg theft. In 2004 and 2005 all the eggs were stolen, but after volunteers mounted a guard, 14 successfully hatched the following year. This distinctly patterned black and white wader with its characteristic long up-curved beak is the emblem of the RSPB and more than any other species symbolises the bird protection movement in the UK. Having been absent for 100 years, avocets returned to Britain in the 1940s and their increase in numbers represents one of the most successful conservation and protection projects. However with only around 900 breeding pairs in the UK it can ill afford to lose eggs to the despicable thieves.

To the right is one of the best vistas to be seen from the Essex coast. The flat expanse of Hadleigh Marsh, with a backdrop of Plumtree Hill and the romantic remains of Hadleigh Castle. Every few minutes one of C2C's cheerful little blue trains scampered across the marsh, adding colour and movement to the scene. Its interesting how trains so often enhance a view, whilst cars nearly always have the opposite effect. A tractor, plough or perhaps a post van could add to a country scene, but a stream of traffic would spoil it. A busy road is an intrusion, but a railway that's been there for the best part of two centuries, doesn't seem out of place.

As I sat in the sunshine eating my chocolate bar the only sounds were of the wind and the metallic 'kowk kowk' of a lone coot in the borrowdyke. Then peace was shattered by an over friendly jack russell, who sniffed first my rucksack, then me, culminating in a distinctly unpleasant lick of my face. I pushed him off, but his lady owner appeared to think his behaviour was totally justified because I had food in my bag.

Hadleigh Castle is the most important late-medieval castle in Essex and along with St Peter's Chapel and Southend Pier, one of the county's most famous coastal buildings. Although largely ruined, its tumbledown state and lofty site overlooking the Thames estuary add to the sense of romance and history. Construction was begun in 1230 by Hubert de Burgh the 1st Earl of Kent and Justiciar of England (Chief Minister), using Kentish ragstone cemented by mortar containing a large proportion of cockleshells. However, in 1232 it was confiscated by King Henry III after de Burgh had been removed from office and imprisoned in Devizes Castle. He soon escaped and joined a rebellion led by Richard Marshall, 3rd Earl of Pembroke, which probably wasn't the best course of action if he hoped to persuade the king to let him have his castle back.

Henry continued the building work and substantial additions were made in the mid 14<sup>th</sup> century by Edward III. It is mainly these extensions which remain today. In its prime the castle was not only a fortress standing guard over the Thames, but with extensive apartments, it was a royal residence to which the king bought his hunting parties to Essex. In 1551 Edward VI sold the castle for £700 to Lord Rich of Leez Prior in Chelmsford (the founder of Felsted School), who allowed much of the stone to be taken for building several churches. By the 17<sup>th</sup> century neglect and landslips had left the castle in ruins, as it was in 1829 when painted by John Constable. The picture, which now hangs in the Yale Centre for British Art, New Haven, USA, is far from the painter's typical gentle country scene, the stormy clouds an image of loneliness reflecting his grief following the death of his wife.

Today the castle looks much as it did when immortalised by Constable, with the three storey south east tower still standing, plus the remains of another tower, sections of the curtain wall and foundations of various buildings including the great hall and kitchen. Now cared for by English Heritage, visitors can wander round the castle ruins at any time and without charge.

With the weather now perfect, that ideal mix of blue sky, fluffy cotton wool clouds and a gentle breeze, the stretch from Leigh to Benfleet was one of the most pleasant of the whole walk. I'd done the walk a number of times before using the inland path by Hadleigh Castle, but never along the sea wall. This gave the combination of good views inland and creeks on the left looking at their best with the sun shining and tide high. For a change I wasn't the only one to be enjoying the path, and a dozen or so others must have passed by, most but not all accompanied by dogs of varying size. It reminded me of the path from Wivenhoe to Colchester, with proximity to population and good weather bringing out the locals.

Beyond Two Tree Island is Benfleet Creek and opposite this

Hadleigh Castle

Canvey Island. Having seen some real sea with waves earlier today, it was now back to the familiar creeks and marshes that make up most of Essex's coast. Hadleigh Castle County Park includes the section of sea wall from a low water crossing point at the tip of Two Tree Island, to just before Benfleet. Run by Essex County Council, the park's mix of scrub, grassland and woodland attracts a good range of birds and its sunny south facing slopes are one of the best sites in the whole county for butterflies.

The park ends near Ferry Road, where a line of boats were tied up in the creek, one of which, the Gladys, has been converted into a small bar. Benfleet Motor Yacht Club has its headquarters along here and on the opposite bank is Benfleet Yacht Club. Just before the station is the bridge to Canvey, which was built in 1973, replacing the original 1931 swing bridge that was the first permanent route to the island. Prior to this access was by ferry, or across stepping stones at low tide. Adjacent to the bridge is a concrete flood barrier, part of the defences designed to prevent a repeat of the loss of life in the 1953 flood.

With more to be seen of the island next time, I finished today's walk at Benfleet station. This interchange for buses to Canvey is one of the busiest on the Shoeburyness line and has the benefit of some fast peak hour services to London, the quickest taking just 32 minutes non stop for the 29 miles from the capital. My 18 minute ride to Upminster was a welcome contrast to the three hour journeys from the wilds of North Essex. The section from Chalkwell to Benfleet had been one of my favourites of the whole walk, yet despite living so near, I'd been as guilty as most of the county's population in ignoring our coast. With stations every mile or two it is so easy to walk a length of this coast, enjoying the fresh air, scenery, history and wildlife. A circular walk from Benfleet to Leigh, outward via Hadleigh Castle, lunch in one of Leigh's many pubs and return along the sea wall, would make an excellent outing for a sunny day.

# PART SIX

## Benfleet to Purfleet

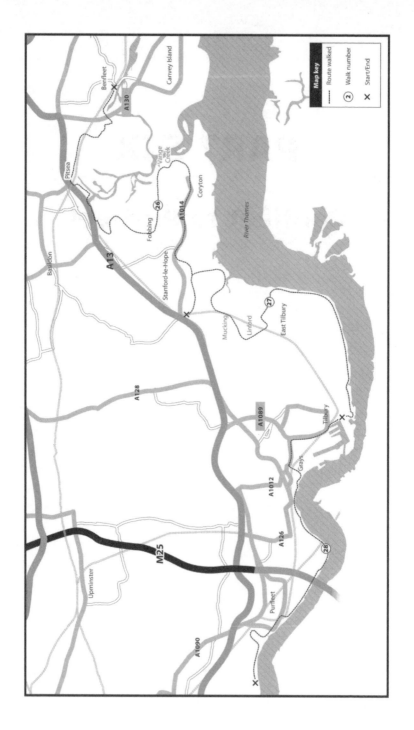

**ESSEX COAST WALK**

CHAPTER TWENTY-SIX

# BENFLEET to STANFORD LE HOPE

(14 miles)
21st April

With a short train ride taking me straight to the coast and just a road to cross from Benfleet station, I was by the water early today. A path runs alongside the creek, passing some ramshackle wooden jetties where there were more wrecks than seaworthy boats. An ugly metal fence on the right, adorned with signs warning that this was a hazardous area surrounded the land by the railway. The path came out at the edge of a field, but then gave no indication as to where it continued. However after following a succession of little tracks by the creek, I came out at the other end of the field by a sewage works. A few yards beyond here the path completely disappeared, the only way through being to duck under some hazard tape and onto a motorbike scrambling track. Not the best place to walk when muddy or if the bikes are out. After a short distance however I was able to make my way down to the creek again, where there's a narrow path, although sea weed underfoot showed that it is covered at the highest tides. I didn't realise at the time, but this little section was to set the pattern for the whole day.

Turning right at the concrete bridge that carries the A130 to Canvey, I headed away from the coast. Whilst it looked possible to carry on along the sea wall, there isn't a path signed or shown on the map. I'd studied it carefully and concluded that even if I could continue along the embankment, a full circuit of Bowers Marshes would be blocked by various unbridged channels. There is however a path on the opposite bank, running the full 14 mile circumference of Canvey, probably the most well known Essex island, albeit not with the best of reputations. At 7.1 square miles it is the 6th largest in England and its population of 37,473 (2001 census) the 4th biggest.

Contrary to popular belief, there's more to Canvey Island than oil storage and caravans. It is the unlikely location for what has been called 'England's rainforest', an area with one of the highest levels of biodiversity in Western Europe. The 240 acre site on the western corner of the island, now known as Canvey Wick, was once earmarked for a huge oil terminal. It was covered with thousands of tonnes of silt dredged from the Thames, but with the discovery of North Sea oil the terminal was never built and the land abandoned. Now home to more than 1,300 species, including 32 on the endangered 'red list', it has more wildlife per square foot than any national nature reserve. Two insects, the morley weevil (sitona cinerascens) and canvey island ground beetle (scybalicus oblongisculus), were thought to be extinct in the UK until being found here.

Nearly all our population of the five-banded digger wasp can be found on Thames estuary brownfield sites such as Canvey Wick. This brightly coloured wasp lives alone in burrows and collects weevils from flowers, which it feeds to its young. The very rare hedychrum niemalei, a kleptoparasite ruby-tailed wasp, lays its eggs in the burrows so that its larvae can steal the weevils intended for the digger wasp's young. Each link in the chain is critical. No flowers = no weevils = no digger wasps = no hedychrum.

What is almost as incredible is that the Government wanted to concrete over the site and turn it into a business park. It was only in 2005, after a three year fight by local residents and the charity Buglife, that the site was given SSSI status. The first brownfield site to gain such protection specifically for its invertebrates, it is now managed by English Nature.

Archaeological evidence shows that Canvey was occupied by early man, with Neolithic axes, a Bronze Age bracelet and Iron Age pottery all having been found on the island. The Romans settled here and the Danes arrived in the 9th century, but were defeated at the Battle of Benfleet. They sailed up Benfleet Creek under command of King Haesten, but were beaten by Saxon forces led by Edward, son of King Alfred. Charred timbers from Viking ships were found in Benfleet when the railway was constructed.

The first sea wall was built around the island by Dutch engineers in the 1620s and people began to move onto the reclaimed land. Many of the 300 Dutchmen stayed on and were given land as payment for their work. Two of their distinctive octagonal cottages remain, one of which is now a museum. The sea wall is virtually the only part of Canvey that is above sea level, hence it has always been prone to flooding.

The 31st January 1953 was the worst night in the island's history. Driven by gale force winds, the storm surge which caused devastating floods across Eastern England, reached Canvey just after midnight. The sea wall was breached at 1 a.m., but the warning system was haphazard. The fire brigade were sent out to alert people with sirens sounded and maroons fired, hoping that the islanders would become curious enough to get out of their beds and look outside. Some did and were evacuated, but others heard nothing above the howling wind and only knew of the danger when the water crashed into their homes. Some woke when icy water lapped over them, but others sadly never woke at all. The water was 20 feet deep in places and by morning 58 islanders had lost their lives and 10,000 were homeless.

After crossing a small wooden footbridge the path ran along the edge of a field and I was back in the countryside, although the roar of traffic from the A130 made for a poor comparison with the quiet of Dengie or Hamford Water. A sign at the field boundary indicated that the path went right, but the more trodden route went left. Dutifully I went right, but it turned out that the other way was a short cut. The next stretch was a wide strip of grass between drainage ditches. Nice if you looked left to the bright yellow field of rape, or right to a meadow, but not so pleasant with Cleanaway's huge Pitsea Tip ahead or the noisy Canvey road behind. The zig zags continued through fields, one with a mass of dandelions in the corner, not as bright as the rape, but more natural and hence pleasing to the eye.

By now I should have been at the bridge which crosses the railway by Rookery Farm, but was actually at Great Mussels barn. A layer of manure on the floor and a 'country smell' indicated that unlike many farm buildings I'd seen, this was still very much in use. Indeed just the other side were a herd of cows who all stopped eating to watch me pass. The track turned right, soon passing through a gate, where signs indicated that I shouldn't have gone this way – 'Private Property' and 'Keep Out'. Passing under a bridge, where a burnt out car reminded that this was close to urban Essex, I rejoined the path on the north of the railway. The diversion hadn't added any distance to the route, or taken me further from the coast, so other than being private, had proved equally satisfactory.

I stopped to look at St Margaret's Church, which I'd seen many times from the train and had often wondered if it was still used. The present stone building was built by Sir John Giffard in the 14$^{th}$ century, with the tower added during the Tudor era, but there has been a church on this site since Saxon times. Its isolated position some distance from the nearest house, let alone village, is probably explained by the church having been built between the two manors of Bowers; Earls Fee and Bowers Hall. Constructed of

St Margaret's Church

Kentish ragstone, but with traces of Roman tiles and Tudor brickwork, this is an attractive church, and one that we are fortunate still stands to hold weekly services. During the 18th century it was used as a barn and in 1829 much rebuilding was required after the church became dangerous due to some graves having been dug too close to the foundations and the vaults collapsing. In 1855 St Margaret's was used for only four services a year, but a proposal to abandon it and build a new one in the village wasn't carried out. More recently it was found that woodpeckers had made 40 holes in the wood of the steeple. This was repaired thanks to a grant from Cleanaway, who also contributed to major repairs to the roof and walls in 2002.

For the next mile I was back by the railway, the path running along the edge of a field newly planted with wheat, then scrubland where horses grazed. A narrow path between new houses and the railway brought me into Pitsea. The town is dominated by a most ugly concrete flyover carrying the A13, beneath which is a huge Tesco store and large car park. I popped into Tesco to buy a drink, the kiosk outside Benfleet station having been shut, but an irresistible force drew me upstairs to the café. Somehow I found myself with a plate of sausage, beans and chips.

Pitsea, once a small village, but now swallowed up by Basildon, doesn't have the best of reputations. Its 1970s concrete centre, a haunt of Essex teenager with his baseball cap and Estuary English, is badly in needed of regeneration and many consider it the ultimate 'Chav Town'. Even its one building of interest, the 13th century church of St Michael, fell into ruin and just the tower remains as a landmark on the hill. Pitsea is not a town in which I wished to dwell long.

Although not signposted, the path continues opposite the railway station entrance. I followed a lady and her dog over the railway crossing and was once more back on the marshes. Three horses lay resting by a gate and I walked around them to save interrupting their afternoon snooze. Running parallel to the A13, the path was far from quiet, although it was good to be close to water again, by the pools and salt marshes of Pitsea Creek.

The map shows the path going north of the small industrial estate at Vange Wharf, but where this ends at Gouldings Farm the way forward was blocked. There was no path, just a fence around the farmhouse, with notices advising of no right of way. Unable to proceed by the route clearly shown on the O.S. map, I walked back round the industrial estate and onto the sea wall. With the tide high the creek and marshes made a pleasant view, deserted of course, although less than a mile from the busy concrete jungle of Pitsea. Although no path was shown on the sea wall, it was easy walking, however just as I began to think that it might be possible follow the embankments as far as the Thames, a fence blocked the way. Too high to climb and with spikes extending into the creek one side and borrowdyke the other, there was no way through.

Retracing steps once more to the industrial estate, the only option was to cross the railway and walk alongside the A13, which with the noisy traffic and rough going on the verges (no pavement), was far from enjoyable. Taking the first opportunity to leave the road, I found a foot crossing over the railway and climbed over a gate that clearly hadn't been opened for years. There was no path the other side, but a barbed wire fence was falling down. Stepping over this I worked my way along between hedge and fence, however the gap soon became too small and I had to turn back.

The next railway crossing had barriers, giving access to Marsh Farm and the few houses around it. Beyond the farm it was only a rough track. I was overtaken by a taxi followed by a rather posh car, with its rear window smashed and a Transport for London Aware sticker on the bit of glass remaining. The vehicles continued very slowly down to Marsh House, an isolate dwelling on Vange Marshes.

An old concrete building, probably of military origin, appeared to still be used for some kind of army games. A tank was parked outside and shooting targets lay in the doorway. A sign warned 'Mines Keep Out', in jest I hope. After passing the largest and smelliest pile of manure seen on the whole walk, I reached what the map showed as a three way footpath junction. To the left should have been the other end of the path that was blocked at Gouldings Farm, although there was no indication of its existence here either. At right angles heading south there was a path, but close study of the map had shown that like those near Hullbridge, this was one of those coastal paths that cross a channel of water. No footbridge was marked so I assumed to follow this route would have meant turning back after a mile, or very wet feet. The path I wanted headed southwest across a field where sheep were grazing. I say the path, but other than a little arrow on the gate, there was absolutely no indication of any walking route through the field.

Nevertheless I went this way and was proved to be correct on finding a wooden footbridge over a ditch at the far side. The bridge was, shall I say, in need of attention. Leaning at a worrying angle and with various pieces loose or dropped off, it was a matter of some doubt as to whether it would support my weight. Stepping very gingerly, I felt movement beneath, but was mighty relieved to make it across and not be dumped in the stagnant ditch water below.

An arrow showing that the path ran around the next field was to be the last sign for a while. The next bridge was longer, but thankfully in a better state, however once over it any semblance of a path had gone. In front of me were two enormous fields, one with peas just germinated and the other wheat. According to the map the path ran alongside the latter, but of course there was none to be seen. The edge of the pea field looked easier going, so I chose this option as far as the track that ran up the hill to Whitehall Farm. I could have taken this, then the road into Fobbing, but instead crossed to the cornfield hoping to find a path. Again there was none so I resorted to following tractor tracks near the edge. As these curved to the left at the end of the field I realised it was taking me in completely the wrong direction. Hopping carefully across the rows of plants, I made my way to the edge of the field, looking for a way through to the next one. Progress was however thwarted by a drainage channel, 10 yards wide and covered with reeds. I continued to skirt round the field looking for a way through, cursing Basildon Council for their upkeep of footpaths. In remote parts of Essex I'd generally found paths maintained, stiles in order and bridges safe, but here, with many more people living nearby, no one bothered.

Sitting down for a minute I got out the map and considered options. I could struggle back through the cornfield and take the track to Whitehall farm, but this would add a mile or more and mean that much of today's walk would be on roads. Alternatively I could carry on heading in totally the wrong direction and hope to find a way across the water. I decided on the latter, but with no way across after a couple of hundred yards got out the map once more and considered a third option – walk back to Basildon and go home. Twice more I walked on a bit, then stopped again, now on the verge of giving up. Then a chink of light appeared. The drainage channel narrowed for a stretch, with the far bank only about five yards away. The reeds provided possible footholds, although clearly wouldn't hold my weight. Crossing would be possible here, but only if I was prepared to get wet. How wet couldn't be known until the operation was completed. Unlike some of the crossings I'd declined on other walks, this one didn't appear to have deep mud, so I went for it. Leaping from clump to clump, the reeds slowed my sinking and completion with legs wet only to the knees had to be rated as a success. In fact the worst part was the final dive sending me sprawling headlong onto the far bank, hands outstretched in a patch of stinging nettles.

Obviously there was no path on this side and with boots squelching it was back to finding tractor ruts that headed in roughly the right direction. I could have done with a compass, but Fobbing church standing on its hill provided a suitable beacon. Eventually I found a footpath sign and a real path. Hoorah! To the left was the path I'd declined because it crossed an offshoot of Vange Creek and to the right a clear path heading towards Fobbing. The sign also showed a footpath heading back the way I'd come from the A13, but it was quite obviously having a laugh.

After a brief stop and celebratory ham roll, I resumed, taking the left hand option where the path split, rather then Marsh Lane which ran up to the road. Then I encountered the next obstacle. A stile took the path into a small field, in the corner of which stood six large cows, each one instantly stopping their munching and staring hard as I approached. The look in their eyes was quite clear – Enter our field at your peril. The instant my left foot touched the stile they stepped forward. Six pairs of eyes said – Come on then, make my day. Now my wife is petrified of cows, a fear that goes back to a walk near Fambridge many years ago when we were chased by a large herd. I've always told her not to worry. They're more scared of us and all that. However, with six of the beasts facing me, each weighing half a tonne or more and seemingly intent on inflicting bodily harm, I was inclined to think she was right. I had visions of my battered body being found several days later, and headlines of 'Mystery Death of Walker'. Only the cows would know the whole story. Still, one mustn't give in to irrational fears (although logic did say they were bigger, faster and angrier than me), so over the stile I went. My pace was unusually swift as I walked along the edge of the field – right at the edge. Don't look back I thought. Ignore them and they'll ignore you. I managed about thirty yards before turning to take a glimpse, just in time to see the grey one at the front start the charge. With the head start maybe I could have reached the end before they did, but with six animals approaching at an increasing rate of knots I wasn't going to hang around. One hand on a post, I swung myself over the barbed wire fence and out of range. The next week I read in the newspaper that a 42 year old woman walking in Suffolk had been found dead in a field, trampled by a herd of cows. No longer shall I consider fear of bovine animals as in any way irrational.

An easy footpath ran through a cornfield and after a short delay to deal with a broken bootlace, I was soon in the village of Fobbing. This used to be close to the river, but after the floods of 1953 the creek was drained and sealed by a dyke. Now a conservation area, Fobbing is an attractive and quiet village, although this has not always been the case.

In 1377, with England's coffers empty and the Barons tired of paying for the Hundred Years War, John of Gaunt imposed a new tax on every adult; the Poll Tax. Initially four pence per person and intended to be a one off tax, it was so successful that it was repeated three times. The Baron's liked the tax, as they were acting as collectors so were able to cream off a proportion for themselves, but the peasants found it increasingly hard to afford and many hid to avoid payment. When the Thomas Bampton arrived in Fobbing and summoned folk from this village, Stanford and Corringham to pay their dues, those who turned up were told that they had to pay extra to cover those who hadn't. Incensed, they refused to pay and led by Thomas Baker, drove Bampton and his men from the village. Sir Robert Belknap, a Chief Justice, was sent to calm the situation, but he too was attacked. By now word had spread and peasants all over Essex and Kent were rioting, wielding scythes, axes, and knives, with manor houses burnt down and records of debts destroyed. Some unpopular landowners were killed, some captured and made to act as servants, while others fled. Watt Tyler was appointed as leader and as the people moved on London, the Poll Tax was defeated. A memorial to the Peasants Revolt was erected at Fobbing in 1981, commemorating the 600th anniversary of the uprising that showed the ordinary people of England will not tolerate unfair taxation. They say one of the benefits of studying history is that we can learn and not repeat mistakes. Almost exactly six hundred years on, Margaret Thatcher thought she knew better.

A short detour up the hill took me to St Michael's church. Underneath this is a network of tunnels, once used by smugglers to whom the lofty tower acted as beacon as they sailed up the creek. Like St Margaret's earlier, the church was locked, so I was unable to donate towards the £25,000 a notice said was urgently needed to restore the 100 year old organ. The well kept churchyard looks out across the marshes and I sat for a while enjoying the views.

Returning down the hill I took the footpath on the right signposted to Iron Latch, although no such place is shown on the OS map. The paved path started by running through a rockery, blue with the flowers of forget-me-not, and seemed more like a garden tour than a footpath. Apparently the garden was created and tended by a local lady, purely to give pleasure to those who walk through.

Turning left on Footpath 191, the remains of one of the country's smallest independent public railways could be seen. The 2¾ mile Corringham Light Railway ran to the Kynoch explosives factory at the remote Shell Haven, carrying workers on the 12 minute ride across the marshes and goods back to a junction with the main line at Thames Haven. Built in 1901, the line was busy during the First World War, and although soon afterwards the explosives works closed, the factory and railway were taken over by coal merchants, Cory Brothers of Cardiff. Their business was expanding into oil and Shell Haven seen as an ideal place for a storage depot, eventually to become the Coryton refinery. Despite passenger numbers dropping to 30 a day, the line survived through the 1930s and was very active in moving goods throughout the next war. Although a passenger service was reinstated in 1945, its days were numbered and the last train ran on 1st March 1952.

I headed due east across Fobbing Marshes, into the wind which was blowing the opposite way to usual and bringing with it a slight chemical odour from the refinery. Walking was at last easy on a grassy embankment and although after taking a left hand fork the path became quite diffuse, map reading wasn't required, with my destination the large bulk of Fobbing Horse Flood Barrier. This impressive structure protects Pitsea and Canvey, the barrier being lowered at times of risk.

A five foot concrete wall protects the marshes from Holehaven Creek (the same stretch of water that becomes Vange Creek then Pitsea Creek as it heads inland). Across the water another flood barrier crosses East Haven Creek and joins Canvey to the mainland. Behind this was the far side of the Cleanaway tip. A fence across the sea wall bars access to the mouth of the creek,

Fobbing Horse Barrier

protecting the oil installations from casual walkers, or those with more sinister intent (or at least those with sinister intent who can't climb fences). The path all the way round the refinery was closed in the 1970s after the IRA planted a bomb here, which fortunately failed to explode.

There is however a path across the marshes, coming out by a roundabout at the refinery entrance. This took me past a small lake, beside which I found the Dave Moore Bird Hide. Showing surprising, but I hope justified trust, this was unlocked and contained a pile of bird books and even binoculars, which visitors were welcome to use. An entry in the log from a visitor earlier that afternoon recorded eight species – willow warbler, shelduck, mallard, black headed gull, canada goose, black tailed godwit, curlew and teal.

A flame burned on one of Coryton's two flare stacks and as I got closer the roar grew from the mass of pipes, tanks and reactors of this huge chemistry set. Originally the Cory Bros storage deport and now owned by Petroplus, but previously by BP and before that The Vacuum Oil Company (who became Mobil), the refinery came into operation in 1953. It now has a refining capacity of 10 million tonnes per year. Currently around 36% of its output is petrol, 27% diesel and the remainder fuel oil, kerosene, lubricants, bitumen and LPG. Four million barrels of crude oil can be stored on the site (that's 140 million gallons or 636 million litres – an awful lot of oil), which is supplied by tankers holding up to 250,000 tonnes that berth at one of the refinery's five jetties. Products are moved by road, water, rail and pipeline, the site being by the start of the UKOP Thames/Mersey pipeline, which carries 7.5 million tonnes per year between refineries and to distribution depots.

Next to Coryton was the Shell Haven refinery, a 2,000 acre site with five jetties and capacity for 4.6 million tonnes per annum. Despite major investment in 1992, the refinery closed in 1999 and is now the proposed site for London Gateway, a huge container port with capacity for 3.5 million container movements a year. Up to ten ships will be able to berth along the 3,000 metres of quay, with the land around being developed as a business and logistics park. Local and national organisations, including English Nature, opposed the development, on the grounds that it will affect the 33,000 birds who winter on the mudflats, is not in accordance with national and international nature conservation policy and will adversely affect local residents with noise, traffic and pollution. The Government however gave the go ahead, but as with airport expansion, no one seems to look at the wider picture of whether it is really necessary to transport so many things around the world.

Although I was now almost at the Thames, it still wasn't going to be possible to walk by the river. The oil installations block access, so the only way forward was on The Manorway, the A1014 access road to Coryton. Fortunately on one side there is a cycle path, which a sign informed was dedicated to Chris Collins 'a much respected colleague'. After a mile two paths are marked on the map, one to Fobbing and the other to Corringham. The latter looked to be marginally longer than the road, but hopefully more pleasant, away from the noise and paved surface that was aching my feet. Alas, I should have known better. There was a sign, but it pointed straight across a field sown with corn. I walked half way round the perimeter, but couldn't see a path in the next field, so gave up and returned to the road.

A ship on the Thames a mile south reminded that I was near the coast, even if I'd seen very little water today. Two cyclists passed me, chatting as they rode home from work, something that with tankers thundering by would be pretty much impossible without the cycle path. I started counting the tankers. From 5.35 to 5.45 nine left and two returned to Coryton, a rate of 66 an hour.

Mesolithic hunter gatherers once roamed the marshes here, their flint tools found by archaeologists 10,000 years later. Over 2,000 'Potin', the earliest known British coins, were found at Corringham. Dating from the 1st century BC, these indicated trade with the Roman Empire prior to its invasion. Now in the shadow of the oil installations, Corringham isn't the most interesting of Essex towns and in many ways is just a part of the larger Stanford-le-Hope. Its two mills have long since gone and the one building of historical interest is St Mary's Church, with a tower dating from Norman times. Like many places of worship I'd seen along the walk, it has survived difficult times, falling into disrepair after the population was drastically reduced by the Black Death. However, by the 15th century things had improved, a spire being added to the tower, the roof replaced and for the first time seating provided for the congregation. Damage from a Second World War bomb was repaired and St Mary's remains the focal place of worship for the parish of Corringham.

Glad to leave the main road, I turned left into the High Road, which is actually a small lane running through the countryside.

This was a pleasant walk in early evening sunshine, passing Oak Farm, then turning right into Rainbow Lane. From here it was another mile to Stanford-le-Hope station and the 18.38 back to Upminster. I'd been walking for 8¼ hours, a long time for what is just 7¾ miles by train, but with all the ins, outs and dead ends it had been almost double the length on foot. Proper maintenance of footpaths and less private signs could open up the marshes for the many thousands living close by. They should be an asset for all. I can see why the couple I'd met at Maylandsea said that these paths were the worst on the whole of the southern English coast, but it wouldn't cost a fortune to put them right.

# CHAPTER TWENTY-SEVEN

# STANFORD LE HOPE
# to TILBURY

(13 miles)
7th May

Summer at last! Just shorts and T shirt today, and a pleasant change for the weight in my bag to be from bottles of drink, not waterproofs. For a mile I retraced the last part of the previous walk along Corringham Road, Billet Lane and past the Crooked Billet pub. Then continuing straight on where Rainbow Lane turns sharp left, a track took me over the single line railway that serves Thames Haven and to the river – the first time I'd seen the Thames since Leigh. A short section of concrete sea wall soon gave way to a grassy bank, which curved around a little sandy bay. Not quite the Cornish Riviera, but nicer than you'd expect for the Thames. I sat for a few minutes to enjoy this unexpectedly pleasant bit of coast – just me and a lone curlew poking about by the water.

With no salt marsh, the next section of wall was right by the river. A farmer was spraying his crops in the field to the right. He stopped the tractor, disappeared behind it for a moment, then returned adjusting his trousers. Ahead cranes were unloading barges full of London's rubbish for Mucking Landfill Site. A fifth of the capital's rubbish comes here, the river saving 440 lorry journeys each day. A dozen small yachts were moored outside what I assumed to be Mucking Creek, although my map failed to name it. This few miles of coast falls between two of the large scale Explorer Maps, so I had to make do with the Landranger 1:50,000 (1 ¼ inch to mile) version, an issue that was 20 years old.

It was a shame to be going inland so soon after finding the coast, but I had another creek to negotiate. The path is shown heading away from the creek, but another one, not marked on the map, stayed by the water. Again this was surprisingly attractive. A little area of marsh with a pair of shelduck swimming on one of the little pools seemed far too nice for Mucking. The path ended abruptly at Mucking Sluice, so I stopped for an early lunch, not expecting to find another good eating spot for a while.

There was no obvious way onwards, so after returning to the main path I went left along a high embankment looking across some small lakes, where a couple sat bird watching. Seeing a path on the left I followed this until it completed the circumference of the field, taking me back to the embankment. Not used to the smaller scale, I'd misread the map and turned left too soon.

Back on the correct route I joined a road, a continuation of the footpath I'd twice left in error. This took me past The Warren Fishery, which is run by Shell Club Angling Section, and comprises four lakes, Main, Square, Match and Tench. These are stocked with specimen sized fish of most species, with carp at over 30 pounds and catfish over 50 pounds. The water's record pike is 39lb, but one at 50lb was found dead in 1995 and would have been the British record had anyone been able to catch it. A 4lb 13oz crucian carp was caught in the Main Lake, which also would have been a record had it been registered, but to do so required killing it, something that fortunately for the fish, the angler decided against.

A sign by Tench Lake warned 'Deep Water – No Swimming'

accompanied by a drawing of an unfortunate, but just too law abiding person, waving their arms around above the water and about to drown. Sometimes you simply have to break the rules.

Footpath 38 heads off to the left just before a railway bridge and runs on a low embankment through Stanford Warren Nature Reserve, an Essex Wildlife Trust property. This 41 acre reserve, which has been created on old gravel workings and a former sewage works, now encompasses what are said to be the largest area of reed beds in the county, although Old Hall Marshes also makes this claim. These provide excellent cover for reed buntings, reed and sedge warblers, all of which breed here. Cuckoos often use the warblers as hosts for their eggs, which as the chicks grow, and with the former bird almost three times the size of the 'adoptive' parent, must come as a bit of a shock to the Mummy warbler. To encourage strong stem growth and slow the drying process, in winter the Trust carry out some cutting and removal of decaying reeds, all part of the largely unseen management that helps maintain such biodiversity across the county. Part of the reserve is rough grassland and here adders, which are surprisingly common along the Essex coast, can often be seen.

The path ends at the hamlet of Mucking, now with a population of less than a hundred, but in Victorian times a thriving village with shops, a large rectory and the mediaeval church of St John the Baptist. In earlier times there was an extensive Saxon settlement here, with more than 230 buildings, mostly sunken huts, but also timber halls which may have been occupied by higher status families. The fourth century village was discovered by crop marks in the soil in 1959 and a major archaeological dig undertaken prior to the site being excavated for gravel. The rectory and church are now private residencies, a sign on the closed gates advising that written permission is required to visit the graveyard.

With no access possible in front of the landfill site, it was to be road walking for a while, with another diversion away from the coast. Just past the railway crossing however a fallen down footpath sign confirmed that the short cut shown on my map still appeared to exist, and although there was no sign of a path along the edge of the meadow, it was easy walking to a stile at the other end. Then it really was roads for a couple of miles. Fortunately these weren't too busy, although every few minutes peace was shattered by a rubbish truck leaving a cloud of dust in its wake.

I was surprised to see a museum sign and even more so that is was apparently open. Walton Hall Museum has blacksmiths, saddle makers, printers and wheelwright workshops, a collection of memorabilia and bygone farm implements, housed in the restored 17th century farm, plus a working bakery where visitors can make their own bread. It also houses the National Motor Roller Collection, ('steam' rollers, not as my wife thought, mobile phones!) claiming to have the largest private collection in England and possibly the world. My initial thought that such a claim may require the ownership of two or maybe three vehicles was dispelled by a whole line of assorted road rollers standing proudly behind the children's playground. I was prepared to pay my £4 for a quick look round, although have to confess to a greater interest in the tea room than the rollers, but two signs inside contradicted the one at the entrance, so by a majority of two to one the museum was closed.

Turning left into East Tilbury Road, I passed through the village of Linford. Here the small church is still open. It is shared between Methodists and Catholics, and appears to be thriving, the 1900 building having been refurbished in 1998. After pausing for an ice cream at Linford Stores, most welcome on this hot afternoon, I was soon able to leave the road, taking a path on the left immediately after East Tilbury station. This ran alongside Gobions Park, a nice new park with skateboard ramps, cycle track and a basketball court, plus play area with safe rides on a cushioned surface. In our day parks consisted of a slide, selection of swings, roundabout and highly dangerous climbing frame, all standing on hard tarmac, covered with little bits of gravel waiting to graze the legs of any falling child.

The path continued alongside a field of bright yellow rape. At the boundary fence of Mucking Tip an old sign with a large hole in it informed that footpath 147 was diverted, the 450 acre landfill site out of bounds to walkers. However a 3 year extension to the site's license will end in 2010 (it will then be full) and the whole area will be restored as a country park. Heading down towards the river I passed another walker – a real one, going at a good pace with a big rucksack. We exchanged greetings, but I wished I'd stopped him for a chat.

I paused for a few minutes on reaching the river. Although the sky was cloudless, with a haze over the Thames the few trees rising from the low lying Cliffe Marshes opposite gave it an eerie, desert island appearance. From here it was to be sea wall all the way to Tilbury, sometimes right by the water and sometimes behind salt marsh. I watched a kestrel hover over a patch of marsh, moving its position every minute or so, but failing to spot any lunch.

The concrete sea wall loops inland just before Coalhouse Fort, but I followed the low grassy bank next to the river, glad of the cooling breeze coming off the water. Completed in 1874, Coalhouse Fort was one of many defences built following the recommendations of a Royal Commission in 1860, in response to the perceived threat of invasion from France and concern that the new iron clad warships could sail into the capital unhindered. Construction work was overseen by Colonel Charles Gordon, later to become General Gordon of Khartoum, who apparently used to patrol up and down the river in a boat shouting instructions to the builders through a megaphone. It wasn't however until World War Two that the fort was to see action in defending the realm, with two anti-aircraft guns mounted on its roof. Coalhouse was also used in the highly secret work of monitoring ships leaving the Thames for the effectiveness of their 'degaussing' equipment; electrical cables fitted around the hull to neutralise magnetic fields and protect against magnetic mines. Cables were laid on the river bed to measure the magnetic field and WRENs working in the fort used flags or lamps to communicate with ships if adjustments were required.

Coalhouse is one of the few 'Palmerston Forts' to have retained its original architecture and is considered to be one of the best examples of a casement fort in the UK. However for many years it was virtually abandoned, a target for the more adventurous vandal who preferred the challenge of scaling its walls to the more routine smashing of bus shelters in Grays. Although Thurrock Council had purchased the fort in 1962, their plans to develop it as a riverside amenity stalled, but change of fortune came in 1983 when the Coalhouse Fort Project took over the lease. Their long term aim is 'to preserve, restore and maintain the fort for the benefit of the public'. Progress is slow but steady, although failure to make the finals of the BBC Restoration programme and gain funding was a set back. Coalhouse is however open to the public on a number of days each year, with volunteers leading guided tours. It is also used as a location for film and TV productions, with an episode of Prime Suspect, the external shots of the prison in Batman Begins and a Gary Newman pop video all filmed here.

On the foreshore just beyond the fort is a strange looking hexagonal tower. Disguised as a water tower and marked as such on some maps, this is actually the remains of an early radar tower, built to watch out for enemy aircraft. For the next three miles there is a named footpath along the river bank; The Two Forts Way, linking Coalhouse and Tilbury forts. The first section, running for about a mile as far as the small creek on East Tilbury Marshes, was opened in 2003. A wide tarmac path, this is accessible to disabled and cyclists, but the narrow earth path on the next section to Tilbury Power Station made much nicer walking. With nettles almost as tall as me close by on either side and a mass of wild

Radar Tower - Coalhouse Fort

flowers, the approach to the power station was surprisingly attractive. However if the next stage of the Way is also to be almost a road, walking will be less enjoyable. As has been found in some National Parks, a fine balance has to be sought between making countryside accessible to all, but without spoiling from the experience for the majority.

Just before the power station I found a most unusual beach. Formed from what appeared to be clinker from the power plant, it was covered with broken glass and ceramics, their edges all ground smooth. My wife makes mosaics from 'sea glass' and pottery, so we often pick it up from the shore on our travels, but I'd never seen anything like this amount in one place. The beach was more white and coloured from the ceramics, than grey from the clinker. The glass wasn't the tiny pieces you usually find on a beach, but large sections of bottles and a few whole ones – an old blue Milk of Magnesia bottle and a brown marmite jar. What was striking about the pottery was that it was obviously quite old, mostly with floral patterns in light blues, greens and pink, plus a few brown pieces. They were the type of plates and cups that our grandparents might have had. I collected some pieces and we looked more closely when I got home. Some had names printed on them – Amersham Hotel, Theodore Hotel France and part of a rhyme about 'Wee Jolly Elf'. But how had they got here?

At first we thought they must have been washed up from the river. Had a ship sunk or lost its cargo? Possible but it didn't seem very likely. Was it to do with the power station? Did they throw old crockery into the furnaces as part of the process? Again unlikely. After much research we discovered the true source. The land by the river here used to be a land fill site. It closed many years ago, but erosion of the bank has unearthed some of its contents. Most had long decayed but the glass and china remained. A few weeks later I took my wife to look and she brought some china back to research. There were pieces from well known makes – Wedgwood, Spode, Minton and Stourport. Most seemed to be from the 1930s, but some was probably well over a hundred years old and possibly late 18th century. All discarded many years ago and now lying by the river, an interesting piece of history and another secret of the Essex coast.

Surprisingly one can walk in front of Tilbury Power Station, steps going over the sea wall to a concrete path right next to the river below. It seemed strange to be just a couple of feet from the water, rather than looking down from above. Originally oil fired, but later converted to coal, the station produces 1,400 megawatts of electricity, powering up to 1.4 million homes. As part of the Government's renewable energy obligation, sulphur free coal is now co-fired with biomass fuels from renewable sources, such as sawdust, wood and palm kernel. Whilst this reduces fossil fuel consumption, the plant still uses almost 2 million tonnes of coal a year, although delivery by sea uses the least environmentally damaging form of transport. The current plant which was built in 1956 is due to be replaced by a £1 billion state of the art 'cleaner' 1,600 megawatt station, by 2014. Whilst NPower describe the new plant as 'cleaner' and 'more environmentally friendly', $CO_2$ emissions will only be 22% lower per unit, although it will designed to use carbon capture and storage technology when this becomes commercially available. Many environmentalists oppose the building of new coal fired power stations, pointing out that they appear to be justified on the basis that future advances in technology will make them cleaner, and that we would be better to invest in renewable energy sources. I don't pretend to be an expert but tend to agree.

A bridge runs across the sea wall to the terminal where the Celorina of Basle was unloading its cargo of coal. With the tide high the path here was under water, so I had to follow the least attractive bit of coast walk so far. First I climbed the steps over the sea wall and negotiated an overgrown path through stinging nettles, then ascended steep metal steps up to a covered walkway. This cage takes the walker under the pipes and over the road which link the plant and terminal. Scenic it is not! More like part of a prison than the coast path. However on descending the other side I found a sudden and unexpected improvement. A Wildflower Community Meadow, planted by NPower in the grounds of the power station.

Hopping over the sea wall I resumed once more on the concrete path by the river, where little areas of marsh provided patches of colour amongst the grey industry. Further out a cormorant sat on a buoy waiting for his tea to swim by. People may say that this part of the Thames is desolate, but like most places, if they care to look there is still natural beauty to be seen.

The path crosses to the landward side of the sea wall, allowing the walker to enjoy the approach to Tilbury Fort and the surrounding meadows. This is where many people mistakenly believe Queen Elizabeth addressed her army before the expected invasion of the Spanish Armada. In fact the low lying land was far too marshy for an army to camp and in 1588 the place we now know as Tilbury didn't exist. It was a couple of miles away at West Tilbury that she delivered the famous words 'I know I have but the body of a weak and feeble woman; but I have the heart of a king, and of a king of England'.

Much older than Coalhouse, construction of Tilbury Fort was started by Charles II in 1672, following a disastrous attack by the Dutch on the English fleet in the Medway. It took 13 years to build, much of the labour being 'pressed' from nearby towns. An earlier D-shaped blockhouse built in the time of Henry VIII was retained inside the fort's walls. Now under the care of English Heritage, it is one of the best preserved bastioned fortifications in Britain and other than some 19th century modifications, which included demolition of the blockhouse, is in largely the same condition now as it was in the late 17th century.

With the river on one side and protected by two moats, a ravelin (triangular fortification outside the bastions) and a redan (V shaped fortification angled to expected point of attack), the fort held powerful artillery, commanding both the river and surrounding land. Perhaps due to its power the fort was never threatened and its only military success was in the First World War, when anti-aircraft guns on the parade ground shot down a Zeppelin airship. There had however been bloodshed back in 1776, when a cricket match between men from the Kent and Essex sides of the Thames ended in rioting. Guns were seized from the guardroom, one man bayoneted and a sergeant shot trying to regain order. At the outbreak of World War Two the fort's chapel was converted to a Gun Operation Room. It controlled the anti-aircraft defences for the Thames and North Medway, until command moved to Vange in 1940.

Most visitors would arrive by river, so the Water Gate was given an impressive decorative façade, making a striking entrance to the fort, while the Landport Gate was relatively plain. Those arriving to look round what is a most extensive and interesting building, still pass through its triumphant arch and into the large parade ground. Guns from various eras remain positioned around the fort, providing enjoyment to many a child. Both times I've taken my youngest son he's come away having 'blown up' every ship for miles around. Equally exciting to the young and perhaps also the not so young, are the dark passages leading to the 19th century magazines. One of two much older magazines, which once held vast quantities of gunpowder, now houses an exhibition tracing the fort's role in the defence of London. One of the highlights of the Essex coast, Tilbury Fort is well worth a visit.

Just past the fort is The World's End, a famous Essex pub. Of typical white weatherboard construction, it was rebuilt in 1788 and was known for many years as the Ferry House. From the here there is another short section of path on the river side of the wall, where a family with two young children played on the beach. Their two pit bull type dogs came out of the river to greet me, shaking themselves dry and looking generally evil. Of course they're the most gentle animals and would never hurt anyone, as the distraught parents always tell the world when one day their dog savages a child. Why anyone should want to keep such creatures is beyond me (unless of course it's the small willy compensation syndrome again).

Climbing over the wall for the final time, I was now at the Port of Tilbury. Of particular interest to me was the Gravesend ferry, our

Tilbury Fort

route to Kent for many a childhood outing, which involved several trains, the boat and sometimes ending with a bus ride where I'd invariably be sick! There has long been a ferry at this point, possibly as far back as Roman times and certainly in the 13th century when pilgrims used it on their way to Canterbury. It remains the lowest public crossing point of the Thames. There is a story that Charles I once used the ferry accompanied by the Marquis of Buckingham and an aide, all three in disguise. They paid the ferryman with a gold coin, which he thought suspicious, so called the military. It was only when Buckingham removed his false beard that they realised they had arrested the Lord Admiral.

Steam paddle steamers took over from sail in 1855. From 1862 when purchased by the London Tilbury and Southend Railway, until 1984 when the British Rail's Sealink was sold to Sea Containers, the ferry was run by railway companies. Currently the service is operated by The Lower Thames and Medway Passenger Boat Company, with subsidies provided by Thurrock and Kent Councils. Just one vessel is now used, running every 30 minutes, and patronage is a fraction of its earlier years, but the ferry still provides a vital link between the two counties. There have however been threats to close it, and in 2001 operations briefly ceased due to problems with operators and doubt over Thurrock Council's commitment to funding, but at present it seems secure.

From 1927 a car ferry also ran, until the opening of the Dartford Tunnel in 1963 made it largely superfluous. It closed a year later. It's hard to believe that until then all the cars and lorries heading to Kent and beyond had to travel either through London, or on secondary roads and via the ferry. In these days before the M25 far fewer goods were driven all over the country; from port to distribution centre, to supermarket, to home, picking up 'food miles', one of the things that is going to have to stop if we are to combat Global Warming. Proposals were put forward for a tunnel linking with the Chatham and Dover Railway in 1881, but lack of funds meant it was never built. What a benefit this would have made though, linking the railways of Kent and Essex and allowing trains from the rest of England to the south coast ports to bypass London. Of course there is now a tunnel, but this is not linked to the rest of the railway system, carrying just Eurostars and eventually high speed trains from Kent to London.

The floating landing stage from which the ferry departs is now partly a car park and the old walkway to Tilbury Riverside Station, fenced off and derelict. This afternoon the 22,000 tonne Marco Polo was berthed at the adjacent cruise terminal, passengers sitting on the sun decks as it prepared to sail for a seven day cruise around UK. Paying up to £2099, they were to be calling at Guernsey, the Scilly Isles, Dublin & various Scottish islands.

Originally named Tilbury Fort, Tilbury Riverside Station was opened in 1854, enabling the London Tilbury and Southend Railway to offer cheap fares via the ferry to Gravesend, then a 'seaside' resort, in competition with the South Eastern Railway's direct trains from London. Boat trains with restaurant cars used to run from St Pancras to connect with liners, but as planes replaced ships for international travel and the Dartford Tunnel reduced ferry usage, the station's days were numbered. Being on a spur off the main line, trains had to reverse before continuing their journeys on to Southend, an operational difficulty that contributed to the station's demise. What was once a hub of activity became a largely deserted outpost. That I was one of only 55 people to submit written objections to the proposed closure illustrated the low level of usage and the last train finally ran on 29th November 1992. A replacement bus now runs (my wife has driven it occasionally), but as is always the case when a railway closes, even fewer people use it.

The platforms and tracks were taken away and a metal wall erected along the open side of the station hall. The impressive station building, with a distinctive turret clock tower and weather vane on its roof, is Grade II listed, so fortunately could not be demolished. For a while part of it was used as a social club known as the 'Bomb Crater', but eventually the station was boarded up and left to decay. I wandered in, keen to see what had become of this historic building, which in my youth we used to pass through two or three times a year. The old restaurant has now been refurbished as Tilbury Riverside Activity & Arts Centre and the cavernous main hall is a car park. With its high roof, history and atmosphere, this cathedral like interior through which so many travelled on their journeys around the world deserves more. It could be a museum, a concert hall, an exhibition centre, but a car park – No!

The square brick built ticket office, where returning boat passengers booked their tickets to London and beyond, still stands alone in the centre of the hall. Inside it has been gutted, but could easily be restored. The waiting rooms where those arriving from warmer climes sat awaiting their trains, are still open, empty and with radiators hanging off the wall, but again restorable. The gentlemen's toilet where my young brother once asked why there was a chocolate machine is still there, the sign in place but a fence preventing entry. I assume the 'chocolate machine' has long gone. The platform signs are still in place and a Network South East Poster from 1990 hangs on the station wall. What a pity that a more fitting use cannot be found for a building with such history, but also such potential.

Tilbury has a reputation as the sort of place one would only move to if they can't afford a house anywhere else. A reputation typified by the infamous skinhead gang from the late 1970s, the Tilbury Trojan Skins, who were immortalised as extras in the Pink Floyd film 'The Wall'. They still organise reunions in the working men's club and apparently remain fiercely patriotic, although no longer violent. The town's reputation cannot be helped by it having elected a BNP councillor, or by the sort of dogs I saw on the beach, but maybe things are changing? Perhaps the Arts Centre, the Two Forts Way, the Community Meadow and the restoration of Coalhouse Fort are a sign of a new interest in culture, wildlife and history of the town, which will put to bed its reputation as being the khazi of Essex.

The final 20 minutes were the least enjoyable of the day, heading inland along the busy A1089, with huge lorries trundling to and from the Zeebrugge Ferry terminal. Tilbury Town station, a mile from the Thames, was originally named Tilbury Dock and is opposite the main dock entrance. A purely functional building, with none of the romance or architecture of Riverside, this was the end of today's walk. A walk which had given far more interest, history and nature than one would have expected for a stretch of river that gets such bad press.

# CHAPTER TWENTY-EIGHT

# TILBURY to PURFLEET

(13 miles)
6th June

The general public aren't really supposed to walk round Tilbury Docks. However if a man in walking boots and carrying a rucksack wanders in nonchalantly while the security people are talking to someone else, he may find himself inside the docks. If the walker hopes to find his way to the sea wall he may however be less successful.

The docks are huge. After half an hour's walking I'd seen no water and just the top of a couple of ships. The map showed a path running on the sea wall towards Grays, but getting to it wasn't proving easy. I turned into one road but a security man popped out of a hut, asking if I was crew. He didn't seem to comprehend my request for directions and suggested I should ask at reception. Then two men pulled over in a van. They understood the map, but said there was no way out of the docks, other than to walk over the lock gate at the far end. The driver said it's six miles round the docks. He knew because he did it for a fun run, but it wasn't much fun, (from the size of him I could see why!). They advised that I'd have to walk back to the main entrance and follow the road to Grays. I wandered around a bit more, asking two other workers, but whilst neither really seemed to understand what I was trying to do, the message was still the same – there's no way through, go back to the entrance.

Turning back reluctantly, I took out my camera and notebook, no longer worried about attracting attention, however no one seemed bothered. Security here isn't exactly strict. My walk back was more leisurely, taking time to comprehend the scale of the place. Construction started in 1882, with the docks eventually covering 450 acres of marshland. The largest lock on the Thames provided access to 56 acres of enclosed water in huge docks 10 metres deep. Laid end to end the network of railway sidings would have run from London to Colchester. The riverside is dominated by the enormous grain terminal with capacity of 100,000 tonnes and the ability to discharge 2,000 tonnes per hour. In 2002 the facility handled over 500,000 tonnes of exports (wheat, barley, oats, peas, beans and rapeseed) and 300,000 tonnes of imports (wheat, maize and soya beans). Maybe if wheat wasn't sent both ways it could have been a bit smaller. Opposite the terminal and amongst all the containers and constant noise of lorries, was a mass of red poppies. A splash of natural red in a very man made environment.

Nearer the entrance is the large Finnforest depot, handling timber, one of the main cargoes passing through the docks. Opposite at the Freightliner depot I watched a huge gantry crane load three containers onto a train. Originating from Italy, Germany and Mexico, one could only guess at what might be inside them. Two electric locomotives stood humming quietly by the buffers, waiting for their turn to take the goods on the next stage of their journey.

A security man stopped me as I walked out the gate, asking where I had come from. Upminster didn't seem to be an acceptable answer. He obviously didn't understand my explanation about the coast path, but let me go on my way, his job having been seen to be done. So 3 miles and 1½ hours later I was back where I'd started. Whilst I'd failed to get through to the river, it had been an interesting walk around one of the UK's three major ports.

The A1089 really isn't a very nice road. Too many lorries. A sign showing Asda just off the roundabout drew me away from it. The pull of the supermarket café had got me again. Justified by the next two miles being along roads with nowhere to stop and eat my ham roll, I had an early but rather mediocre lunch of roast chicken. On resuming I found that I could have sat on a seat where the pavement comes away from the main road, cutting the corner as it heads towards Grays. Well I could have eaten my lunch there, but I'd have been sharing the seat with a couple who were reading the underwear pages of a clothes catalogue.

Continuing along the A126 through Little Thurrock, I paused to photograph the parish church of St Mary the Virgin. The attractive building dates from the 12$^{th}$ century, although was extensively 'restored' in Victorian times. I noted two pubs, The Ship and The Traitors Gate, both which would probably have provided a better lunch than Asda. Turning right after the Catholic church of St Thomas of Canterbury, I was at last heading south, towards the river. Just before the railway bridge is The Recreation Ground, home to Grays Athletic FC. My eldest son saw his first West Ham match here. A friendly on a baking hot day, which the Hammers won 3.0. Sadly Grays are planning to move to a new stadium and yet another traditional old ground close to the centre of the town will be lost.

Where Bridge Street turns sharp right I continued straight on along Manor Way and into Grays Beach Riverside Park. The centrepiece of its various attractions is a huge sandpit, once a swimming pool, which holds Britain's biggest play galleon. In front of this is Grays Beach. Shingle not sand, and most definitely river not sea, but given the location, not an unattractive stretch of foreshore.

Climbing the steps over the sea wall I walked along the beach.

Before heading upstream I went left to investigate the path by Tilbury Docks. Was there a way through? The path runs on the river side of the sea wall, but stopped abruptly at a high wall topped with barbed wire. So this was the answer. The huge grain terminal was just over the sea wall and I'd been no more than 200 yards away this morning, but had now confirmed that however lax the security staff may be, there's no way through the docks to the coast path.

For a few minutes I watched the activity on the jetty as a ship unloaded its cargo, then wandered back along the pebble beach. Here there were the usual bits of glass, tin cans and assorted rubbish, but more unusually, quite a few coconuts. From the grain jetty to Purfleet the path stays by the river, an interesting and surprisingly varied walk. Just after Grays Beach is Thurrock Yacht Club, a far less exclusive affair than some of those I'd seen on previous walks. Founded in 1946 as a 'club for working men', this claims to be one of the most inexpensive yacht clubs in Britain, although it has to be said that its location is hardly the most salubrious.

The path goes around Grays Town Wharf, which has recently been refurbished. Flats have been built on both sides as part of redevelopment of the whole river frontage. The wharf dates back to medieval times, the earliest known reference being a complaint of unreasonable tolls in 1228, by the Prior of the Hospital of Jerusalem in Clerkenwell, against Richard de Gray, Lord of the Manor of Thurrock. Exclusive rights to provide boats for the passage of goods and people, and to charge wharfage fees, made up a fair proportion of the Lord of the Manor's income. The first ferry to London was recorded in 1302 and by 1637 Grays could be reached from capital on every tide, although in order to access the wharf it was probably necessary to change to a smaller boat in midstream. However in 1841 a 400 foot long wooden pier was built to extend the adjacent Pier Wharf and the new steamers could now call. By 1850 25,000 people a year were being carried between Grays and London, although trade soon collapsed when the railway opened in 1854.

For about a mile the river frontage is of new houses and apartments, which have replaced the old warehouses and factories. The waterfront, which is now opened to those wishing to walk, fish, or just sit and watch the river, was once a hive of activity. Thriving establishments brought work and prosperity to the town. Barges were made or broken, factories manufactured products such as lard and oil drums, and coal, timber and oil were brought ashore. Some towns have chosen to renovate their waterfronts, but Grays seems to have largely started again.

One of the few old buildings that remains is The Wharf pub. Once the haunt of seafarers and wharfmen, its main clientele is now apparently the Essex chav. A handful of drinkers were sitting at tables outside, although the advertised riverside views have been rather spoiled by the heightened sea wall. On the next quarter mile of riverbank I counted nine shopping trolleys lying partly submerged in the mud. The water may be cleaner, the waterfront gentrified, but some Essex habits die hard. In contrast a pair of shelduck by the river's edge stood out clean and bright against the dull mud, something that wouldn't have been seen in the old days of the polluted Thames.

Homes now gave way to heavy industry and the Nustar oil terminal. With two jetties, 53 tanks and storage capacity of 311,000 cubic metres, this handles a range of petroleum products. A rare footpath sign directed me up steps and over the sea wall, where for a short distance the first grassy section of the day made a pleasant change from concrete underfoot. However the industry continued. Gibbs Wharf is operated by Foster Yeoman who bring limestone for processing from their quarries in Scotland and Somerset. The path runs inland for a short distance, just a low fence separating it from the car park of the next installation, a petrochemical plant. Workers smoking in several bus stop type

Some Essex Habits Die Hard!

shelters stared at me as if the sight of a walker was a rare occurrence. I was surprised that smoking was allowed anywhere with so many tanks of flammable material stored here.

Most of the sites are still very much working, but one stood derelict. It appeared to be some sort of grain hopper, with several silos fed by a long conduit running up from the river. Every window on the site was broken and it looked just the sort of place where a body would be found in The Bill or Taggart. Once busy, this was now industrial archaeology. Atmospheric and not beautiful, but nevertheless interesting, although I doubt anyone will think of preserving it.

Back to the river, alongside all this heavy industry a cormorant dived repeatedly into the still water. Footpath 170 became 141 and took me over the sea wall once more. For about a third of a mile the river side of the wall was totally covered with graffiti. This wasn't just tags or slogans, but real art of a high standard. It had clearly been organised with each artist allocated a length of about ten yards. I'd missed a similar section of 'legal graffiti' on the sea wall near Grays Beach. This had been painted in 2007 and included a memorial to two young men who'd been killed earlier that year trying to spray tube trains at Barking. I'm pretty conservative when it comes to both art and graffiti, but enjoyed this colourful free gallery by the river.

For a mile the industry stopped and it was back to nature. Over the wall used to be West Thurrock Power Station, which was built on the marshes, but closed in 1993. Its stockpile of nearly half a million tonnes of coal was taken to Tilbury's power plant by Rhine barge. Left to nature once more, it is now an SSSI, with over 1,200 species living here. However, as a brown field site protection from development is difficult and despite much protest, permission was given to build a huge lorry park and warehouse on part of the area.

One bit of marsh that is safe from the developers is the salt marsh at Stone Ness. Outside the sea wall only wildlife want to use it. At the tip is Stone Ness lighthouse, a red metal tower, 44 feet high, with a wind generator on the top. Established in 1885, the light is visible for 9 miles, warning shipping of this rare bit of land protruding into the river.

I sat by the river for a while to eat my second lunch of the day. The wind was picking up, bringing little waves that splashed on the stony beach. Some of the marsh plants were flowering and others equally beautiful, so many shades of green. If I kept my eyes downwards this could have been back on one of the rural estuaries, but lifting my gaze showed that I was actually in the shadow of the Queen Elizabeth II Bridge. Lorries trundled over on their way to Kent, a large tanker, the Fure Nord, was unloading

Old Grain Terminal Near Grays

oil at the wharf opposite and the next oil terminal was yards away. Essex is full of nature, but in some places you have to look harder for it – to concentrate on what is close, look for the detail and not allow the eye to be blinded by the huge man-made structures that dominate.

For a while there was a choice to walk either side of the sea wall.

Naturally I chose the river side, but at the Vopak oil terminal had to climb a steep metal ladder to get back to the landward side. Anyone unhappy with heights would be well advised to stay to the right of the wall. There didn't used to be a path under the QE2 Bridge and few know it's there now. We once had an employee living in Grays who for some reason decided to walk to our Purfleet factory. He set out early, but arrived late, not due to the length of the walk, but because he'd been arrested for trespassing under the bridge.

The bridge is impressive when you drive over or view it from a distance, but from underneath I could see the true scale if it. The central span is 450 metres long and suspended 65 metres above the Thames, allowing at least 57½ metres clearance for ships below. Its 112 cables contain 1,500 tonnes of galvanised steel and the whole structure used 145,000 cubic metres of concrete. The towers are 190 metres high and its length including the approach viaducts is 2872 metres (1.7 miles). When opened in 1991 it was Europe's largest cable-supported bridge, but the 856 metre Pont de Normandie in France has considerably exceeded it and by just 6 metres, the second Severn Crossing is now the UK's longest.

Close to the bridge are the circular ventilation shafts of the Dartford Tunnels. Situated directly above the tunnels, these contain huge fans which extract polluted air through their large chimneys. The first tunnel opened in 1963 and was expected to carry 2 million cars a year. However usage in the first year was double this and it was soon realised that a second tunnel was needed. This opened in 1980 and the two bores now carry 27 million northbound vehicles each year. There had been many previous plans to build a tunnel under the Thames, the first as long ago as 1798, which was to link Tilbury with Gravesend. This got no further than digging a vertical shaft, with neither the engineering or funding being adequate to complete the job. In 1938 they got as far as building a pilot tunnel of 12 foot diameter. It was planned that the full-scale tunnel would be

Queen Elizabeth II Bridge

ready for use by 1942, but work was abandoned due to the outbreak of war.

The section from the bridge to Purfleet must be a contender as the least scenic stretch of coast path in the whole country. Whilst it doesn't have the caged walkway of Tilbury Power Station, this is longer and the high sea wall prevents any view of the river. All there is to see is the industry on the right. Lafarge Cement with a network of conveyers carrying sand from the wharf and depositing it in huge graded heaps. Pura Foods, producing over 300,000 tonnes of edible oil each year and including the world's largest margarine factory. Purfleet Thames Terminal, which handles 250,000 trailers, containers and tanks per year, including the import or export of 400,000 cars. I climbed a ladder to look over the sea wall and watched containers being loaded onto the Clemantine, one of the huge RO-RO ships that operate four daily services to Zeebrugge and two to Rotterdam.

This last walk was very different to the previous 27. There is probably more industry in these five miles of river front than the rest of the Essex coast put together. It wasn't what you'd call pretty and I wouldn't have wanted it to go on for many more miles, but it was interesting. Not however the sort of place you'd want to go for a Sunday afternoon stroll. It was just as deserted as virtually all the rest of the county's coast. Not because it's inaccessible, but presumably because people either don't want to walk here or don't realise you can. I didn't expect to be able to walk by the river in front of all these huge industrial sites, but Thurrock Council (I presume it is them to thank) have done an excellent job in putting the route together. Much of the path has probably been there since the sea wall was built, but now all the links are there – steps over the wall and tunnels under jetties. Like so much of the Essex coast it's just a shame so few people bother to come out and see it.

Finally the huge Esso fuel depot, which distributes around 15% of the company's fuel in the UK, filling 250 tankers a day. Truckers protesting at rising fuel prices targeted the depot in 2001, blockading the entrance and delaying tankers, although it was the resultant panic buying that caused garages to run dry. An attempt to organise a similar protest in 2007 resulted in just one demonstrator turning up at Purfleet. June Walker, a 61 year old pensioner from Rainham, said she had no connection with the

England's Least Scenic Coast Path? - Purfleet

haulage industry, but objected to paying '£57' to fill up her Peugeot 307. Greenpeace also protested at the depot in 2001, calling the company 'the world's number one global warming villain', and blaming it for George Bush's refusal to sign the Kyoto climate treaty. At dawn on 25th July 57 volunteers broke into the site, 5 of them dressed as tigers. A 100 foot banner reading 'Stop Esso – Stop Bush' was unfurled and the entrance blocked with two customised containers bolted to the road. Protestors climbed pylons, occupied roofs, lighting towers and refuelling points, bringing the depot to a standstill. It wasn't until 8pm that the last protestor was removed – a hot and exhausted 'tiger' who'd spent 15 hours sixty feet up a lighting mast. Police described the demonstration as 'peaceful', but 41 activists were arrested.

No one wants to pay more for fuel, but it is a finite resource and prices will inevitably rise as stocks reduce and the remaining reserves become more difficult to extract. The only way to put off the day when we have no petrol, no diesel and no plastics, is to reduce the rate at which we use oil. Bowing to pressure the Government may succeed in getting more oil released to bring down the price, but what will the lorry drivers do when there is no more diesel? Time can only tell that it was Greenpeace who were right.

The industry ended with a derelict area, now earmarked for new housing as part of the Thames Gateway project. Development is taking place along both banks of the river from Tower Bridge to Thurrock and Bexhill, building houses and infrastructure. In Purfleet they plan to put up 3,400 new homes, create 2,700 jobs, quadruple the population and give the town a proper centre. At the moment it is spread out, with few facilities. All very laudable you may say, but not only do they want to build on derelict areas, but also existing industrial units – including our glue factory. Manufacturing industry is no longer wanted. Not only do we have to contend with a declining market, with competition from the Far East and lack of Government support, but now they want to kick industry out of its traditional roots. To quote Dave Amis from East Thurrock Independent Working Class Association, 'Sure there will be plenty of jobs created but most will be low skilled, badly paid and demanding a 'flexible' attitude towards work – that means long and anti-social hours.' Local people are asking when homes will be built for Thurrock families who've been on Council waiting lists for years. Unfortunately as has already been seen at Grays, no one wants to build cheap houses. Much of the reason for the national housing shortage is the increasing number of people living alone. The sensible solution would be to build smaller and lower cost housing, requiring less land per person. However there's more money in posh houses and apartments, so that is what's built.

At the Vopak Cornwall Site, where various gases are stored, the path went inland, coming out onto the road through a gap in the fence. A small sign advised that this was temporary and gave no indication that one can walk all the way to Tilbury Docks. Turning left I passed Botany Terrace, six old brick terraced houses and one of the remnants of the old Purfleet village, then followed a sign for Thames Path, around the front of the Royal Hotel and back to the river. Originally Wingrove's Hotel, the name was apparently changed after the Prince of Wales, later to become Edward III, visited to sample its famous whitebait dinners.

Purfleet was once an important military location housing the Royal Gunpowder Magazines, which moved here from Greenwich in 1760, as it was considered too risky to keep so much gunpowder close to London. Five magazines were constructed, each of which could hold 10,400 barrels, with a garrison of soldiers guarding the site. They remained in use until 1960, when the land was sold to Thurrock Council for housing. Four were demolished, but one remains. It is the last of its type

Royal Gunpowder Magazine - Purfleet

in the world and a Grade I Scheduled Ancient Monument. The magazine now houses a heritage centre, containing a large collection of military artefacts, plus various exhibits relating to the area's history. This includes a small exhibition about Purfleet's most famous resident – Dracula. In Bram Stoker's 1897 novel the Count buys a house named 'Carfax', which the book says was in Purfleet and it was from here that Dracula wished to carry out his vampire activities. In Victorian times the area was a popular tourist attraction and it is thought that Stoker was probably introduced to the town as one of the many Londoners who came here by train to enjoy the waterfront, country walks and tea rooms.

Another short detour inland took me over the Mar Dyke, a small tributary of the Thames. This and the River Darent opposite in Kent, were once a single river, but were cut in half when the glaciers forced the Thames southwards during an Ice Age 450,000 years ago. The footbridge across the river has a length of railway track running across it, remains of the narrow gauge line that used to transport munitions to and from magazines of either side of the Mar Dyke.

And so to the final section of Essex coast – Rainham Marshes, another part of the county that is being transformed. This has long been a haven for birds, but the public was denied access for over 100 years. Apart from the military virtually the only people venturing onto the marshes were those torching cars or dumping rubbish. Then in 2000 the RSPB bought the marshes from the M.O.D. and set about the long task of restoring them to their former glory. The area had once provided high quality grazing and arable land. Many signs of military activity remain, although the RSPB removed a hundred years of accumulated rubbish and unexploded ordnance before the reserve could be opened to the public. Much of the 15 miles of ditches had to be unblocked to allow movement of water, with sluices built that allow the water level adjustment to maximise available habitat. This has particularly helped the water vole, with the reserve now considered to hold the densest population in the country and a sizable proportion of the UK's total. The benefits for birds of the RSPB's work are already being seen, 188 species being recorded in 2007.

The marshes were threatened in the 1980s when they were considered as a site for Euro Disney, but conservationists helped thwart the plans. More recently long viaducts have been built across the northern edges, carrying the A13 and High Speed Channel Tunnel Link. The latter of these is by far the more graceful, with Eurostar trains sweeping across its curves at 140mph. Now safe from development, there are hopes that when Cleanaway's landfill site at the Rainham end of the marsh closes in 2012, the whole area may become London Riverside Conservation Park.

The Visitor Centre is a most unusual building. It reminded me of an oil rig. The designers had to meet a complicated brief from the RSPB, requiring it to be carbon neutral, vandal proof and of course functional. Piles were sunk 19 metres into the ground to allay concerns from the Environment Agency about the weak Thames Wall, which has burst its banks on several occasions. There is a dry moat with drawbridges to provide security from vandalism that had been rife in the area. The building has a natural stack ventilation system, with passive solar heating (no fans) and rainwater is harvested for the toilets. The large windows let in plenty of light and allow visitors extensive views across the marshes. It also serves an excellent chocolate cake.

I chatted to Howard Vaughan, one of the RSPB's information officers, who kindly agreed to send me some information on the reserve. He pointed out exactly where the boundary lies between Essex and the London Borough of Havering, so the end of my walk was in sight. Unfortunately by now it was raining. I looked

RSBP Visitor Centre – Rainham Marshes

round the shop for a while, but as it showed no sign of stopping, eventually set off along the last section of sea wall. A few people were wandering round the wooden walkways of the reserve to my right, but as usual I was the only coast walker. It seemed right that after miles of Thames industry the last mile was back by the marshes that make up so much of the County's coast. Soon the path dropped below the embankment and I'd had my final sight of the river. And then, opposite the old rifle range targets, I reached the end – 305 miles from Manningtree and I had completed the Essex coast walk.

So there I was, standing in the pouring rain on the marshes at the end of Essex. A line on the map, but nothing on the ground to show its significance. There had been no sign to welcome me to the county back at the Stour and nothing here to show I was leaving it. It seemed right to stop and reflect for a while, but with rain falling I just took a quick photo and set off towards Rainham and home.

Once out of Essex things took a turn to the bizarre, but I shall save this tale and a few reflections for my final chapter.

# CHAPTER TWENTY-NINE

# REFLECTIONS

I could have turned back and walked to Purfleet station, but it seemed more fitting to cross the marshes and head on to Rainham. A town that is known as Rainham Essex, to differentiate from Rainham in Kent, but has been outside the county's official boundary for more than 40 years.

Within yards of leaving Essex the rain started to get heavier. Soon it was torrential. The path became a stream with running water two or three inches deep. I'd only bought a light waterproof and was soon soaked to the skin. A cycle path runs from the RSPB centre to Rainham, so at least the route through the marshes was obvious. Every 200 metres little sign posts indicated the number of kilometres to each end of the path and I gratefully counted them down. With nothing to see but rain, I kept my head down and with a bit of mental arithmetic used the markers to calculate that my walking speed was 3 ½ miles per hour. The path crosses the access road to Cleanaway's tip, although by now this was more river than road. The rain was still pouring down, heavier here in Greater London than at almost any time during 28 walks through Essex.

Once off the marshes I followed a sign for Ferry Lane for a few hundred yards before realising it was going the wrong way. Then

I worked out why I was so confused. Rainham always used to be south of the A13, but the new A13 runs the other side of the town, so I had to cross it. With the rain showing no sign of abating, it was back to the roundabout, right towards the A13 and under the viaduct. Here there were roadworks, no path and lots of mud. The roundabout was completely covered with water and I dodged spray as cars whooshed through it. It took several minutes waiting before a gap in the traffic allowed me to cross the slip road.

Still unsure if I was going the right way, I was at least on a pavement and could see the railway line that would guide me to the station. Then a car pulled over. An elderly gentleman wound down the window and told me he was lost. Could I tell him the way to Upminster? As soon as I said that was where I was going to catch the train to he almost pleaded with me to get in. This time I didn't decline the lift. The walk was officially over and anyway I was doing him a favour. I put my coat on the back seat, trying not to get his car wet, but he was too grateful to have a guide to mind. He'd taken his niece to Elm Park and got hopelessly lost because roads were flooded on the way back.

I took him onto the A13 and for a moment he worried we'd go onto the M25. I assured him this wasn't necessary, but I don't think he was used to big roads. Telling him to take the next slip road off the three lane A13, he asked me if it was on the right or left. This successfully negotiated we headed through Aveley. He didn't exactly go slowly and I can't say it was the safest I've ever felt in a car. As we approached one junction I had to remind him of the need to give way, and he assured me that he wasn't a bad driver, but I had a feeling we wouldn't have stopped without my warning. He didn't want to tell me how old he was because it might worry me.

He was very interested in my walk and as we chatted it turned out he lived only a mile from us. Out of politeness I said there was no need to drop me home, as I wouldn't want him to get lost again and as we approached Upminster he agreed this would be a good idea. He really was worried about getting lost a mile from his house. We agreed he'd drop me at the bus stop. He pulled into a car park so that I could put my coat on in the car rather than get wet when I got out. It was still pouring with rain. As we were almost home he decided it was OK to let on that he was 83 and had had a cataract operation 6 months ago. It was then that he noticed he hadn't put the car lights on. We carried on into the town centre and I got out for the bus. He shook my hand and thanked me profusely. As he was heading away from Upminster when he'd stopped me I've no idea where he'd have ended up. Now I understand why you sometimes read stories of people driving onto the wrong motorway carriageway. But what a nice old gentleman.

So I started with breakfast on the Norwich express and ended with a lift from a very kindly, but very lost old man. In between I'd walked the banks of six rivers, passed seaside resorts, major ports, power stations, oil refineries and seen a bit of sea. So there's the first observation – only around 10% of the mainland Essex coastline actually faces open sea. Harwich to Dovercourt, Walton to Point Clear and Bradwell to the Crouch, although for most of the last section there is a mile of impenetrable salt marsh separating sea from path. The lower reaches of the Stour, Blackwater and Thames estuaries are wide enough to almost count as sea, but it was still rare to hear the splashing of waves as I walked.

It is the often remote and winding sea walls and salt marshes of the estuaries that I shall remember most. Mile after mile of what some may see as boring and monotonous, but is in fact a constantly changing vista. An expanse of mud when the tide is out, but swirling water as it comes in. Beautiful in sunshine, mysterious in mist, but never the same.

But in many ways it is a changing coast and I'd caught just a fleeting glimpse – a brief moment in a long history. Nature has always been changing the shape of the coast. Drastically at first, the ice ages moving the rivers and depositing the clay that man now extracts. Then more subtlely, but always trying. Man has lived here for thousands of years, but it's only in the last few hundred that he too has altered the coastline, rather than live with what nature has provided. Building of sea walls and draining of marshes has changed the very outline of the coast, but now nature is fighting back. It isn't viable for us to try to protect all the land, especially as we cause the planet to warm and sea levels rise, so now we're starting to let the sea back in. We are beginning to realise that it's better to work in harmony with nature rather than to fight it.

A good proportion of the coast is designated as nature reserves. The RSPB, English Nature, local councils and most of all the Essex Wildlife Trust, do sterling work in protecting wildlife; plants, animals and birds. Such reserves are an increasingly necessary oasis as habitat is lost elsewhere and many species are growing in number as a result, but even in these reserves nature is not left alone. A helping hand is required to manage the environment, working with nature to provide the best conditions for biodiversity. Most of us are aware of the various charities that protect wildlife, but it wasn't until I walked through reserve after reserve that I realised how much has to be done to enable populations to flourish.

Over many centuries small settlements became villages, but for hundreds of years growth was slow. It is only in the last 200 years that most of the towns have appeared. Small villages became thriving seaside resorts, as first ships then railways bought trippers. Most settlements had their own wharf and there were many little ports along the coast. Gradually though most of the smaller ones fell into disuse, centralising in Harwich and Tilbury, two of the largest ports in the country. Local industry built up, then mostly closed, with petrochemical plants virtually the only large scale installations remaining. As the UK manufacturing industry declines and we import more and more goods, new and larger port facilities are required. Farmland is lost to housing, golf courses or country parks, but we bring more food across the ocean that could be grown in England. Parts of the coast became a dumping ground, with much of the rubbish coming from London, but space is running out for landfill. Another way has to be found to dispose of rubbish, or better still produce less in the first place. Land which has been an ugly scar on our coastline is now returning to recreation, claimed back for the people of Essex.

Many towns have now realised that times have changed and so must they. Seaside resorts are being spruced up and waterfronts revitalised. Mostly this is being done sympathetically with old buildings tastefully renovated, but more 'affordable' housing should be included. Sea views shouldn't just be for the wealthy. Thankfully most of the redevelopment is recent, so we have relatively little 1960s concrete, but how many of today's buildings will still stand centuries later? How many will enhance the landscape as so many of the county's churches, mills and cottages have done for hundreds of years? Probably the only modern building I saw that had real beauty was the QE2 Bridge and that was built with a lifespan of just 120 years.

In the mid 18th century a coast that relied on the water for its links with the outside world found it was served by a network of railways. Roads improved so most of the barges, coasters and local ferries were no longer needed. Although car ownership grew rapidly during the 20th century, Essex was fortunate that some of its key rural branch lines escaped closure. Partly thanks to servicing docks and a nuclear power station respectively, the Harwich and Southminster lines survived. Brightlingsea and Maldon were less lucky. As I found, the rural buses are reliable and friendly. Whilst some of the services are sparse, there were just enough to enable me to accomplish my aim of using public transport for every walk. However passengers were few and if we are to reduce car usage there must be viable public transport alternatives. Buses must run more frequently and somehow their image needs to change. Neither rising petrol prices nor environmental concerns are enough to persuade most people to leave their car behind, but we have to achieve this. Trains are more popular and reopening the line to Maldon would fill a major gap in the county's transport. But would it spoil the town as London workers moved in, house prices went up and local people could no longer afford to buy?

Some of the county's more remote outposts have changed comparatively little and hence have a special charm. Too inaccessible for commuters, they have remained as communities rather than dormitory towns. They have no need to be twee for tourists and are far more self-contained than many larger, but less remote settlements. The local bus, the Post Office, the village shop, pub and school are crucial to these villages. It will be a shame if either short sighted removal of services, or misguided development, cause these communities to change forever.

So what changes are to come? There will surely be more 'managed retreat'. The line has to be constantly defended or allowed to break, and Essex has shown that the latter can work to the benefit of both man and nature. Essex is fortunate that much of its coastline remains unspoilt and as conservationists gain the upper hand, there now seems little prospect of developers being allowed to ruin it. There will be battles and no doubt the occasional loss, but the biggest changes we are likely to inflict will be from global influences. If climate change proceeds as many predict, rising sea levels could swamp much of our low lying coastal land. It will simply be uneconomic to protect all the land against the increasing storms that climate change will bring. The outline of our coast will change as we decide which bits to protect and where to allow the sea to take over the land. Not just the parts man claimed over the centuries, but potentially huge areas, including whole towns and villages. A coast that has transformed slowly over centuries could alter beyond recognition. Just as we learn to work with nature on a local scale, our global demand for growth at all costs would lead to more change than anything seen since the Ice Ages.

Whilst rising sea level is the most obvious consequence of global warming on our coast, it may be other effects that cause the greatest change for us all. Increasing sea temperatures are already being blamed for declining numbers of phytoplankton, the single cell plants that produce half the world's oxygen and form the bottom of food chains supporting most marine life. Increasing extremes of weather, with many more droughts, floods, hurricanes and cyclones, will make it harder for the world to feed its population, with greater risk of major displacement of people, political conflict and even war. Changes in ocean currents caused by melting ice could drastically affect the earth's climate. The Gulf Stream allows us to swim in sea at same latitudes that Canada has polar bears, but if this were to shutdown life in Britain would be very different to that today.

However, not only do we have to consider the effects of climate change, but also the impact of reducing stocks of the very materials that are causing the change. Reserves of oil, gas, coal and metals are becoming depleted and increasingly more expensive to extract. Eventually we will have to go back to ways of life that rely far less on non sustainable resources. Once more it will become the norm to work close to home, to grow our own food or buy local produce, to make do and mend rather than purchase more and more consumer goods and to use public transport. Mills, wharves and railways that were discarded in the 20th century, may come to life once more, as fossil fuels become increasingly expensive. Land will return to agriculture and communities to a way of life that is sustainable. So the coast of Essex will change. Whether mankind across the world can modify his activities so that we can adapt to sustainable living in a gradual and managed way, or whether they will be forced upon us by depleted resources or catastrophe, remains to be seen.

I set out expecting to walk on the sea wall all the way from Manningtree to Purfleet, but one of the frustrations of the walk was having to regularly leave the coastline. Diversions inland provided variety, but I'd rather have had the choice. Sometimes docks or industry were legitimate reasons, but in other places it just seemed that walkers weren't wanted between expensive houses and the sea. There is a welcome trend towards opening up the countryside, but 'Freedom to Roam' still has a long way to go. It would require relatively little expenditure for virtually the whole of the Essex coast to be accessible and I hope that our Councils will work towards this.

My second frustration came from the footpaths themselves. Poor signing, non existent, or overgrown paths and sometimes badly maintained infrastructure. The quality of paths was something that varied considerably along the coast. Signing was often haphazard and a map usually essential, but other than around Basildon, stiles and footbridges were generally in good order. With this exception, the paths close to towns and villages were usually OK, but it was the more remote and less used ones that gave the most problems. And this indeed was the problem. Lack of use allowing vegetation to grow so that sometimes walking became a chore not a pleasure. A self perpetuating problem, to which the answer has to be encourage more people to walk.

One of the surprises was how few people walk on the Essex coast. Mostly it was only near towns and villages that I saw anyone, and there were a number of sections where I was probably the only person walking all day. Our country parks are well visited, but the wilder and less sanitised parts of the coast are largely ignored. Its unique coastline is one of the county's greatest assets, yet few venture out to enjoy it. Maybe the majority do prefer a short walk round a country park, with its car park, visitor centre and ice cream van, but perhaps some, like me, would find they preferred the coast if only they gave it a try.

I chose to walk the Essex coast because it was convenient, but soon found it had so much to offer. That was the biggest surprise and the greatest delight. I'd expected a relatively dull walk, with occasional places of interest. What I found was that if you look for it every little part is interesting. It has a long and fascinating history, varied and plentiful wildlife, some fascinating geography, but most of all, the Essex coast is remarkably beautiful. Even if the far view is lacking, a look downwards will so often provide beauty – a butterfly, a bird, marsh flowers or just the grasses. Small things that are so easy to miss when looking at a 'view'. Essex doesn't have the stunning splendour of great cliffs, hills or bays, but its beauty is more gentle. Sometimes you have to look, but it's always there and what's more it's on my doorstep. My first thought on completing the walk was that I wanted to turn round and do it all again. Hopefully I may have encouraged a few others to appreciate our coast and maybe next time I won't be quite so alone out on those sea walls.